The Declining Importance of Race and Gender in the Labor Market

The Declining Importance of Race and Gender in the Labor Market

The Role of Employment Discrimination Policies

June E. O'Neill
Dave M. O'Neill

The AEI Press

Publisher for the American Enterprise Institute

WASHINGTON, D.C.

Distributed by arrangement with the Rowman & Littlefield Publishing Group, 4501 Forbes Boulevard, Suite 200, Lanham, Maryland 20706. To order, call toll free 1-800-462-6420 or 1-717-794-3800. For all other inquiries, please contact AEI Press, 1150 Seventeenth Street, N.W., Washington, D.C. 20036, or call 1-800-862-5801.

Library of Congress Cataloging-in-Publication Data

O'Neill, June.
    The declining importance of race and gender in the labor market : the role of employment discrimination policies / June E. O'Neill, Dave M. O'Neill.
        p. cm.
    Includes bibliographical references and index.
    ISBN 978-0-8447-7244-8 (cloth : alk. paper) — ISBN 0-8447-7244-5 (cloth : alk. paper) — ISBN 978-0-8447-7246-2 (ebook : alk. paper) — ISBN 0-8447-7246-1 (ebook : alk. paper)
    1. Discrimination in employment—United States. 2. Discrimination in employment—Government policy—United States. 3. Discrimination—Law and legislation—United States. 4. Labor market—United States. I. O'Neill, David M. II. Title.
    HD4903.5.U58O54 2012
    331.13'30973—dc23
                            2012019621

Printed in the United States of America

Contents

ACKNOWLEDGMENTS   ix

LIST OF ILLUSTRATIONS   xi

INTRODUCTION AND SUMMARY   1

PART I: FROM EMANCIPATION TO THE 1964 CIVIL RIGHTS ACT

1. FROM EMANCIPATION TO THE CIVIL RIGHTS ACT:
    SOCIAL AND ECONOMIC PROGRESS   9
    Lincoln's Great Promise: Emancipation and Reconstruction   10
    Sources of Upward Mobility: Migration and Education   12
    Racial Differences in Economic Status   15

2. TITLE VII OF THE 1964 CIVIL RIGHTS ACT:
    LABOR MARKET DISCRIMINATION BECOMES A FEDERAL CRIME   20
    Federal and State Government Antidiscrimination
        Efforts before 1964   21
    Developments That Shaped the Civil Rights Act and Title VII   24
    The 1964 Civil Rights Act and Title VII   27
    Changes in Antidiscrimination Law and Policy after 1964   29

PART II: IMPLEMENTING ANTIDISCRIMINATION POLICY:
THE OFFICE OF FEDERAL CONTRACT COMPLIANCE PROGRAMS
AND THE EQUAL EMPLOYMENT OPPORTUNITY COMMISSION

3. THE OFFICE OF FEDERAL CONTRACT COMPLIANCE PROGRAMS
    AND ANTIDISCRIMINATION ENFORCEMENT   43
    Procedures and Concepts for Determining Discriminatory
        Behavior   44
    Targeting Contractors for Compliance Review   45
    Outcomes of Compliance Reviews   50

Effect of OFCCP on Discrimination: Evidence from Compliance
Reviews *52*
Effect of OFCCP on Discrimination: Evidence from Court
Cases *56*
New Rules, New Complexities *59*
Conclusion *60*

4. THE EQUAL EMPLOYMENT OPPORTUNITY COMMISSION
AND ANTIDISCRIMINATION ENFORCEMENT   **62**
Charges against Employers Brought by Individuals *64*
Enforcement through Litigation by Type of Discrimination *71*
Conclusion *117*

PART III: ANALYSIS OF PROGRAM EFFECTS

5. ACCOUNTING FOR CHANGES IN THE BLACK–WHITE WAGE GAP   **123**
Overview of Major Sources of Change in the
Black–White Wage Gap *124*
1940–60: The Decline in the Black–White Wage Gap
before Title VII *134*
1960–80: The Black–White Wage Gap Continues
to Decline Post–Title VII *143*
After 1980: Stagnation in the Black–White Wage Gap *158*

6. ACCOUNTING FOR CHANGES IN THE GENDER WAGE GAP   **162**
Skill Differentials between Women and Men *164*
Why the Gender Gap Narrowed After 1980 *175*
Conclusion *176*

7. EFFECTS OF AFFIRMATIVE ACTION ON THE ECONOMIC STATUS
OF AFRICAN AMERICAN AND WOMEN WORKERS   **178**
Effects of the OFCCP on Occupational Upgrading *182*
Effects of the OFCCP on Relative Wages *185*

PART IV: MEASURING LABOR MARKET DISCRIMINATION TODAY

8. LABOR MARKET DISCRIMINATION AND WAGE GAPS IN THE 2000s   **195**
Wage Differences between Minorities and Whites *197*
The Gender Gap in Wages *223*
Conclusion *243*

NOTES	251
REFERENCES	269
CASES CITED	279
INDEX	283
ABOUT THE AUTHORS	293

Acknowledgments

This study began as part of a series of evaluations of government agencies commissioned by the American Enterprise Institute. Marvin Kosters, the director of the series, approached us about writing on the agencies that were charged with implementing antidiscrimination law—the Office of Federal Contracting Programs (OFCCP) and the Equal Employment Opportunity Commission (EEOC). These agencies are relatively small and perhaps mysterious to the average American, but they deal with the important issue of labor market discrimination and often employ controversial methods such as affirmative action. We agreed to take on the study, but soon realized that it could not be effective without broadening the topic. In order to make judgments about the effect the government agencies may have had on remedying discriminatory pay differentials, it is necessary to analyze the roles played by other forces that influence pay gaps, such as education and work experience. It is also important to examine how pay gaps changed in the years before the passage of the 1964 Civil Rights Act and before the creation and strengthening of the OFCCP and EEOC in the 1960s and 1970s. As often happens with complex topics, the scope of work grows, so what began as a standard evaluation of government agencies became a major study of the change in racial and gender pay differentials over many decades and the role of government involvement in this change—which includes not only the agencies but the legal and judicial establishments.

We thank Dr. Kosters for setting us on the right path with extensive comments in the early stages of the study. We were ably assisted in the early stages by Andreas Lachnit. The extensive statistical analyses were proficiently conducted by Mei Liao and Wenhui Li. Financial support was received from the American Enterprise Institute, the Olin Foundation, the Weisman Foundation, a PSC-CUNY award, and the Wasserman Department of Economics and Finance at Baruch College. We are also grateful for the assistance of Jacquie Pfeffer-Merrill, who edited the manuscript.

List of Illustrations

Figures

5-1   Black–White Wage Ratios, 1939–2010   *125*

5-2   Trends in Real Hourly Earnings from 1940–80
       of Men and Women by Race and Education   *136*

5-3   Female Labor Force Participation Rates by Race:
       1954–2010 (Ages 25–54)   *152*

5-4   Male Labor Force Participation Rates by Race:
       1954–2010 (Ages 25–54)   *155*

5-5   Percent of Men Who Worked at Some Time during
       the Year, by Race and Education: 1967–2009   *156*

5-6   Trends in Real Hourly Earnings from 1979 to 2010
       of Men and Women by Race and Education   *161*

6-1   The Gender Gap: Female–Male Wage Ratios (1955–2010)   *163*

6-2   Labor Force Participation Rates by Sex: 1948–2010
       (Ages 25–54)   *165*

6-3   Labor Force Participation Rates over a Working Life
       of Cohorts of Women Born in Selected Time Intervals,
       1886 to 1965   *169*

8-1   Average Hourly Earnings of Asian, Black, and Hispanic
       Men as Percent of Hourly Earnings of Non-Hispanic
       White Men, Full-Time Workers Ages 25–54, 1979–2010   *198*

8-2   Average Hourly Earnings of Asian, Black, and Hispanic
       Women as Percent of Hourly Earnings of Non-Hispanic
       White Women, Full-Time Workers Ages 25–54,
       1979–2010   *203*

8-3   Employment Status of Women and Men with Children
       by Age of Children, 2009   *224*

Tables

1-1   Educational Attainment by Race at Ages 25–29, 1920–60   *15*

1-2   Labor Force Participation and Characteristics of Workers
        by Race and Sex, Ages 25–54   *16*

1-3   Black–White Wage Ratios by Sex, Region, and Education,
        1940 and 1960   *18*

3-1   Office of Federal Contract Compliance Programs (OFCCP)
        Performance and Program Statistics   *51*

4-1   EEOC Charges Received under Title VII by Type
        of Discrimination Claimed   *66*

4-2   EEOC Charges and Resolutions under Title VII   *67*

5-1   Educational Attainment of Men and Women
        by Race and Age, 1940–2009   *128*

5-2   Mean AFQT Percentile Test Score of Men Ages 19–21
        by Race and Education   *131*

5-3   Changes in the Wage Differentials by Education, 1940–2010:
        Wage Ratios of College Graduates to High School Graduates;
        High School Graduates to High School Dropouts   *133*

5-4   Trends in Wage Inequality: Changes in Hourly
        Wage Ratios between Different Percentiles of the
        Wage Distribution, 1979–2009   *134*

5-5   Black–White Wage Ratios by Age, Education, and Region,
        1940–60   *135*

5-6   Occupational Distributions of Black and White Men
        and Women, 1940–80 (Percentage Distributions)   *138*

5-7   Black–White Wage Ratios for Men and Women by
        Education and Region, 1940–2000 (Ages 25–54)   *144*

5-8   Male Black–White Weekly Wage Ratios in the South
        and the Non-South by Education, 1940–2000,
        Ages 25–54   *149*

5-9   Female Black–White Hourly Wage Ratios in the South
        and the Non-South by Education, 1940–2000,
        Ages 25–54   *151*

5-10   The Change in the Hourly Wage Ratio between
        Black Women and White Women and Black Women
        and White Men, 1960–80 and 1979–2009   *153*

6-1   Percent of Women in the Labor Force by Marital Status
       and Age   167
6-2   Proportion of Years Worked since Age 18
       by Employed White Women   170
6-3   Educational Attainment of Men and Women:
       Percent of All Persons and of Workers Completing
       High School or More and College or More
       (Ages 25–54), 1940–2000   172
6-4   Women's Share of Bachelor's, Master's, and Doctor's
       Degrees in Selected Field of Study: 1972–2009   174
6-5   Percent of First-Professional Degrees Earned by Women
       in Dentistry, Medicine, and Law: Selected Years,
       1949–50 through 2008–9   175
7-1   Percent of Workers Employed in EEO-1 Reporting
       Firms by Federal Contractor Status and Race and
       Sex of Worker   181
7-2   Relative Occupational Advancement of Protected Workers
       in Federal Contractor and Non-contractor Firms
       (1970–1980)   183
7-3   Does Employment in the Federal Contractor Sector
       Increase the Wage Rate of Protected Groups?
       Results from Regression Analysis (2000)   188
8-1   Minority/White Wage Ratios for Detailed Racial and
       Ethnic Groups of Men (Ages 25–54) before and
       after Controlling for Skill-Related Characteristics   200
8-2   Minority/White Wage Ratios for Detailed Racial and
       Ethnic Groups of Women (Ages 25–54) before and
       after Controlling for Skill-Related Characteristics   204
8-3   Selected Characteristics of Men by Race (NLSY79)   207
8-4   Explaining the Black–White and Hispanic–White
       Wage Gaps Among Men   209
8-5   Explaining the Male Black–White and Hispanic–White
       Wage Gaps at Different Education Levels   211
8-6   Selected Characteristics of Women by Race (NLSY79)   217
8-7   Explaining the Black–White and Hispanic–White
       Wage Gaps among Women   218

8-8   Explaining the Female Black–White and Hispanic–White
       Wage Gaps at Different Education Levels *219*

8-9   What Working Situation Would Be Ideal for You?
       Results from a 2007 Pew Research Center Survey *225*

8-10   Average Hours Spent per Day in Child Care, Work, and
       Other Activities by Age of Youngest Child, for Employed
       Women and Men Ages 20–44 Reporting Time Use on a
       Weekday, 2003–2004 Annual Averages, ATUS Data *226*

8-11   Selected Characteristics of Men and Women (NLSY79) *231*

8-12   Explaining the Gender Wage Gap: Female-Male Hourly
       Wage Ratios (NLSY79) *233*

8-13   Selected Characteristics of Men and Women by
       Marital Status (NLSY79) *236*

8-14   Explaining the Gender Wage Gap: Female-Male Hourly
       Wage Ratios by Marital Status (NLSY79) *238*

Appendix

7A-1   Regression I: Industry/Region Cross-Sectional Model:
       Dependent Variable—Log Hourly Rate of Pay
       in 2000, by Sex and Race *189*

7A-2   Regression II: MSA Cross-Sectional Model:
       Dependent Variable—Log Hourly Rate of Pay
       in 2000, by Sex and Race *190*

8A-1   Means and Partial Regression Coefficients of Explanatory
       Variables from Separate Log Wage Regressions for Black,
       White, and Hispanic Men Ages 35–43 in 2000 (NLSY79) *245*

8A-2   Means and Partial Regression Coefficients of Explanatory
       Variables from Separate Log Wage Regressions for Black,
       White, and Hispanic Women Ages 35–43 in 2000
       (NLSY79) *246*

8A-3   Means and Partial Regression Coefficients of Explanatory
       Variables from Separate Log Wage Regressions for Men
       and Women Ages 35–43 in 2000 (NLSY79) *247*

8A-4   Explaining the Source of the Gender Wage Gaps
       (NLSY79 in 2000) *249*

Introduction and Summary

In his Saturday morning address to the nation on March 12, 2011, President Obama deplored what he saw as widespread gender discrimination in pay, citing a statistic that women earn only 75 percent as much as men. He invoked that figure to bolster support for the Paycheck Fairness Act, a bill that promises to raise women's pay.[1] But discrimination against women cannot be simply inferred from the 75 percent pay comparison because it does not compare women and men with equivalent labor market productivity. It simply compares the pay of female and male workers without taking account of the facts that explain the disparity, such as the facts that women on average have had considerably less continuous and full-time work experience than men of the same age and choose different types of jobs. Women freely make these choices, often for reasons related to the need to accommodate work with family responsibilities.

The president is not alone in misusing data on wage gaps. Advocacy groups and the media often misuse statistics to exaggerate the extent of racial and gender discrimination in employment and thereby influence legislation and litigation. Yet the real story to be told is one of declining discrimination and the rising economic status of minorities and women in America.

For the past fifty years, the federal government has been committed to ending racial and gender discrimination in the labor market. We examine the historical roots of discrimination and the evolution of government concern with the problem. We also show how the implementation of antidiscrimination policy lost its moorings as special interest groups, the legal establishment, and the agencies charged with implementing antidiscrimination policy distorted the concept of discrimination and developed increasingly more intrusive rules and regulations. What began as a clear policy to advance equal employment opportunity, as specified in Title VII of the 1964 Civil Rights Act, changed into requirements for employers to

1

implement racial and gender preferences, practices that were specifically prohibited by Title VII.

Have these policies worked? The increasingly more elaborate efforts of the agencies charged with implementing antidiscriminatory practices cannot be linked to significant and sustained improvements in the economic status of minorities or women. The black–white and female–male wage gaps have narrowed considerably over time, but the timing of those improvements suggests that other economic and social forces were the major factors underlying changes in the earnings of minorities and women. One exception to this general finding is the increase in the relative wages of African American workers in the South following passage of Title VII of the Civil Rights Act of 1964. The sheer momentum of the Act and its enforcement by federal officials served to end the extreme racial segregation and other openly discriminatory practices of Jim Crow in the South.

Today, in the second decade of the twenty-first century, it is apparent that wage differentials still exist between racial and ethnic groups and between women and men. We find, however, that labor market discrimination is not an important reason for these differentials. Our conclusion is based on an extensive analysis of data on wage differentials between minorities and whites and between women and men. The wage differentials observed are largely explained by differences in work-related skills. Skill differences also account for the lesser-known reverse wage gaps for minority groups such as Asian men and women, who earn significantly more than their white, non-Hispanic counterparts.

This is not to say that all employers and workplaces are free of prejudice. In our review of cases brought to the Equal Employment Opportunity Commission we found reports of individual situations involving blatant discrimination against members of minority groups and women. But such cases are relatively rare and can be effectively prosecuted using the law enforcement provisions of the original Title VII. There is no need for continuing the policies requiring racial and gender preferences that came into effect after the passage of Title VII.

This book has four parts, each divided into chapters. Part I covers the historical developments that followed Abraham Lincoln's Emancipation Proclamation. Chapter 1 describes the changes in the social and economic conditions of the black population in the years between emancipation and the passage of the 1964 Civil Right Act. At the time of emancipation most African Americans were newly freed slaves living in the rural South. After a brief period of Reconstruction, the federal government withdrew, leaving African Americans to face a hostile world of inferior segregated schooling, segregated labor markets and public accommodations, and without protection from the violence to which they were all too often subjected. Yet they were able to make significant gains in educational attainment. Those educational gains, combined with migration out of the South, eventually translated into remarkable increases in earnings. Yet even as late as the early 1960s, blatant racial segregation in most aspects of life was still the order of the day in the Jim Crow South. African Americans still did not have equal access to the ballot box and still did not have equal protection under the law.

In chapter 2 we examine the development of federal government involvement in labor market discrimination from the time of the Roosevelt administration through the drafting and passage of Title VII of the 1964 Civil Rights Act, and we review the important changes that were subsequently made to the original provisions of Title VII by the Courts and by Congress. "Disparate impact discrimination" was added to the lexicon of unlawful discrimination and put on a par with intentional discrimination. Affirmative action procedures, which are essentially quotas, became routine. The potential for such changes in the meaning of discrimination had been anticipated by the senators who drafted the Civil Rights Act and who added strong language to the original Title VII specifically prohibiting them. But the language inserted in the Civil Rights Act was not enough to deter either "disparate impact" or affirmative action.

Part II focuses on the operations and enforcement procedures of the two major agencies charged with implementing the federal government's antidiscrimination policy. Chapter 3 considers the Office of Federal Contract Compliance Programs (OFCCP) and chapter 4 considers the Equal Employment Opportunities Commission (EEOC). Together, these two chapters provide an extensive survey of civil rights litigation. The detailed study of the activities of the two agencies shows the direction of government antidiscrimination policy and how it has evolved over time, as well as providing evidence for evaluating their potential effectiveness in combating labor market discrimination.

In Part III we use empirical analysis to identify the effects of federal anti-discrimination activity on changes in the relative earnings and employment of protected groups. This is a difficult task, because many factors other than changes in federal enforcement activities influence wage levels and wage differentials, such as changes in the economy and changes in the skills of workers. In chapter 5 we examine data covering the period 1940–2000 to determine how well the timing of enforcement landmarks correlates with changes in racial wage differentials after accounting for changes in skill differentials, migration and changes in the wage structure in the economy. We find that the black–white earnings gap declined sharply in the period 1940–60 when government antidiscrimination activity was essentially absent. We also find evidence that, although the passage of Title VII of the 1964 Civil Rights Act had an immediate effect of narrowing the racial earnings gap, especially in the South, subsequent activities of the EEOC and OFCCP do not appear to have had any sustained effects.

In chapter 6 we examine data covering the period 1940–2000 to determine how well federal antidiscrimination enforcement efforts correlate with changes in gender wage differentials. We find no perceptible effect of federal antidiscrimination policies on the gender wage gap. In contrast to the relative rise in wages of black men following the passage of the Civil Rights Act, no change is observed in the wages of women relative to those of men after passage of the Act, although the relative wages of black women rose sharply when compared to the wages of white women. Nor do we find that the activities of the EEOC and OFCCP had measurable effects on reducing the gender pay gap, which started to narrow only after 1980. We attribute the narrowing in the gender wage gap to slowly evolving changes that led to increases in women's lifetime work experience and work preparation.

In chapter 7 we analyze cross-sectional data that allow us to test specifically for the effect of the OFCCP on the relative earnings of black workers and find no perceptible effect.

In part IV (chapter 8) we address the question whether current differentials in earnings between minority and white workers and between women and men reflect an important degree of discrimination. Using data from the 2005 and 2010 American Community Surveys, we estimate the relative earnings of African American workers as well as those of Asian and Hispanic workers by specific national origin, adjusting for basic measures of skill (education, immigration status, and English-speaking ability). We examine racial and ethnic differentials for men and for women separately. We find that most of the observed differentials are explained by skill differences. For some groups, lower earnings are largely the result of lower educational and skill attainment. Groups with a high percentage of recent immigrants have lower earnings in part because of language difficulties. In the case of Asian groups, high levels of education more than compensate for problems related to immigration.

We then turn to data from the National Longitudinal Survey of Youth, which contains unique detail about skill differences, including scores on the Armed Forces Qualification Test and detailed information on lifetime work experience. With this rich dataset, we investigate in more depth the sources of the wage gap between blacks and white non-Hispanics and between Hispanics and white non-Hispanics. We analyze these differentials separately for women and men and find that the various wage gaps are fully explained once we account for more refined measures of skill. These results imply that deprivation related to education and family are more serious obstacles to the attainment of racial equality in earnings than current labor market discrimination.

The gender gap in wages, by contrast, is mainly related to choices that women make between home and the workplace. Working women have typically had as much education as male workers. But in recent years women have been acquiring more years of education than men, at both the college and post-graduate levels, and that education gives them greater access to higher-paying occupations. Yet, women also value time spent with their children and, as a consequence, are more likely to work part-time, to take more career breaks than men, and therefore to accumulate fewer years of continuous work experience. Occupations and job situations that allow for part-time work and convenient schedules pay less. For reasons such as these, childless women who never marry earn more than married women and as much as similarly situated men.

Our main conclusion is that government intervention to ensure equal opportunity has often morphed into vain attempts to impose equal outcomes. We find that it is not employment discrimination that is holding back groups with lower earnings. When lack of skill is the problem, it is counterproductive to compel employers to hire or promote workers that they view as unsuitable for the job. The paperwork and affirmative action regulations that firms now face are costly to implement. They interfere with the operation of the labor market and are an impediment to economic growth. Moreover, the requirement of racial and gender preferences in employment that are the basis of affirmative action and disparate impact rulings can have undesirable effects on minorities. They reduce the incentive to obtain the human capital needed to increase socioeconomic status and reduce the significance of the accomplishments of those minorities who did not require special standards to compete.

PART I

From Emancipation
to the 1964 Civil Rights Act

1

From Emancipation
to the Civil Rights Act:
Social and Economic Progress

A century separates Lincoln's 1863 Emancipation Proclamation and the Civil Rights Act of 1964, two landmark government actions that sought to bring full citizenship and equality under the law to African Americans. The constitutional amendments that followed the Emancipation Proclamation gave the African American population a measure of basic rights as citizens, enabling them to make considerable progress in education and earnings despite the violent repression and legal racial segregation that they faced in the Jim Crow South.

Several attempts were made to challenge segregation in the Courts, including the infamous *Plessy v. Ferguson* Supreme Court decision, which upheld racial separation in the provision of public accommodations. None succeeded until the 1950s when the Supreme Court ruled in *Brown v. Board of Education* that forced segregation in public schools was unconstitutional.

Yet, the African American population in the South was still essentially disfranchised in the early 1960s. After *Brown* the integration of the public schools proceeded, but not without bitter confrontation, while other public accommodations remained legally segregated in the South.

In this chapter we examine the progress of African Americans after emancipation, focusing on the changes in the relative social and economic status of African American men and women before passage of the 1964 Civil Rights Act. In the next chapter we consider the political and legal developments leading up to the Act as well as the conflicts that arose in the years after its passage when the intent of the Act to guarantee equal opportunity was replaced by a goal of equal outcomes.

Lincoln's Great Promise: Emancipation and Reconstruction

With the Civil War still raging, Abraham Lincoln published the Emancipation Proclamation on New Year's Day 1863. The Proclamation provided that "persons held as slaves within said designated States, and parts of States, are, and henceforward shall be free." The "designated States" were all those in Confederate territory still in rebellion, so, as a practical matter, the Proclamation had only a limited effect on freeing the slaves.[2] But the spirit of the proclamation was a powerful step forward. During his campaign for re-election Lincoln called for constitutional emancipation. Slavery was finally abolished nationwide with the passage of the Thirteenth Amendment in 1865; former slaves were granted full citizenship with the citizenship clause of the Fourteenth Amendment in 1868; and they were granted the right to vote with the Fifteenth Amendment in 1870.

Several crucial rights flowed from the Emancipation Proclamation and the subsequent constitutional amendments that clarified those rights. The Fourteenth Amendment guaranteed citizenship to all persons born or naturalized in the United States and thereby overturned the Supreme Court's 1857 *Dred Scott v. Sandford* ruling that African slaves and their descendants (even those who had been freed) could not be citizens of the United States. The Fourteenth Amendment's due process and equal protection clauses in theory offered former slaves protection from attempts by southern states to restrict the migration of former slaves. Although the Fourteenth Amendment did not automatically bring about "equal protection" for the African American population in the southern states, it did bring a modicum of protection to the rights of African Americans. Most important, the education of African Americans could no longer be treated by any government as a crime, as decreed by the slave codes in much of the antebellum South. Moreover, any locale that provided public schooling was required to provide schooling for African Americans, and that schooling was expected to be "equal."

It proved difficult to implement these legal provisions in the South. The Civil War had devastated the South. Southern whites were embittered by the changes brought to their way of life. Even if southern whites had been sympathetic to the plight of the African American population, their economic circumstances would have made it economically difficult to undertake a program of economic development. There was, however, a brief Reconstruction

Period when the federal government provided military protection and, through the Freedmen's Bureau, helped the African American population to take advantage of their new political rights and economic opportunities.

Efforts by the Union to provide education to the black population actually started during the Civil War when Union forces, after securing a southern city, encouraged missionary societies to open day schools for blacks (Welch 1973, 52). The Freedmen's Bureau intensified these efforts during the period 1865–70; it financed construction of an estimated 4,250 schools and turned to the church for staffing. The Bureau contributed 60 percent of the revenue for these schools; churches provided 25 percent and tuition and donations the remaining 15 percent. As a result, about 5–7 percent of black children in a given year received instruction.[3] Reconstruction lasted only until the late 1870s. Once the federal troops were withdrawn and the eyes of the world turned elsewhere, the southern states ushered in an era of extreme racial separation and repression. Still hostile to the idea of former slaves as free men, white southerners used their political power to establish explicit regulations, collectively known as "Jim Crow," that imposed racial segregation in almost all public facilities. The Ku Klux Klan and other racist groups enforced Jim Crow through violent intimidation, including lynchings, of African Americans and whites who defied its provisions. To maintain a white monopoly on political power, southern states essentially disfranchised African American citizens by instituting poll taxes and other requirements to vote that the African American population could not meet.[4]

Although Jim Crow laws and regulations clearly violated the principle of racial equality in the Fourteenth Amendment, the Supreme Court upheld the constitutionality of a Louisiana law mandating separate railroad cars for black and white passengers within the state in its 1896 *Plessy v. Ferguson* decision. The nearly unanimous opinion famously declared that racial segregation of public transportation did not violate the Constitution as long as the accommodations provided to both races were "equal." The lone dissenter, Justice John Marshall Harlan, wrote: "Our Constitution is color-blind and neither knows nor tolerates classes among its citizens."[5] Harlan's words would be echoed almost seven decades later in the 1964 Civil Rights Act. In the meantime, "separate but equal" remained the legal justification for racial segregation of public facilities. Although the Supreme Court's 1954 *Brown v. Board of Education* decision held "separate but equal" provision of public education unconstitutional,[6] the *Brown* decision did not extend to voting or to other public facilities and accommodations. Jim Crow continued to reign in the South.

Sources of Upward Mobility: Migration and Education

Although African Americans faced considerable obstacles in Jim Crow, they were able to improve their economic circumstances markedly in the century after emancipation. The two most important sources of upward mobility were migration and education.

Migration. In every census between 1790 and 1910, about 90 percent of the African American population was found to be living in the South (Taeuber and Taeuber 1966). It was not until World War I that any significant African American migration to the North took place. Several factors contributed to the low rates of black migration out of the South in the early decades of the twentieth century. Initially, African Americans lived in rural, often isolated areas of the South. They lacked information and resources to fund a move to the North and lacked basic education to compete for industrial jobs at a time when hordes of European immigrants were coming to America.

During World War I immigration was curtailed and the sharp increase in demand for labor by northern wartime industries opened opportunities for black migrants to the North. At the same time, conditions in agriculture deteriorated in many parts of the South when the boll weevil destroyed massive numbers of acres of cotton. The decline in agricultural prospects increased incentives to leave the South. After World War I immigration resumed for a few years, only to be cut off again in the early 1920s. By that time, an increasing number of African Americans had attained levels of schooling and resources needed to migrate and find a job. In addition, the friends and relatives who were already living in northern cities with established black communities could assist fellow African Americans in settling and in finding jobs. Although black migration to the North slowed during the Depression of the 1930s, it resumed and intensified during World War II and the decades that followed.

Education. Before the Civil War, public education was not generally available for the white population in the South. Moreover, after the war, the

South was a poor and backward region for many decades. The availability of educational resources consequently was lower in the South than in other regions of the country. Thus even white southerners had fewer schooling resources and lower levels of educational attainment than northern whites. But, within the South, the provision of school resources to blacks lagged far behind those available to whites in spite of the seeming requirement of the Fourteenth Amendment that states could not deny "equal protection of the law" to any person within their jurisdiction.

In the early years of the twentieth century the contributions of such philanthropists as Rockefeller and Peabody provided a significant boost to the advancement of public education for African Americans in the South. Beginning in 1913 the Julius Rosenwald Fund provided major funding, contributing an estimated 15 percent of the money spent on school construction for African Americans in the South over the period 1913–32. Nonetheless, at the end of the Rosenwald building program, the per pupil value of black school property was barely one-fifth as great as that of white schools, and other indicators of racial differences in school quality were similarly large.[7]

Yet despite the formidable barriers, the education of African Americans advanced—slowly before World War I and more rapidly after the war. In 1890 only half of black children ages 10–14 in the United States were enrolled in school, compared to 85 percent of white children. By 1910, 69 percent of black children ages 10–14 were enrolled in school, compared to 91 percent of white children.[8] The black–white enrollment gap nationwide partly reflected the fact that most African Americans lived in the South, and within the South they mainly lived in non-urban areas where enrollment rates lagged behind those in urban areas. In urban areas in the South 77 percent of black children were enrolled in school in 1910.[9] With increased urbanization within the South, migration out of the South, and increases in the provision of public schooling, particularly within the South, the school enrolment rates of African American youth increased such that by 1950 the difference in enrollment rates of African American and white children had become quite small.[10]

Enrollment rates, however, are only a rough indicator of actual education obtained, because attendance during the year and promotion rates differed widely by race. For example, in 1920, the average African American enrolled in school in the South attended school only 86 days compared to 113 days attended by southern whites and 147 days attended by enrolled students (of all races) outside the South.[11] Moreover, there were huge racial and regional gaps in other measures of school resources, such as class size and the qualifications and salaries of teachers.[12] However, provision of school resources (and likely of school quality) improved greatly for African Americans in the years after 1920, and provision of such resources increased faster for blacks than for whites. By 1953, the year before *Brown v. Board of Education* ruled that it was unconstitutional for schools to be segregated, the black–white differential in school resources had narrowed dramatically.[13]

The relative improvements in school resources for African American children eventually translated into relative increases in the years of schooling obtained by black adults and a narrowing of the racial gap in educational achievement. In 1920, approximately 45 percent of the black population ages 25–29 had completed fewer than five years of schooling while only 13 percent of whites had such low attainment (table 1-1); in the same year, only 6 percent of blacks had graduated from high school while 22 percent of whites had done so. Over the next few decades the gain in black educational attainment was remarkable. By 1940 the percentage of African Americans with fewer than five years of schooling had dropped to 27 percent; by 1960, that statistic had fallen to just 7 percent. Increasingly, black youth were attending and completing high school. By 1960, the proportion of 25–29-year-old blacks who had completed high school had increased to 39 percent, which still lagged behind the 64 percent graduation rate for whites. Only a small percentage of the population attended and graduated from college in the years before 1960. Nonetheless, the proportion of African Americans (ages 25–29) who had completed college increased from 1.2 percent in 1920 to 5.4 percent in 1960. White college completion rose from 4.5 percent to 12 percent over the same period.

Once African Americans gained access to schooling, their basic skills, as measured by literacy, increased rapidly. The illiterate percentage of 40-year-old black men declined from 75 percent in 1880 to 14 percent in 1940 and to 6 percent in 1960 (Smith 1984). Among 40-year-old white men, those percentages were 8 percent in 1880, 2 percent in 1940, and less than 1 percent in 1960. The narrowing of the gap in educational achievement is truly remarkable, and particularly so if one considers the roadblocks to African

TABLE 1-1
EDUCATIONAL ATTAINMENT BY RACE AT AGES 25–29, 1920–60

	% with less than 5 years of elementary school		% with 4 years of high school or more		% with 4 years of college or more	
	White	Black	White	Black	White	Black
1920	12.9	44.6	22.0	6.3	4.5	1.2
1940	3.4	27.0	41.2	12.3	6.4	1.6
1950	3.3	16.1	56.3	23.6	8.2	2.8
1960	2.2	7.2	63.7	38.6	11.8	5.4

SOURCE: *Digest of Educational Statistics 2006,* table 8 at http://nces.ed.gov/pubs2007/2007017.pdf

American progress created by the end of Reconstruction and the passage of the notorious *Plessy v. Ferguson* decision.

Racial Differences in Economic Status

As table 1-2 shows, black workers faced two serious disadvantages in terms of ability to earn an income, although the degree of disadvantage declined considerably between 1940 and 1960. One disadvantage was simply residence in the South, a low-wage, undeveloped region that offered even more limited opportunities for African Americans than for whites owing to racial segregation and prejudice. In 1940, about 73 percent of black workers, both male and female, lived in the South. As a result of mass migration, the percent of black workers living in the South declined to about 55 percent by 1960. Only about 24 percent of white workers lived in the South in 1940 and that percentage rose to 27 percent by 1960.

A second disadvantage was the relatively low level of education of African American workers. As discussed above, one of the tragedies of slavery was the withholding of education from slaves, a crime that was continued by the inadequate schooling opportunities available to southern African Americans after the Civil War. In 1940, 85 percent of African American male workers had not gone beyond the eighth grade in school; by 1960, the percentage of black male workers with eight or fewer years of schooling fell to 55 percent. In comparison, in 1940, 54 percent of white male workers

TABLE 1-2

LABOR FORCE PARTICIPATION AND CHARACTERISTICS
OF WORKERS BY RACE AND SEX, AGES 25–54

	Men				Women			
	Black		White		Black		White	
	1940	1960	1940	1960	1940	1960	1940	1960
% of Population in Labor Force	92.3	88.7	95.0	95.3	44.3	53.4	26.1	39.9
% Living in South	72.8	54.5	25.0	26.8	73.0	55.8	22.6	26.7
Years of School Completed (% Distribution)								
0–8	84.6	55.3	54.3	27.2	76.3	44.9	37.7	21.0
9–11	8.2	21.5	17.9	21.2	11.2	24.4	18.6	21.6
12 or More	7.2	23.2	27.8	51.6	12.4	30.7	43.7	57.4
12	3.9	14.7	15.2	28.3	6.7	19.1	25.0	36.8
13+	3.3	8.6	12.6	23.3	5.8	11.6	18.7	20.5

NOTE: Estimates are based on public use files of the 1940 and 1960 decennial censuses.

had eight or fewer years of schooling, and, by 1960, this percentage had dropped to 27 percent. Over the 1940–60 period, the percentage of black male workers who had completed high school increased from 7 percent to 23 percent. The percentage of white male workers who had completed high school also increased considerably over the same time period, from 28 percent to 52 percent. In percentage terms the gain in schooling made by black men exceeded the gain made by white men over this period, and consequently the racial gap in education narrowed.[14]

A major factor in narrowing the overall wage gap was the mass migration of African American men from the South to other regions of the country (see table 1-2). African Americans who moved to the North were able to take advantage of the higher pay and likely reduced racial barriers to employment. The exodus of African Americans also may have contributed to rising pay in the South, since it reduced the supply of labor to occupations and industries that had employed African Americans, putting upward pressure on wages. The wartime demand for labor also would have led to pressure to employ African American workers, even in the South. Thus, despite the barriers erected by Jim Crow, the black–white wage ratio rose 13 percentage points in the South between 1940 and 1960 among 25–54 year old men (from 42 percent to 55 percent). The gain outside the South for the same age group was not nearly as large—the wage ratio rose only from 63 percent to 72 percent.

It is difficult to determine the extent to which discriminatory barriers were a feature of the labor market outside the South in the early 1960s. The experience of African Americans in northern industry is difficult to generalize.[15] Many of the states outside the South had passed fair employment practices legislation. The passage of such legislation may reflect a lower level of discrimination outside the South, and such legislation in turn may have diminished prejudice in the workplace.

Both region of residence and educational attainment are bound to have an effect on wages. In table 1-3 we show the black–white earnings gap in 1940 and 1960. The data for men and women are shown separately. Three observations stand out: the large racial gap in earnings in 1940; the much larger gap in the South than outside the South; and the impressive narrowing of the gap between 1940 and 1960, even before the passage of the Civil Rights Act.

In 1940, the earliest year for which comprehensive national data are available from the decennial census, African American men (ages 25–54) earned a weekly wage that was only 45 percent as much as the average weekly wage of white men. The wage gap differed considerably by region. In 1940, the male black–white wage ratio was 42 percent in the South and 63 percent outside the South, a 21 percentage point difference. Between 1940 and 1960 black men experienced larger gains in earnings than white men, raising the black–white wage ratio from 45 percent to 61 percent nationwide. Some of the gain in relative earnings is attributable to the narrowing in the education gap between blacks and whites. But significant gains were made even among those with about the same education level. Thus among men with eight or fewer years of schooling, the black–white wage ratio rose from 48.5 percent to 67.3 percent.

Turning from men to women, it is important to note that both African American and white female workers had more education than male workers of the same race in both 1940 and 1960. The attainment of black women

TABLE 1-3
BLACK–WHITE WAGE RATIOS BY SEX,
REGION, AND EDUCATION, 1940 AND 1960

	Men			Women		
	Black–White wage ratios		Percentage point change	Black–White wage ratios		Percentage point change
	1940	1960	1940–60	1940	1960	1940–60
Total, Ages 25–54	44.9	61.2	16.3	40.5	66.4	25.9
By Region						
Non-South	63.0	71.7	8.7	59.1	78.0	18.9
South	42.1	55.0	12.9	34.9	58.8	23.9
By Years of School Completed						
0–8	48.5	67.3	18.8	44.7	61.4	16.7
12	55.6	68.1	12.5	53.2	75.6	22.4

NOTE: Wages of men are weekly wages. Wages of women are hourly wages. Wages calculated from the decennial censuses, Public Use Microdata Set (PUMS) 1940–1960. The wage sample is restricted to those who worked full-time and 26 weeks or more during the year.

workers increased sharply between 1940 and 1960 as the percentage with four years of high school or more rose from 12 to 31 percent. White women workers had completed more schooling than African American women in both 1940 and 1960. But the gains of white women were not as large as those of black women, and the differential in education narrowed.

Like African American men, African American women experienced large wage gains between 1940 and 1960. In 1940 the hourly earnings of black women were only 40.5 percent as much as those of white women.[16] By 1960 that wage ratio had increased to 66.4 percent—a much larger gain than that made by men. The same set of factors that influenced the relative earnings of black men also affected women—migration to the North, the narrowing of the gap in education, and the opening of opportunities that emerged as a consequence of World War II. It is notable, however, that the increase in the black–white wage ratio between 1940 and 1960 is larger among women than men within both the South and outside the South and is particularly large among those with twelve years of schooling. We explain the reason for the larger gain for black women in chapter 5. But here we note that black women moved ahead faster than white women because they had accumulated more work experience.

Although the black–white wage gap narrowed considerably between 1940 and 1960 among both men and women, a significant pay differential remained, particularly in the South. Within the South, open racial segregation was still a potent force in employment, restricting access to occupations and industries. Studies of the textile industry in the South, for example, have related the low rate of black employment in southern textiles to prohibitions on blacks and whites working indoors together (Donohue and Heckman 1991; Wright 1999).[17]

The seeds of change, however, had been sown by the early 1960s. Martin Luther King's stirring oratory brought more supporters to the cause of ending Jim Crow. The Freedom Riders and sit-ins in the South brought increased public attention to the wrongs of the Jim Crow South, and the savage beating of students in Birmingham ordered by the notorious Bull Connor and the murder of Medgar Evers further heightened the appreciation of the need for reforms in the South. As the civil rights movement gathered political support, momentum built for passage of a law that would enshrine equal civil rights for all. This movement culminated in the passage of the 1964 Civil Rights Act, which, among its other aspects, marked the first major effort of the federal government—endorsed by both Congress and the President—to address explicitly discrimination in employment.

2

Title VII of the 1964 Civil Rights Act: Labor Market Discrimination Becomes a Federal Crime

The Emancipation Proclamation promised freedom, and the Thirteenth, Fourteenth and Fifteenth Amendments to the Constitution granted citizenship and basic rights to the newly freed slaves. But in the decades that followed, the federal government made little effort to protect the African American population from violence and persecution in the South. Nor did the federal government take measures to prohibit labor market discrimination anywhere. Indeed, for much of the time the federal government facilitated racial discrimination in employment, education, and the provision of private and public services. The 1896 Supreme Court *Plessy v. Ferguson* decision legitimized racial segregation in all of these areas when it ruled that "separate but equal" provision of services did not violate the Constitution. President Woodrow Wilson ordered racial segregation of the federal civil service in 1913, a practice that remained entrenched even after it was barred in 1940 (Graham 1990; Wolgemuth 1959).

The dismantling of government-protected racial segregation was finally begun by President Truman in 1948 with his executive order to end segregation in the military; and in the same year, President Truman issued an executive order guaranteeing fair employment in the civil service. Then, in 1954, the Supreme Court declared in *Brown v. Board of Education of Topeka* that state-imposed segregation in public schools was a violation of the Fourteenth Amendment. But *Brown* applied only to the provision of public education and, in the southern states, segregation continued in the labor market as well as in other aspects of life.

We begin this chapter with a review of the federal government's efforts to combat employment discrimination in the two decades before passage of the 1964 Civil Rights Act. We then discuss the debate that raged over the formulation of the Act and summarize the most important provisions of Title VII of the Act as originally framed, passed, and signed into law by President Johnson in 1964. We then take up subsequent modifications to the law that significantly changed its interpretation and enforcement. Those modifications reflect a very different concept of illegal employment discrimination from that articulated by Congress in 1964. What was clearly intended to be a goal of *equality of opportunity for individuals* was transformed into a goal of *equality of results for groups* obtained by special preferences. The current debate over civil rights policy is closely tied to the sharp difference in philosophy underlying these two divergent goals.

Federal and State Government
Antidiscrimination Efforts before 1964

The conscience of America was not indifferent to the plight of African Americans and some efforts to combat discrimination in employment were undertaken by the federal and state governments starting in the 1940s. Some of those efforts introduced ideas and mechanisms that influenced the provisions of the Civil Rights Act as well as later developments.

The Roosevelt administration, generally on the side of liberal thinking in other matters, had nonetheless acquiesced to a segregated military. But in 1941, confronted with the threat of a massive March on Washington to protest racial discrimination in the armed forces, President Roosevelt issued Executive Order 8802 in which he said "there shall be no discrimination in the employment of workers in defense industries or Government because of race, creed, color, or national origin". He later established the Fair Employment Practices Committee (FEPC).[18] The FEPC was directed to address discrimination in federal employment, except for the military, as well as in defense contracting. This executive order, like its successors, focused exclusively on firms holding government contracts. There was no presumption that the Fourteenth Amendment, which prohibited states from denying African Americans due process in legal and political contexts, also applied to private employment contracts. But when it came to federal contractors, one could argue that it was legitimate for the executive branch, which was responsible for ensuring the performance of the work, to specify some of the conditions under which the work was carried out. The executive order affirmed the requirement for nondiscrimination in government contracts but, not being approved by Congress, lacked the authority to issue penalties for noncompliance. Unable to issue penalties, and as only a small, part-time committee, this first FEPC lacked the power to check labor market discrimination. However, it held hearings and listened to complaints, even venturing into the South, and ultimately made enough noise to stir resentment by those with vested interests in current labor practices (Graham 1990, 10–2).

This first FEPC was to be replaced in 1943 by a new Committee on Fair Employment Practice authorized by Roosevelt's Executive Order 9346. This executive order was more strongly worded than Executive Order 8802, exhorting all employers and unions to eliminate discrimination. Its jurisdiction was broadened to include all "war industries" and it was authorized to "conduct hearings and issue findings of fact." The new Committee on Fair Employment Practice was given significantly more resources than its predecessor in the form of a larger staff and field offices. But it too had no enforcement powers. Over the five-year period 1941–6, fourteen thousand registered complaints were received; about a third were successfully resolved, although in the South that proportion was much lower (Graham 1990, 12). Although the FEPC operated under the cover of a "war emergency," the ire of Congress was eventually aroused by what was regarded as yet another expansion of presidential power by the Roosevelt administration and of federal intrusion into the operations of private firms. Although defenders of the FEPC attempted to establish a permanent commission, Congress voted to defund the FEPC in 1946 (Graham 1990, 12–6).

Although it turned out to be only a temporary institution, the FEPC served as an inspiration for fair employment commissions at the state level. These had a better chance to combat labor-market discrimination because they were created by state legislation with the authority to establish enforcement agencies with punitive powers. Empowered by state law, they investigated complaints, held hearings, pursued reconciliations, and sometimes issued "cease and desist" orders backed by the threat of fines and imprisonment should the case go to court. New York State pioneered state-level enforcement of fair employment practices when it established the State Commission Against Discrimination in 1945.[19] The New York example was followed by New Jersey and several other states in the latter half of the 1940s.

By 1960, fourteen states, all outside the South, had enforceable antidiscrimination laws. Many more states passed such laws in the 1960s and 1970s. The procedures followed were roughly similar to those practiced today by the Equal Employment Opportunity Commission. For example, over its first two decades of operation in New York State, the Commission Against Discrimination received close to 9,000 complaints. About 20 percent were shown to have probable cause, 60 percent were dismissed for lack of sufficient substantiation, and the rest were subject to further investigation or resolved without any enforcement action. Only a tiny proportion (0.3 percent) ever went to a hearing and of those only a small proportion were subject to a cease-and-desist order (Graham 1990, 22). Similar outcomes are reported for the twelve states that adopted FEPCs over the period 1945 to 1961. It is difficult to evaluate the effectiveness of the FEPCs in improving the economic status of African Americans.[20] No southern state had such laws, and it was in the South where the problem of discrimination was most severe.

As these developments were taking place at the state level, antidiscrimination policy gained some momentum at the federal level in the late 1950s. During the Eisenhower administration Congress passed the Civil Rights Act of 1957, which established the Civil Rights Division in the Department of Justice and created the U.S. Commission on Civil Rights. The commission then, as now, was charged with collecting statistics and other information on discrimination. The first group of commissioners, a group of six prominent individuals, held hearings on voting rights in Montgomery, Alabama (despite interference from George Wallace, then a Circuit Court judge) on the implementation of *Brown v. Board of Education* in Nashville and on other issues in various cities. Although the commission was never given enforcement powers, their findings and recommendations were publicized and drew attention to the issue of civil rights.

Small steps to put more effort into the policing of federal contractors began in the Eisenhower administration with the appointment of Richard Nixon, then vice president, to chair the President's Committee on Government Contracts.[21] The committee gathered statistics on the racial composition of workers employed by federal contractors in various cities. Some pressure was brought to bear on contractors to hire more black workers. The committee considered a policy resembling the affirmative action practices later adopted by the Office of Federal Contract Compliance that require contractors to supply statistics on the minority composition of their employees with timetables for addressing underrepresentation. However, this policy emerged only at the end of the Eisenhower administration and was not implemented. A decade later, a similar policy was introduced as the Philadelphia Plan in President Nixon's administration.

John Kennedy became president during a time when the issue of civil rights was becoming increasingly explosive. Following in the footsteps of his predecessors, he addressed the issue by signing Executive Order 10925 and set up a new President's Committee on Equal Employment Opportunity (PCEEO) to be chaired by Vice President Lyndon Johnson. The Kennedy order is noteworthy mainly for the mention of the term "affirmative action," which had not been used before in an executive order.[22] However, the context in which it was used merely reaffirmed the goal of requiring non-discriminatory behavior by federal contractors: "The contractor will not discriminate against any employee or applicant for employment because of race, creed, color or national origin. . . . The contractor will take affirmative action to ensure that applicants are employed, and employees are treated during employment without regard to their race, creed, color or national origin." Nothing is said about requiring special preferences, goals, or timetables.

Kennedy's PCEEO was more effective than its predecessors. Aggressive pressure from the National Association for the Advancement of Colored People (NAACP) and the specter of huge defense contracts going to firms with low minority hiring propelled Kennedy to appoint highly energetic staff to direct the activities of his PCEEO. As we discuss below, the PCEEO had an important role in the desegregation of Lockheed Corporation, which set the stage for further desegregation of the labor market.

Developments That Shaped the Civil Rights Act and Title VII

Against the backdrop of dramatic, often bloody confrontation between segregationists and advocates of racial equality in the South, the growing civil rights movement put increasing pressure on the federal government to enact antidiscrimination legislation applicable to all firms, not just defense firms, and to provide the resources needed for enforcement. Contributing to the momentum was the increasing support for ending discrimination in the general public.

In addition, a number of events motivated Congress to pass a civil rights act and shaped key provisions. We discuss three of those events: the Lockheed desegregation agreement; growing demands for racial employment quotas to redress a perceived decline in the relative economic status of African American workers; and an Illinois judgment against Motorola, involving a job screening test that led to the rejection of an African American job applicant.

Desegregation at Lockheed. In 1961, Lockheed Aircraft was awarded an unprecedented billion-dollar government contract to build the giant new C-141 jet transport at its plant in Marietta, Georgia. Although this plant was built with federal funds, on federally owned land adjacent to an airbase, Lockheed maintained racially segregated washrooms and eating places at the plant. Moreover, African Americans made up only about 4 percent of the Lockheed workforce. Most of the black workers were in unskilled jobs; the few semiskilled black workers belonged to a segregated African American local of the International Association of Machinists (IAM). The white local of the IAM controlled the apprenticeship program and excluded African Americans.

However, three days after the award was announced, President Kennedy issued his executive order establishing his President's Committee on Equal Employment Opportunity. Perceiving an opportunity, Herbert Hill, the labor secretary of the NAACP, confronted the Kennedy administration with a demand to end the blatantly discriminatory practices at Lockheed's Marietta plant. The demand had particular force because Hill had extracted a public pledge from the new administration to cancel the contract of any employer who refused to comply with the administration's ban on discrimination.

The response of Lockheed was striking and unexpected. Despite its location in the Deep South, the company quickly dismantled its segregated facilities and dealt with other disparate treatments of African Americans. The Lockheed capitulation raised the real possibility that a federal law prohibiting labor market discrimination everywhere in the United States would be accepted by businesses in the South in the face of large and enforceable penalties for discriminatory practices (Graham 1990, chapter 2).

A Rise in Black Unemployment and a Call for Quotas. In the early 1960s the civil rights movement became impatient with a perceived lack of progress in raising the relative economic status of African Americans. In the summer of 1963, Secretary of Labor Willard Wirtz (a labor economist by training) testified before congressional committees that black unemployment had been rising significantly relative to that of whites and the Census Bureau released a report indicating that the relative income of blacks had stagnated since World War II. These reports fueled assertions by activists that African Americans were losing ground and in turn tended to shift the rhetoric of the debate away from the demand for equal non-discriminatory treatment and towards a call for compensatory measures. A drumbeat for quotas began to be heard from some quarters of the civil rights movement (Graham 1990, chapter 4). As we show below the vision of quotas caused a defensive reaction among southern and some northern legislators that directly affected the provisions written into Title VII of the Civil Rights Act.

Motorola and the Battle against Testing of Applicants for Jobs. A third development involved a 1964 decision by a hearing examiner of the Illinois Fair Employment Practices Commission (FEPC), who ordered that Motorola discontinue its use of a general ability test to screen its applicants for jobs that involved checking for flaws in television sets. Motorola had rejected an African American job applicant based on his poor performance on the test. However, the reason for the disallowance of the test was not that it was a "pretext" for prejudice against blacks on the part of Motorola's management, but that the test was unfair to "culturally deprived and disadvantaged groups" because it did not take into account "inequalities and differences in environment." This ruling by a state FEPC led to a huge outcry throughout the business community. *New York Times* columnist Arthur Crock asserted that if Title VII of the 1964 Civil Rights Act, then under consideration in Congress, were to be interpreted in this way, it would mean that "a Federal bureaucracy would be legislated into senior partner-ship with private business with the power to dictate the standards by which employers reach their judgments of the capabilities of applicants for jobs, and the quality of performance after employment whenever the issue of 'discrimination' is raised" (Graham 1990, 149-50). There was quick action on the Senate floor. Texas Senator John Tower drafted an amendment to Title VII that would negate the Motorola judgment. The amendment passed in the Senate and was incorporated in Title VII.

The 1964 Civil Rights Act and Title VII

After a lengthy and acrimonious debate, Congress passed the Civil Rights Act of 1964, the first comprehensive civil rights bill since the post–Civil War era. The eleven titles of the Act barred discrimination based on race, color, religion, or national origin in many areas including voting require-ments, use of motels, restaurants, and other public accommodations. One of its key sections is Title VII, which is concerned with discrimination in the labor market.

Title VII prohibits discrimination in all aspects of employment and compensation based on race, color, religion, national origin, or sex.[23] It established the Equal Employment Opportunity Commission (EEOC) to investigate complaints of discrimination. The discrimination outlawed by the original Title VII is what has come to be called "disparate treatment" discrimination—intentional discrimination against minorities and women in the labor market. Thus a firm that denies equal treatment in hiring, promotion, or pay to an equally qualified worker, solely on the basis of his or her race or sex, can be found guilty of a felony and subject to fines and other punishment.

One important provision of Title VII addressed the concern raised by the Motorola case that an agency created by the Act would have the power to oversee employee requirements set by employers for private firms even if they were not found to be discriminating. Title VII of the 1964 Act states explicitly that hiring and promotion decisions based on ability tests cannot be considered discriminatory if the intent and use of the test are to deter-mine the appropriate skill level of applicants and not to deny employment to a worker because of race or sex. In the words of the Act:

> . . . nor shall it be an unlawful employment practice for an employer to give and to act upon the results of any professionally developed ability test provided that such test, its administration or action upon the results is not designed, intended or used to discriminate because of race, color, religion, sex or national origin. (Title VII, section 703h)

The objective of Title VII was to eliminate barriers to protected groups created by the prejudices of firms. The Act would not insulate protected groups from the give-and-take of labor market forces but only from discriminatory behavior of employers. Although job tests may not be perfect predictors of performance, it would have been a significant change from accepted practice to regulate how employers screen potential employees so long as screening tests are not being used with the intent of discriminating against protected groups.

A second important provision of Title VII addresses the concern that the Act would be used to sanction quotas to achieve racial balance. The Act explicitly rules out the use of racial or gender preferences:

> Nothing contained in this title shall be interpreted to require any employer . . . to grant preferential treatment to any individual or to any group because of the race, color, religion, sex or national origin . . . on account of imbalance which may exist with respect to the total number or percentage of persons of any race, color, religion, sex or national origin employed by an employer . . . in comparison with the total number or percentage of persons of such race, color, religion, sex or national origin in any community, State, section or other area, or in the available work force in any community, State, section or other area. (Title VII, Section 103)

But as we discuss in detail below, despite the explicit provision that Title VII should not be used to impose quotas on firms that are not discriminating against individual African Americans, the executive orders that followed the 1964 Act authorized federal contract compliance agencies to require firms to pursue proportional representation of minority groups.

One issue that was bound to be raised about the Civil Rights Act was its constitutionality. Since no one had ever argued that the Thirteenth or Fourteenth Amendments barred individuals from practicing segregation on their own property, how could Congress now impose this behavior on individuals? In the famous case *Heart of Atlanta Motel v. United States*, the Supreme Court ruled that the 1964 Act was a reasonable use of the Commerce Clause by Congress to regulate interstate commerce because the motel was in an area close to major interstate highways that catered extensively to interstate traffic. They argued that by refusing to provide accommodations for black individuals the hotel was interfering with interstate commerce. Although *Heart of Atlanta* only challenged Title VII indirectly, it is doubtful that any constitutional challenge to Title VII would have been successful.[24]

Changes in Antidiscrimination Law and Policy after 1964

In the years after the passage of the 1964 Civil Rights Act, actions of Congress and the judiciary changed the scope of the law and altered the meaning of unlawful discrimination. The agencies charged with implementing Title VII also adopted policies in conflict with the original aim of the Act. We discuss several of the significant court cases in later chapters. Here we note a few overarching developments, including the new requirement that employers make "reasonable accommodation" for the religious practices of their employees and the important change in the concept of discrimination to include "disparate impact."

Legislative Changes Made by Congress. The 1972 amendments to Title VII expanded the scope of the law, extending coverage to state and local governments, to educational institutions, and to firms with as few as fifteen workers. The powers of the EEOC were significantly strengthened, as it was given the authority to initiate litigation, a power formerly reserved to the Department of Justice. The law also added the requirement that employers "reasonably accommodate" employees' and applicants' religious practices unless doing so would impose an undue hardship on an employer's business.

Other amendments also added older workers (age 40 and older), disabled workers, and pregnant women to the list of groups specifically protected by Title VII. In 1991, amendments were passed that increased the potential monetary awards that individuals could claim as victims of discrimination by adding compensatory damages for pain and suffering to the standard claim of lost wages and attorney fees. The 1991 amendments also restored the requirement to protect workers from the disparate impact of employment practices, a development that followed from the *Griggs v. Duke Power* decision (see below) when *Griggs* appeared to be subject to judicial challenge as in *Ward's Cove Packing Company v. Atonio.*[25]

The most recent legislative change occurred in 2009 when Congress passed the Lilly Ledbetter Fair Pay Act which had the effect of significantly increasing the period—originally only six months—during which a worker could bring a charge of disparate treatment discrimination under Title VII. This Act was named for Lilly Ledbetter, who had waited many years to bring forward a complaint of discriminatory pay for her work as a manager for Goodyear.

Changes Made by the Court: *Griggs* v. *Duke Power* and the Birth of Disparate Impact Discrimination. In 1971, the Supreme Court unanimously ruled in *Griggs v. Duke Power* that Congress did not intend to limit its regulation of testing to situations in which the firm was using testing as a tool to weed out minority applicants. The Court ruled that the 1964 Act in fact requires that tests with a disparate impact on a protected group, unless they can be shown to be significantly correlated with job performance, are prohibited even in the absence of discriminatory intent. In the words of Chief Justice Warren Burger:

> The objective of Congress in the enactment of Title VII is plain from the language of the statute. It was to achieve equality of employment opportunities and remove barriers that have operated in the past to favor an identifiable group of white employees over other employees. Under the Act, practices, procedures or tests neutral on their face, and even neutral in terms of intent, cannot be maintained if they operate to "freeze" the status of discriminatory employment practices.[26]

Burger misstated Congress' aim with Title VII: the goal of Title VII was clearly and simply to keep prejudiced employers from discriminating against protected groups in the labor market. It was not to require firms to lower their standards to accommodate protected groups or to provide preferential treatment to compensate for past deprivation. As discussed above, the Illinois FEPC ruling that Motorola had discriminated by rejecting a black applicant who could not pass a job test because he suffered from educational deficiencies had raised concerns that Title VII would create exactly the situation created by the Motorola case. Those concerns were strongly put to rest by the framers of Title VII.[27] Thus the Supreme Court in *Griggs* appears to have substituted its own judgment as to the plain intention of Congress in framing Title VII.

Why did the Burger Court so radically transform the concept of illegal discrimination? Undoubtedly it was influenced by the fact that Duke Power was a southern firm that had been rigidly segregated by race in the period before the passage of the 1964 Act. Black workers had been restricted to jobs in the labor department—the lowest classification—and were barred from applying for transfer to higher occupational categories.[28] However, Duke Power had dismantled its old system of racial classification on the day that Title VII went into effect (July 2, 1965). It was largely on these grounds that the district court that first heard the case ruled against the plaintiffs. At issue, however, were the firm's educational requirements for advancement. In 1955, Duke Power had instituted a requirement that all new employees hold a high school diploma or equivalent (such as a GED), except for those who were applying for the labor department, for which there was no educational requirement. The high school policy also applied to any incumbent employee who wished to be considered for advancement out of the labor department or the watchman position to higher-level departments. The company claimed that the policy was instituted because its business was becoming more complex and that some employees were unable to adjust to the increasingly more complicated work requirements.

The requirement of a high school diploma or equivalent in 1955 could not have been imposed as a ploy to hide discriminatory intent, since only whites were affected. The company's racial policy barred any black worker from applying for any job other than that in the labor department or from transferring out of that department. It was only after Title VII went into effect a decade later that the opportunity for advancement was made available to black workers. In 1966, one black worker with a high school education was promoted out of labor and into coal handling, and two years later he was promoted to utility handler. Two more black workers fulfilled the high school requirement and were also advanced within the next few years, and a fourth black worker later became eligible for advancement by completing a course deemed equivalent to a high school education.[29]

It would have been difficult to base a charge of discrimination on the high school requirement, since it was originally implemented nine years before passage of Title VII when only whites were affected. In fact, the plaintiffs downplayed the high school requirement. Instead, the focus was on a change in promotion and transfer policies that allowed employees on the payroll prior to 1965 who did not have a high school education or its equivalent to qualify for transfers and promotions by passing two tests (the Wonderlic general intelligence test and the Bennett mechanical test) with scores equivalent to those of the average high school graduate. Moreover, the company at that time instituted a program open to all employees regardless of race that would pay for two-thirds of the cost of education for those who needed to improve their skills to qualify for the higher-level jobs. One might think that by providing the alternative, the company was expanding options for advancement since it was still possible to advance by attaining a high school diploma or equivalent and, as noted, four of the 16 plaintiffs had done so by the time of the Fourth Circuit trial in 1970.

In view of these facts, the Fourth Circuit, with only one dissenting vote, denied relief to the group of four plaintiffs hired after 1965, holding that they had not received disparate treatment, as they were given the same options for advancement as similarly situated white workers.[30] But the problem was more complex for the six workers who were discriminatorily hired into the labor department without any option to transfer out before 1965. For this group the Fourth Circuit held the test requirement invalid because there is no way they could be given equal treatment with similarly situated whites, because some white workers hired at the same time in the past (before 1955) were able to advance without either a high school diploma or passing a test. At that earlier time seniority and supervisors' judgments were the route to advancement for whites. Differences in seniority between blacks and whites hired before 1965 further complicated the issue.

The Fourth Circuit based its ruling on Title VII and concluded that Duke Power could legitimately administer its tests to all applicants even if a larger proportion of whites than of blacks passed the test. The key issue was that blacks and whites were to be offered the same options to take the same test, which would be administered and scored in the same way and met the conditions of Title VII (section 703) that the tests be professionally developed. The circuit court appears to have handled the difficult issues in a fair and nuanced manner.

The Burger Court by-passed Title VII and ruled that tests producing different outcomes for black and white workers were to be regarded as invalid unless they could be proven to be relevant to a particular job. The emphasis on job-relatedness was influenced by EEOC guidelines, which give the EEOC's interpretation of the intent of Title VII. Quoting from Justice Burger's opinion:

> The Equal Employment Opportunity Commission, having enforcement responsibility, has issued guidelines interpreting section 703(h) to permit only the use of job-related tests. The administrative interpretation of the Act by the enforcing agency is entitled to great deference.[31]

Burger had no evidence that the educational requirements were not relevant to performance on the jobs in question. The only evidence asserted by Burger as to the invalid nature of the test was that white workers who were promoted when there were no educational qualifications were found to do well. But no survey was shown in evidence, so we do not know how many did not do well. In fact, the stated reason given by the company for instituting qualifications was that they found that their workers were not up to the changing skill needs of the jobs in the higher-level occupations. The court did not address the fact that Duke Power first introduced an educational requirement when only whites were involved. It would have been foolish for the company to do so if they had no reason for believing that additional education would improve the ability of workers to do the more difficult tasks in the non-labor departments. The alternative to objective criteria for promotion is supervisors' opinions about workers. That could hardly be a viable alternative for a company with a history of segregation.

As we shall show in chapter 4, the concept of disparate impact as the basis of disparate impact discrimination has spread far beyond simple job tests for the selection of applicants. It has been applied to a long list of job-related screening requirements that a prudent employer might use without any discriminatory intent; yet such requirements could have an adverse impact on one or more of the protected groups. If the EEOC rules that the screening device is not a "business necessity," then it cannot be used, even if it is a useful and efficient business practice.

In retrospect it is ironic that the reasonable decision of the Fourth Circuit was ever appealed by the plaintiffs to the Burger Court. If it had not been appealed the concept of disparate impact and disparate impact discrimination might not have been adopted as quickly or decisively. Hugh Davis Graham, in his volume on the civil rights era (1990), reveals that John Pemberton, deputy general counsel for the EEOC, had drafted a letter of advice to Jack Greenberg, who was the chief lawyer for the *Griggs* plaintiffs, advising him *not* to appeal the Fourth Circuit decision to the Supreme Court and instead accept the limited victory. He argued that the tests given by Duke Power (the Wonderlic and Otis) were widely used in industrial and commercial employment, were selected by a professional psychologist who had testified at trial on their behalf, and were precisely the kinds of tests Congress had sought to protect when adopting the Tower amendment (guaranteeing the firm's right to set hiring standards without discriminatory intent). He concluded that "the record presents a most unappealing situation for finding tests unlawful" (Graham 1990, 385).[32]

The Implementation of Affirmative Action and Quotas. The other major departure from the words and spirit of Title VII as passed in 1964 has been the utilization of quotas by the Office of Federal Contract Compliance (OFCC) to achieve affirmative action goals. Quotas have been imposed on federal contractors even in the absence of any direct evidence of discrimination. At issue is the policy of detecting discrimination simply by comparing the statistical representation of protected groups in the employer's workforce with that in the relevant population and the use of hiring quotas to correct deviations from the desired proportional representation of minorities and women. Hiring quotas, referred to as "goals and timetables," are the major tool used by the OFCC to implement its antidiscrimination efforts. As noted, this practice was specifically prohibited by language inserted by the Congress in Title VII.

From affirmative action to quotas. The shift to quotas began in the Johnson administration with Johnson's 1965 Executive Order 11246, which restated the requirements on contractors not to discriminate against minorities in employment.[33] However, Johnson did go further than his predecessors in structuring the monitoring of contracts by designating the Department of Labor as the lead agency for coordinating contract compliance.[34] Willard Wirtz, as secretary of labor, established the OFCC within the Department of Labor to monitor the contracting activities carried out by the various individual government agencies involved in awarding contracts.

The eager new staff of the OFCC attempted to increase minority employment by requiring pre-award scrutiny of bids for contracts. Under the OFCC's plan, all contracts had to be cleared by the OFCC on non-discrimination grounds in advance of any contract award. This plan was frustrated when the Department of Defense, the largest procuring agency, protested the "crippling effects" of delays waiting for OFCC approval (Graham 1990, chapter 11).

One early OFCC success occurred in the construction labor market. After failed attempts to desegregate construction labor markets in St. Louis, San Francisco, and Cleveland, the OFCC plan to oversee contracts eventually did take root in the construction industry in 1967 as the first Philadelphia Plan.[35] That plan marked the beginning of the transition of affirmative action from a tool for preventing acts of discrimination to a tool for assuring a certain representation of a protected group. To achieve this success, the OFCC, along with the EEOC and the U.S. Attorney's Office, joined a plan to integrate the construction trades union developed by Philadelphia's Federal Executive Board (FEB). (The FEB was an interagency board established to coordinate the activities of the various federal agencies operating in Philadelphia and other localities.) Under the plan, the contract compliance committee would provide no numerical target goals or other specific instructions to the bidders to avoid the appearance of setting illegal quotas. Instead, all bidders for a federal contract would be required to submit, as part of their bid, detailed "manning tables" specifying the number of minority workers they pledged to hire in the various trades employed. Bids were tendered before the submissions were reviewed by the committee. The low bidders were only regarded as apparent low bidders until their affirmative action plans were approved.

But the Philadelphia Plan ran afoul of Elmer Staats, the U.S. comptroller general, who declared the plan illegal because it invalidated federal bidding rules. Staats argued that it was unjust to withhold a contract from a low and otherwise acceptable bidder because that bidder failed to have an acceptable affirmative action program when the bidders were not told in advance what an acceptable program would be. By this argument, Staats demonstrated that he at least recognized the difference between monitoring federal contractors for specific acts of discrimination—the purpose of Title VII—and monitoring them to promote specific hiring quotas prohibited by Title VII.

Richard Nixon was elected president only several days before the Staats ruling that the Philadelphia Plan was illegal.[36] Early in the Nixon administration, the new Secretary of Labor George Shultz, with the support of President Nixon, set about strengthening the OFCC and reviving the Philadelphia Plan. He created the new position of assistant secretary of labor for wage and labor standards and appointed Arthur Fletcher to fill the post. The OFCC then became a major office reporting to Fletcher. In the spring of 1969 Fletcher directed the redesign of the Philadelphia Plan.

To avoid the fate of the earlier plans, Fletcher drafted a plan that would both satisfy Comptroller Staats' concern that contractors could not be subject to post-award negotiations of affirmative action plans in the absence of clear guidelines to bidders and avoid specifying numerical guidelines that would violate Title VII's ban on racial quotas. In the redesign, Fletcher countered Staats' objection by openly setting forth guidelines. Fletcher announced the new plan at a ceremony in Philadelphia in June of 1969. The plan was to be put into effect in all major U.S. cities and would establish "specific goals or standards for percentages of minority employees" in construction.[37] In an effort to avoid the appearance of proportional representation, the OFCC assessed local conditions and developed target ranges for minority employment, rather than a single numerical target, for each major construction trade. Five-year targets were set with increasing minority percentages. For example, only 0.51 percent of plumbers and pipefitters in Philadelphia were found to be minorities by the OFCC, which then set a goal of increasing that percentage to a range of 5–8 percent in 1970 and then to 22–26 percent by 1973. These target ranges were devised as a rough average of the 30 percent who were African American in the Philadelphia area and the 12 percent African American representation in the skilled construction trades in 1969 (Graham 1990). Although those goals look like quotas, Fletcher maintained that they were not because contractors would be given a chance to show they had made a good-faith effort to increase the numbers of minorities on their payrolls.

Opposition seeking to derail the Philadelphia Plan came from many quarters—unions, members of Congress, conservative organizations. The most serious threats to the plan pointed to its open requirement to maintain racial balance as a violation of Title VII. The U.S. Department of Labor's Solicitor Laurence Silberman defended the policy with several arguments: that the Fifth Amendment's due process clause that justified desegregation of the public schools in the District of Columbia could be applied in a parallel way to justify the Philadelphia Plan;[38] that the Department of Labor had found blatant and ongoing discrimination in the construction trades and the plan was justified as a way to redress past discrimination; that Congress had shown tacit approval by defeating an amendment proposed by Senator John Tower to make Title VII the exclusive remedy for discrimination; and that the Supreme Court upheld a college's decision to reject a bid for a contract that did not meet affirmative action goals (*Weiner v. Cuyahoga College*) and, in another instance, supported a move by the Department of Justice to dismiss a case against the Philadelphia Plan.[39]

Thus the original justification for an approach using quotas and affirmative action seems to have been that it would force openly prejudiced employers (including certain labor unions) to consider African American workers on the basis of their productivity. Presumably that judgment was made under the assumption that exclusive reliance on the use of Title VII's prohibition of disparate treatment discrimination against individual minority workers would not be enough to change behavior in the federal contractor segment of the economy.

The Philadelphia Plan applied only to the construction trades, but it was soon followed by a broader plan that would apply to all contractors. In early 1970 Secretary Shultz issued Order No. 4, which applied to all contractors with more than 50 employees holding contracts of $50,000 or more. Since Order No. 4 covered 250,000 contractors and 20 million employees in diverse industries, it was impossible to set specific numerical targets for each employer. Instead the order required all contractors to file an affirmative action report within 120 days of signing a contract. Each contractor was charged with analyzing his workforce to identify any underutilization of protected groups—usually meaning a departure from proportional representation relative to the local population. Any imbalance was to be corrected with numerically stated goals and timetables. Failure to do so could result in loss of the contract. In 1970 Order No. 4 was first applied in a number of large cities and eventually was expanded to all government contractors.

It was not until the late 1970s, however, that an agency was given the power and staff to scrutinize the behavior of all federal contractors. In 1978, President Carter consolidated all enforcement operations relating to government contractors in one office within the Labor Department and renamed it the Office of Federal Contract Compliance Programs (OFCCP). The new OFCCP had the organization and authority for universal application of the Philadelphia Plan and took its lead from Order No. 4.

In its own 2003 statement of Executive Order 11246, the OFCCP wrote that:

> Regulations at 41 CFR 60-2.11(b) define underutilization as having fewer minorities and women in a particular job group than reasonably would be expected by their availability. When determining availability of women and minorities, contractors must consider, among other factors, the percent that qualified minorities and women make of the employment in the area in which the contractor can be expected to recruit.[40]

This OFCCP document asserts that goals and timetables are not "quotas," but represent what would emerge if the contractor simply made a "good faith" effort to close the gap between his estimates of availability and his actual hiring of minorities and women.

In this regard it is interesting to note that Laurence Silberman, after observing goals and timetables in action under the Philadelphia Plan for a few years, concluded that they had turned into quotas:

> We wished to create a generalized, firm but gentle pressure to balance the residue of discrimination . . . I now realize that the distinction we saw between goals and timetables on the one hand, and unconstitutional quotas on the other, was not valid (Silberman 1977).

George Shultz, who as secretary of labor was one of the architects of the Philadelphia Plan, also expressed his disenchantment in a 1995 *Washington Post* interview: "It's certainly outlived its usefulness. At the time we needed a 2 by 4 to end discrimination, but the time for the 2 by 4 is gone." He was a supporter of California's referendum to ban most affirmative action policies at the state level. "The problem is," Shultz said, "that affirmative action that you genuinely want to see . . . turns very easily into a quota." Although support for affirmative action as practiced at the OFCCP may be fading, it has not disappeared. Arthur Fletcher, who worked with Shultz to design the Philadelphia Plan, has remained a supporter. In the same *Washington Post* article, Fletcher justified affirmative action as "about ensuring that evils are not committed in the future, not paying for past sins" (Harris and Merida 1995).

In sum, the clear intent of Title VII as originally passed by Congress was to redress intentional discrimination by employers and coworkers—and to do so without interfering with legitimate business practices such as tests to screen potential employees and to do so without imposing quotas on employers. However, the combined effects of decisions taken by Congress and by the courts have brought about disparate impact measures that interfere with reasonable business practices and have burdened employers with de facto quotas. These developments run directly counter to the intent of Congress when it passed Title VII.

PART II

Implementing Antidiscrimination Policy:
The Office of Federal Contract
Compliance Programs and the Equal
Employment Opportunity Commission

3

The Office of Federal Contract Compliance Programs and Antidiscrimination Enforcement

Over the past four decades an elaborate structure has developed for enforcing antidiscrimination policies. During the 1964 debate over the Civil Rights Act, Senator Absalom Robertson of Virginia asked his Senate colleagues, "What is meant by discrimination?" As we noted in chapter 2, the original language of Title VII offered an answer to this question by saying that if an employer's workforce did not mirror local demographics, absent any discriminatory intent, this would not constitute illegal discrimination.[41] Yet over the years Congress, the courts, and the enforcement agencies have increasingly assumed discriminatory intent when a workforce does not provide for proportional representation of minorities and women. The population protected by Title VII has also been expanded to include older workers, pregnant women, and the disabled. In this study, we examine only enforcement efforts relating to discrimination based on race, color, national origin, sex and religion—the original focus of Title VII.

In this chapter, we describe and evaluate the enforcement activities of the Office of Federal Contract Compliance Programs (OFCCP); in the next chapter, we do the same for the Equal Employment Opportunity Commission (EEOC). In both chapters, we focus on the concepts of discrimination that guide them and the implementation procedures that they utilize. We examine the logic of the concepts and enforcement procedures as stated in agency manuals and other guidelines used by both the officials who carry out enforcement and the employers affected by the policies. We also examine available evidence from litigation, including court cases in which firms challenged the agencies' findings of a violation. The court cases help to reveal how the concepts and enforcement procedures are applied in practice.

The OFCCP is part of the U.S. Department of Labor (DOL), and its central office is located in Washington, D.C. Its mission is to monitor all aspects of employment in firms with federal government contracts to insure that they do not discriminate in the hiring, promotion, and pay of their workers. It is not a large agency by Washington standards when measured in terms of budgeted dollars or number of employees. The OFCCP budget for fiscal year 2009 is estimated to have been about $83 million, barely an asterisk in the $2.7 trillion federal budget; the number of full-time equivalent employees is around 700. However, in spite of its small size, the OFCCP has great power to regulate the employment practices of the firms within its domain, which together employ at least one-quarter of the civilian labor force.

Procedures and Concepts for Determining Discriminatory Behavior

The OFCCP focuses its enforcement efforts on three aspects of discrimination in employment: (1) determining if the representation of protected groups in each firm's workforce is at the requisite level as determined by the OFCCP's "goals and timetables" rules; (2) determining if the pattern of wage rates or other forms of compensation reflect discrimination between protected groups and other workers; and (3) determining if certain hiring practices of the contractor (e.g., skill requirements) discriminate against protected workers.

Instrumental to the OFCCP's work is the EEO-1 report, which all contractors and subcontractors with fifty or more employees are required to submit to the OFCCP each year. Each must list the number of its employees by nine broad occupational categories with breakdowns by minority status and sex for each occupation in its EEO-1 report. (The occupational categories are: officials and managers; professionals; technicians; sales workers; office and clerical workers; craft workers; operatives; laborers; service workers.) The EEO-1s provide the data that OFCCP uses to target individual contractors for compliance reviews.[42]

The enforcement process also requires that all firms awarded federal contracts fill out an Affirmative Action Plan (AAP). This document instructs the contractor to compute the "availability" of qualified minorities and women in the firm's "labor market area" and to compare the composition of the available pool with the composition of the firm's current employees. The contractor is also required to specify on the AAP affirmative actions it will take to close existing gaps between actual and required employment of protected groups—its employment goal—and the timetable for getting there. The AAP must be kept on file and updated every year to track the progress in closing gaps and to distinguish when the size of the gap has changed because of changes in labor market area conditions. The AAPs are submitted to the OFCCP only if and when the contractor is selected for a Compliance Review (CR). But if selected, the current maintenance of the AAP becomes an important requirement on which the contractor will be judged.

Once selected for a CR, a contractor is subject to an extensive examination to determine if any OFCCP regulations have been violated. Finally, if a contractor is found to be noncompliant, it must either make the changes dictated by the OFCCP or contest the OFCCP's decision in the administrative courts of the DOL.

To evaluate this process we first take up the methods used to target particular contractors for a CR. We then consider the procedures and concepts used by the OFCCP to evaluate the performance of the individual contractor who is selected for a CR.

Most OFCCP actions against federal contractors are initiated by the OFCCP. Seldom does an individual worker at a firm with a federal contract bring a complaint of discrimination to the OFCCP. When an individual complaint is brought to the OFCCP the case is usually referred to the EEOC, which routinely deals with individual complaints of discrimination. However, armed with the power to revoke a federal contract, the OFCCP can bring serious pressure on a contractor to comply with its findings, even though not a single worker in the firm may have complained of discrimination.

Targeting Contractors for Compliance Review

Only about 5 percent of contractors are subject to a CR in any year. On its website, the OFCCP states that it selects contractors for review based on "multiple information sources and analytical procedures" including the use of a "mathematical model that ranks federal contractor establishments based on an indicator of potential workplace discrimination."[43] However, when the OFCCP's targeting procedures have been challenged in court, it has been revealed that about 15 percent of its targeting is based on subjective factors that it considers indicative of likely discriminatory behavior. For example, it has emerged in court cases that the OFCCP considers banks particularly likely to discriminate against women. As we later show, in some of those rare instances when the OFCCP has been challenged in court, it has faced the charge that its targeting procedures in general, even those based only on quantitative objective data, violate constitutional guarantees against illegal search and seizure.

Unfortunately, the actual details of the selection procedures used by OFCCP are not made available to the general public. The information we provide below was drawn from material provided in a handbook developed by the Equal Employment Advisory Council (EEAC), a private organization that guides firms in meeting their Title VII obligations and developed this handbook specifically to help federal contractors anticipate and minimize the likelihood that they would be subject to a CR.[44]

The EEAC handbook suggests that the OFCCP uses the following procedures to target firms for CRs. First, the OFCCP groups the EEO-1 forms of all the contractors by Metropolitan Statistical Area (MSA). This grouping places each contractor in its labor market area, a relevant factor in evaluating a firm's performance in attaining affirmative action goals. The agency then groups the EEO-1 forms within each MSA by size of establishment. (As we suggest below, size of contractor may be related to OFCCP objectives other than reducing discrimination.) Within each category of MSA and size of establishment, OFCCP computes an index value for each contractor that combines the percentage of minorities in the contractor's total workforce; the percentage that is female; a measure of the difference in occupational distribution between all minorities and whites; and, finally, a measure of the difference in occupational distribution between males and females.

The overall index value tends to be greater the greater the percentages of minorities and females employed and the more favorable their occupational distributions. Those indices are then averaged over all contractors in a size class within an MSA. The selection of a contractor for a CR is based on the ratio of the individual contractor's index to that of the average federal contractor in the MSA—the greater the ratio, the less likely to be targeted for a CR. Contractor firms within a size class that rank low on the index are more likely to be flagged for a CR.

Nowhere does this procedure consider the availability of qualified minorities or women in the contractor's recruitment area. The only factor guiding the OFCCP's judgment of a firm's discriminatory behavior is the contractor's position relative to that of other contractors within the same size group, industry, and MSA. The use of this set of criteria can have odd effects. It will penalize contractors whose utilization of protected categories of workers is below average when compared to other federal contractors in its MSA, even in situations where the same contractor would be above average when compared to all (contractor and non-contractor) firms in the MSA.

Thus, it is possible to have a situation in which all contractor firms within an MSA and industry-size category employ a higher percentage of protected-worker groups than their percentage of qualified workers in the entire MSA. Yet some of those federal contractors will still be selected for a CR. It is also possible that, in some MSAs, most of the contractors may actually be discriminating by the affirmative action standard but that the OFCCP will miss some of them because they have above-average indices when compared only to the other federal contractors in their MSA.

The OFCCP does not provide any explanation for its relative index procedure in any documents available to the public. Its silence on this point may indicate that the procedures for targeting are, in fact, more ad hoc than systematic. It is difficult to find employment data by MSA to estimate the actual percent of qualified minorities in the relevant market for contractors. Use of a procedure that is independent of this information allows OFCCP to employ a method for flagging contractors for a CR with a scientific veneer but that in fact does not provide a good measure of the extent to which contractors are falling short of meeting their affirmative action goals.

The targeting methods just described are inefficient because they make no allowance for *differences across MSAs* in the degree to which federal contractors are falling short of affirmative action goals. Their method can only capture relative differences among contractors *within each MSA*, regardless of how the contractors are doing relative to the actual representations of protected groups within the MSA. Moreover, it should be stressed that the concept of discrimination the OFCCP is attempting to measure is flawed, however measured, because it defines guilt without any direct evidence of discriminatory behavior by a firm. As we discussed in chapter 2, Title VII, as originally passed by Congress, specifically prohibited such criteria.[45]

Given the stated goals of their targeting procedure, one might assume that, in practice, the OFCCP aims to increase the representation of minorities and women in contractor firms by putting pressure on firms that show the indicators of discrimination stated in their targeting formula. However, direct observation of which contractors are targeted for CRs is now impossible, because researchers no longer have access to data on workers in federal contractor firms that also identify the subset of firms subject to a compliance review. Prior to 1980, EEO reports on contractors selected for CRs were available to researchers; a number of studies made use of them to analyze the effects of affirmative action.

Two studies used EEO-1 reports to examine the determinants of selection for a CR among federal contractors. In the first study, James Heckman and Kenneth Wolpin (1976) examined a sample of federal contractor establishments in the Chicago area in 1972. They found no systematic pattern of targeting based on factors such as size of firm or proportion of minorities. Selection appeared to be random. The period covered, however, was in the start-up phase of contract compliance and predated the consolidation of scattered agency activity into the OFCCP.

Jonathan Leonard (1985) studied the incidence of CRs among federal contractors during the period 1974–9, a period of consolidation and growth in the OFCCP. His analysis was based on a national sample of EEO-1 records matched with records of CRs conducted by the U.S. Department of Defense (DOD). DOD is by far the largest contracting agency, and the sample included almost 8,000 establishments in all regions of the country and operating in a broad array of industries. Leonard's surprising finding was that the likelihood of a review was not merely random—it was more nearly perverse. Contractor establishments with no black male employees were much less likely to be reviewed than those with 20 percent or more. None of the 74 establishments with no female employees were ever reviewed. Yet 28 percent of the establishments with 70 percent or more females were reviewed. These unexpected patterns persisted even after multivariate analysis was conducted to control for the possible effects of correlation with region and other factors.

More easily explained is Leonard's finding that large firms were the most likely to be reviewed. Only 3 percent of establishments with fewer than 50 workers were reviewed. This proportion rose to more than 40 percent for establishments with 500–2000 employees and then declined somewhat among the very largest contractors. A focus on large establishments allows an agency to take advantage of economies of scale. In addition, large establishments are likely to maintain better records and employ human resources staffs that make the process easier. Leonard also found that firms employing a large proportion of nonclerical white-collar workers were more likely to be reviewed.

Given the firms that were actually selected by the OFCCP for review, what can be inferred about the OFCCP's targeting procedures? Leonard concluded from his evidence that the OFCCP's version of affirmative action is inconsistent with a program whose primary purpose is to fight the most blatant forms of discrimination and instead can be more usefully thought of as a program to redistribute jobs and earnings to minorities and females[46] (Leonard 1985, 383–4). He supports this interpretation of the results by pointing out that a key characteristic of the establishments reviewed is that they tend to be large employers of white-collar, nonclerical workers. Such workers, he reasons, have had considerable specific training (inelastic supply) and therefore can pressure employers for pay raises. No evidence on earnings increases is given, however. We suspect that the more important reason may be a political one. Large, prominent firms are the ones most easily hit with large settlements, drawing favorable attention to the OFCCP and helping to enhance its own budget. Unfortunately, it is no longer possible for researchers to obtain the data on individual contractors to determine the current practices of the OFCCP. We do not know therefore whether the outcome of targeting is similar to that inferred by Leonard about the OFCCP's practices in the 1970s. It suffices to say that a cloud hangs over the OFCCP's antidiscrimination activities, given at least its past targeting procedures that, in combination with its "goals and timetables" affirmative action approach, clearly violate the original intention of Title VII.

Outcomes of Compliance Reviews

Once the OFCCP has selected a contractor for a CR, its evaluation takes place in two stages. First a mid-level official prepares a desk audit to identify potential concerns. Then, second, a compliance officer (CO) visits the contractor to determine whether any concerns identified in the desk audit rise to the level of a violation of OFCCP rules. If the CO finds the contractor to be in violation of Title VII, he enters into negotiations with the contractor to forge a Conciliation Agreement (CA) that would avoid court adjudication. In a CA, which is essentially a settlement, a firm agrees to OFCCP's demands for changes in its hiring, promotion, and dismissal procedures, or payment of compensation to any employees against whom the firm was found to have discriminated.

Table 3-1 shows data on the number and outcomes of CRs for 1991–2002 and on just the number of CRs for 2004–9.[47] As the table shows, over the period 1991–2009 the annual number of compliance reviews has fluctuated between about 3,500 and 6,500. The percent found to have violations declined from 65–75 percent in the 1990s to a low of 39 percent in 2002. In most years about 97 percent of violations have been settled with a CA.

Only a tiny number of compliance reviews ever reach open adjudication in administrative court, with the consequence that there are few occasions where the actual interpretations used by the COs can be observed and evaluated. For example, in fiscal year (FY) 2000 the OFCCP carried out 4,162 CRs, which covered a subset of federal contractors employing around 1.5 million employees (out of a total of about 35 million in all federal contractor firms). Of the 4,162, 2,320 firms (56 percent of those reviewed) were found to be in some violation of the OFCCP standards. Of these, 1,694 signed a CA without much opposition and another 434 also agreed to a CA but only after the OFCCP filed an Administrative Complaint; 180 who did not agree to a CA but the OFCCP had not yet brought an Administrative Complaint; and 12 (merely 6 percent) that did not agree to a CA and against which the OFCCP brought an Administrative Complaint. Thus in FY 2000, only about 6 percent of complaints against firms were addressed openly in an administrative court that would allow scrutiny of OFCCP procedures. No wonder it is difficult for firms to know how to ensure that they will not be found in violation of Title VII.

TABLE 3-1
OFFICE OF FEDERAL CONTRACT COMPLIANCE PROGRAMS (OFCCP) PERFORMANCE AND PROGRAM STATISTICS

	1991	1992	1994	1996	1998	2000	2002	2004	2006	2009
Compliance Reviews										
Completed Reviews (#)	5,379	4,953	4,179	3,476	3,774	4,162	4,135	6,529	3,975	3,917
With Violations (#)	4,167	3,720	3,124	2,311	2,349	2,320	1,632	N.A.	N.A.	N.A.
Resolved with CA	2,799	2,547	2,262	1,682	1,691	1,694	910	N.A.	N.A.	N.A.
Resolved with NOCD	1,334	1,151	784	603	588	434	671	N.A.	N.A.	N.A.
Not Resolved NACF	0	0	48	11	53	180	45	N.A.	N.A.	N.A.
Not Resolved ACF	34	22	30	15	17	12	6	N.A.	N.A.	N.A.
Employment in Reviewed Firms (000)	2,229	2,150	1,771	1,413	1,377	1,482	1,449	N.A.	N.A.	N.A.
OFCCP Staff										
Total Staff (FTE)	874	841	783	702	754	811	730	749	670	N.A.
Compliance Officers	481	444	394	377	407	453	411	N.A.	N.A.	N.A.

CA = Conciliation Agreement.
NOCD = Resolved with CA after administrative complaint filed.
NACF = Not resolved with CA; no administrative complaint filed.
ACF = Administrative complaint filed.
FTE = full-time equivalent.
Administrative Complaint = Adminimstrative judicial proceedings to enforce violations of a compliance review not resolved with a CA.
N.A. = Not available.
SOURCE: U.S. Department of Labor, Employment Standards Administration, Office of Federal Contract Compliance Programs; Washington, D.C.

Effect of OFCCP on Discrimination:
Evidence from Compliance Reviews

We now turn to a critical examination of the process that the OFCCP examiners use during the CRs. Consideration of these processes shows that concepts used by the OFCCP during CRs are unlikely to attain their stated objectives. The process undertaken during the CR to detect discrimination has three components: whether the contractor is in compliance levels with the OFCCP's affirmative action goals and timetables; whether the contractor engages in discrimination in wage determination; and whether the contractor engages in disparate impact discrimination.

Affirmative Action Goals and Timetables. In its completion of a firm's EEO-1 report, managers must apply concepts and produce empirical estimates that almost certainly cannot be carried out with any degree of accuracy. When conducting a CR, the CO will evaluate *all* contractor estimates for "reasonableness," which calls for considerable tolerance for subjective interpretation by the CO. For example, on the key issue of estimating the contractor's available pool of qualified minorities and women, the manual first directs the examiner to evaluate the contractor's estimate of its "immediate labor market area." To quote from the manual used by the OFCCP:

> In evaluating the contractor's determination of its immediate labor market area, the examiner should consider the following: *the immediate labor market area is that geographic area from which employees may reasonably commute to the contractor's establishment. It may include one or more contiguous cities, counties or Metropolitan Statistical Area* (emphasis added).[48]

But what constitutes a "reasonable commute"? For example, a small federal contractor located in the middle of Long Island, New York may be able to recruit most of its low- and semi-skilled labor force from an area fairly close to its plant. Its workforce would then reflect the national origin and racial composition in that area and would be skewed toward mostly white non-Hispanic workers if the composition of the neighborhood were mostly white non-Hispanic. If the contractor is selected for a CR, the CO may insist that the "immediate labor market area" should also include Queens, the

Bronx, and Brooklyn, boroughs of New York City with a higher proportion of minorities. The CO may believe that the commute involved would be "reasonable." But will the CO consider that the firm likely would need to pay higher wages to induce workers from Queens, the Bronx, and Brooklyn to commute and the effect this would have on business costs?

The OFCCP manual does not address such issues, so we cannot predict how the CO would rule in this situation. Nor were we able to find a court case involving the issue of determining the relevant labor market area. However, what is certain is that the CO has the power to decide what constitutes a reasonable commute, while the contractor would incur large legal costs and risk losing a government contract if it were to challenge a decision requiring recruitment from more distant areas.

The CO also faces the thorny task of evaluating the contractor's estimate of the percentage of workers in the establishment's market who are "qualified" minorities and women. (Recall that this is the same statistic the OFCCP avoids estimating when it carries out its own targeting analysis.) These availability estimates are a key element in deciding whether a contractor is meeting its affirmative action goals and timetables. On this subject the manual offers the following instructions to contractors and COs:

> In assessing these factors contractors should use the best data available. While the most recent decennial Census data normally provides the best detailed information on requisite skills, they become increasingly outdated the more years it has been since the Census was conducted. Also the Decennial Census shows only persons employed in a given occupation at the time the Census was conducted, rather than those with the skills to be employed in that occupation. Therefore the following adjustments to decennial census data are normally needed.[49]

The manual then goes on to explain how even after the contractor obtained the Decennial Census and adjusted the numbers to the relevant year (how this can be done is not explained in the manual apart from the direction that some state employment services keep updated census numbers), the contractor must still further adjust the representation of minorities in the census occupational categories because past and present discrimination has held down their occupational attainments. The manual does not explain how to adjust for this past and present discrimination factor, either.

It is very unlikely that any but the largest contractors would actually be able to carry out any of these data analyses. And even if the requisite census data could be obtained, census data alone cannot determine whether those who self-report themselves as in a particular occupation in fact meet the skill requirements of an individual contractor. Thus, not only does the OFCCP ask contractors to conduct statistical estimation that they may not be equipped to do, but the validity of the basic data is itself highly uncertain. One court case (discussed below) revealed how the enforcement of numerical targets can lead to the imposition of significant costs on contractors without any obvious benefits.

Wage Discrimination. In sharp contrast to the extensive and prolix instructions the OFCCP manual gives its examiners for detecting violations of affirmative action goals and timetables, on the subject of illegal pay differentials it is concise. In the words of the manual:

> The term "Compensation Discrimination" encompasses at least four distinct concepts:
>
> (a) Disparate treatment in pay in relationship to the established range for a job whether at entry or later; e.g. Blacks with backgrounds similar to whites on the legitimate factors considered for initial salary are hired at lower pay.
>
> (b) Discrimination in the opportunity to earn a salary such as discrimination in placement, job assignments, promotion opportunities. The opportunity to work overtime
>
> (c) Equal Pay Act discrimination; i.e. sex based differentials in wages paid for "substantially equal" work
>
> (d) Comparable Worth discrimination (paying different wages for "jobs of 'equal value'"[50]

The manual goes on to say that OFCCP's authority reaches "at least as far" as the first three types of compensation. It says that the '. . .courts have generally been hostile to cases based on comparable worth theory.'"

Note that the official manual does not prohibit the CO from applying the comparable worth concept of discrimination, so it is difficult to tell if the OFCCP is actually utilizing this approach. A complicating factor is that the only official manual available was last updated in 1998.

However, the OFCCP sometimes alters its official procedures through changes that are made public only in the Code of Federal Regulations. This happened in June 2006, when the OFCCP announced a new standard for wage discrimination called "systemic compensation discrimination."[51] This type of wage discrimination occurs when "similarly situated" individuals are paid different wages or compensation. And what determines whether two employees are similarly situated? The OFCCP manual offers this guidance to COs:

> Employees are similarly situated under these standards: if they are similar with respect to the work they perform, their responsibility level, and the skills and qualifications involved in their positions. To determine whether employees are similarly situated under these standards, actual facts regarding employees' work activities, responsibility, and skills and qualifications are determinative.[52]

Thus OFCCP eliminates the term "comparable worth" from its list of types of wage discrimination and substitutes systemic compensation discrimination and defines it exactly as comparable worth is defined—jobs of comparable value or worth as determined by the CO. This kind of language could allow a CO carrying out a CR to determine that a librarian with a college education is equivalent (or superior) to a master electrician and is being discriminated against because she is being paid less.

Disparate Impact Discrimination. Compliance officers, as well as officials called Equal Opportunity Specialists (EOSs), are directed to examine the data on hiring patterns in the contractor's Affirmative Action Plan and to scrutinize screening devices and job requirements for adverse impacts on minorities and women to determine if they constitute disparate impact discrimination.

For example, the CO is told that if flow data on applicants and hires show that minorities and women have lower hire rates (ratios of hires to applicants), then he is to determine if they are illegal by measuring the *statistical* significance of the differential. However, no mention is made of the *practical* significance of the differential, so that the CR rules are loaded against large contractors who typically will have small standard errors to weigh against the observed differentials: a low ratio of hires to applicants in a small firm is less likely to be statistically significant than the same ratio in a large firm. Moreover, the manual gives no guidance on whether the differential in hiring rates was for one month or persisted over a lengthy period, or whether the evidence on stocks of minorities and women employed suggest the flow differentials are misleading as a guide to discriminatory intent. The treatment of situations involving disparate impact discrimination is also very brief and sketchy. The manual simply tells the CO that if he finds that the contractor's job requirements—level of formal education, scores on job tests, etc.—are having an adverse impact on minorities or women, then he is to determine whether they are necessary for the contractor to successfully conduct his business.

The unfortunate and capricious effects of these guidelines are evident in the few CRs that lead to adjudication in court.

Effect of OFCCP on Discrimination: Evidence from Court Cases

As mentioned above, very few CRs ever reach the courtroom where the actual situation is resolved in light of the actual criteria used by OFCCP for determining discrimination. Of those cases that do reach a court, some drag on for years (even a decade), and some appear to involve some of the most trivial issues. But they serve to provide a useful window on how the OFCCP examiners apply the concepts and measures specified by their compliance manual. The cases reviewed from the 1970s forward are available on the DOL's website (www.oalj.dol.gov). We concern ourselves only with the cases involving discrimination against minorities and women (covered by President Johnson's Executive Order 11246), and have selected those that provide sufficient published detail about the facts of the case, the arguments of the OFCCP and the contractor, and the reasoning of the judge in reaching a decision.

The cases reviewed may not be representative of the average behavior of COs, the bulk of whose work never reaches open court challenges. The behavior of the COs revealed in open court does add to our understanding about the manner in which procedures and concepts are enforced: in particular, the court records reveal the ad hoc nature of much of OFCCP's enforcement procedures. In particular, it shows that the OFCCP targets establishments and imposes affirmative action goals and timetables that have no basis in congressional law and are clearly contestable in court.

Court cases to be adjudicated are almost all held in the DOL's administrative law system. The administrative law judges hear only those cases involving complaints against the DOL for the administration of its various programs, including OFCCP actions to check labor market discrimination. The decisions of the administrative law judges can, in principle, be appealed to the federal circuit system; however, we could not find such a case (although in one case the plaintiff made a charge that OFCCP's targeting procedure violated the Constitution). For all practical purposes, the few cases that are appealed are resolved in the DOL's administrative law system. The importance of this restriction on the scope of judicial review is that the constitutional validity of any of the OFCCP's various procedures, such as affirmative action with goals and timetables, is never questioned (EEOC 2006b). Any change in these fundamental provisions must await action from Congress or the president.

The cases we discuss fall into three categories: discrimination in hiring; disputes over targeting procedures; and one case involving the application of required employment levels based on estimates of availability of qualified protected workers.

Cases Involving Discrimination in Hiring. Several cases involve allegations of favoring white men in hiring decisions. These cases all concerned the use of statistical data on hire rates that show differentials in favor of white males over very short time periods but not over longer periods, and in very narrowly defined occupational categories but not in more aggregated data, constituting evidence of illegal discrimination. The OFCCP has brought cases where the time period involved was only three months (*OFCCP v. Greenwood Mills*, ALJ case #84-ofc-39) or where the aggregation of the data was very narrow (*OFCCP v. Interstate Brands Corp.*, ALJ case #1997-ofc-0006).

OFCCP conduct is also questionable in hiring cases based solely on flows of new hires while ignoring data on the stock of minorities employed in the same occupational category for which OFCCP is charging discrimination. (*OFCCP v. Cambridge Wire Inc.*, ALJ case #94-ofc-12). In one case it became clear that the contractor was hiring relatively few minorities because minority workers in his plant were complaining that the entry-level workers were almost totally African American. And even though minorities were being promoted without discrimination to higher-skill jobs, in one instance the OFCCP pursued the case for five years (*OFCCP v. Burlington Industries*, ALJ case #90-ofc-103).

Another type of hiring case involves the employment of women for strenuous work situations: e.g., oil rigger (*OFCCP v. Loffland Brothers Co.*, ALJ case #75-1) and manufacturer of metal products for airplanes (*OFCCP v. Lawrence Aviation*, ALJ case # 87-ofc-11 and *OFCCP v. Jacksonville Shipyards*, ALJ case # 89-ofc-1). In these cases contractors have argued that men are hired more often than women because they better handle physical demands—e.g., heavy lifting—and their retention rates are higher than women's. Such arguments are uniformly rejected by the OFCCP and most of the time by the administrative courts as well. It is difficult to judge the validity of these findings. Not enough detail is given to determine if the firms were guilty of statistical discrimination against female applicants, which is a widely recognized violation of the Title VII of the Civil Rights Act, or whether they screened for strength with tests that are legal in many hiring situations.

Cases Concerning Targeting Procedures. A number of cases have been brought by contractors in which the OFCCP is accused of using subjective elements in deciding which contractors to target, such as claims that "banks tend to discriminate against women." In some court cases, documents have been produced showing OFCCP admitting to making CR selections based on these subjective considerations. Such practices have been challenged by contractors in at least two cases as a violation of Fourth Amendment protections against unreasonable searches and seizures (*OFCCP v. Beverly Enterprises*, ALJ case # 1999-ofc-11 and *OFCCP v. Bank of America*, ALJ case #97-ofc-16). The lower administrative court judges tend to favor the contractors but they are almost always overruled by higher administrative courts.

A Case Involving Availability and Affirmative Action. If any single case illustrates the negative effects that affirmative action might have on the efficiency of resource allocation in the economy it is the *Jacor* case (*OFCCP v. Jacor Inc.*, ALJ case #95-ofc-17). Jacor had entered into a CA in 1991 in which it agreed to make good-faith efforts to hire more minorities and women. Jacor Inc. is a heavy highway construction subcontractor, specializing in crack filling, seal coating, bituminous damp-proofing, and membrane waterproofing. It employs laborers, bricklayers, and cement masons.

But in 1992 Jacor was informed by the CO that it had failed to carry out the specific affirmative action techniques to which it had agreed. Even though Jacor sent recruitment letters to the special sources required, the letters were found by the CO to be inadequate because, although they invited minorities and women to apply, they did not mention specific job opportunities. Jacor then agreed before a judge to undertake more letter writing and also to visit special recruitment sites.

Finally, only the female gap remained; the letter writing and site visits had closed the minority gap. In 1995, five years after the case was brought, Jacor was back in court. But this time, even though Jacor still could not find a single female employee, after finding that Jacor had never stopped making a good-faith effort, the judge threw out OFCCP's case: "It is recommended that the case against Jacor, for violation of a CA entered into in 1991, be dismissed."

Cases Involving Disparate Impact Discrimination. We found only one case, *OFCCP v. U.S. Airways* (ALJ case #88-ofc-17), in which a CO applied the concept of disparate impact discrimination. This case involved an airline that gave language and other tests to new minority applicants for the job of pilot. The CO charged the airline with disparate impact discrimination because it did not require the same level of screening of an "incumbent" pilot who was recalled after a six-year furlough and who had already taken the tests. The judge ruled against the OFCCP in this case.

New Rules, New Complexities

On December 9, 2011 the OFCCP published a Notice of Proposed Rulemaking (NPRM) in the *Federal Register* that would fundamentally alter the affirmative action requirements in section 503 of the Rehabilitation Act of 1973, the legislation that added individuals with disabilities to those entitled to affirmative action.[53] The proposed rule would, for the first time, set a goal that 7 percent of every job group in a contractor's work force be persons with disabilities. In addition, the NPRM advises that the OFCCP is considering a subgoal of 2 percent for individuals with severe disabilities (e.g., totally blind, totally deaf, complete paralysis, severe intellectual disability). At present, under the Americans with Disabilities Act of 1990 (ADA) federal contractors, as are all employers, are required to follow nondiscriminatory practices regarding the disabled. Among other requirements employers must provide reasonable accommodations to the known physical and mental limitations of otherwise qualified job applicants and employees. But the current regulations do not specify any numerical goals for persons with disabilities.

Why then is the current administration calling for these new numerical regulations? In an OFCCP press release, OFCCP Director Patricia Shiu argues that "for nearly 40 years, the rules have said that contractors need to make a 'good faith' effort to recruit and hire people with disabilities. Clearly, that's not working."[54] What the OFCCP ignores, however, are the high potential costs to firms of hiring and "reasonably accommodating" disabled individuals, particularly those with physical disabilities and little education. A number of studies have found that the passage of the ADA in 1990 was followed by a decline in the employment of disabled individuals.[55] The decline could be attributed to the increased costs of reasonable accommodation in view of the uncertainty that a handicapped worker in fact would be able to perform a given job adequately and the increased difficulty of firing a disabled worker under the new ADA restrictions.

The introduction of numerical targets for disabled workers, as proposed by the OFCCP, would add a new layer of complexity to the operation of the already hard-pressed agency. No good data on workers with all the different types and degrees of handicaps are available for the geographical areas in which federal contractors operate. Yet employers who wish to work under a federal contract would likely have to invent some procedure, as would the OFCCP compliance officers.

Conclusion

Whether one examines the professed and actual methods used by OFCCP to target contractors for compliance reviews, the concepts they use to

determine violations of those contractors selected, or their actual interpretations in the tiny number of court cases in which they are challenged,
we can only conclude that the OFCCP is doing little, if anything, to
reduce employment discrimination. When the evidence of this chapter is
combined with the direct statistical analysis we present in chapter 6, this
conclusion appears inescapable

4

The Equal Employment
Opportunity Commission and
Antidiscrimination Enforcement

Unlike the Office of Federal Contract Compliance Programs (OFCCP), which was established by executive order, the Equal Employment Opportunity Commission (EEOC) was established by Title VII of the Civil Rights Act of 1964 as an independent agency to monitor compliance with its provisions. Subsequent legislation, including the 1967 Age Discrimination in Employment Act, the 1990 Disabilities Act, and the 1972 and 1991 Civil Rights Acts, expanded the number of groups protected by its provisions as well as the scope of its enforcement powers. Over the years the concept of discrimination was altered and enlarged to include accommodation of religious practices, disparate impact as well as disparate treatment discrimination, and a wider view of the definition of sexual harassment. The jurisdiction of the EEOC is much broader than that of the OFCCP: its authority encompasses most workers, not only those working for federal contractors. So, in spite of its small size (its 2010 budget was estimated to be only $367 million), the EEOC wields considerable power over the terms of employment and the conduct of business in the United States.

Originally the powers of the EEOC as delimited by Title VII did not include the power to bring suit itself (legal cases were to be referred to the Department of Justice) but included only the power to respond to complaints brought by individuals. (The emphasis on individuals' complaints is in sharp contrast to the OFCCP, which, as we noted in the previous chapter, almost always initiates actions against firms based on its own analysis of the firm's minority and gender composition, without the complaint of any individual employee.) However, in 1972 Congress amended Title VII and granted litigation authority to the EEOC, an authority to be shared with the Department of Justice for two years. That authority included the power to pursue "pattern or practice" suits and generally made it easier for the commissioners to file Commissioner's Charges.[56] The commission soon began to investigate prominent firms.

Still, most enforcement activities of the EEOC are initiated by individuals who believe they have been victims of discrimination and come to the EEOC with a sworn "charge" of discrimination against an employer. Yet, at times, the EEOC has exerted its power and brought actions against firms believed to be guilty of a "pattern or practice" of discrimination. Those actions are often based on a finding that a firm employs a disproportionately low proportion of women or minorities, even when no individual worker has filed a complaint. Sometimes a charge starting with a complaint of discrimination or harassment brought by only a few employees is taken as evidence of firm-wide discrimination or harassment and is broadened into a "pattern or practice" case.

The prevalence of systemic investigations in the overall activities of the EEOC has ebbed and flowed depending on the interest and philosophy of the various EEOC commissioners. Under the stewardship of Chairwoman Eleanor Holmes Norton in the late 1970s, "pattern or practice" investigations were prominent, but after Clarence Thomas took over as chairman in the 1982, such investigations were de-emphasized. More recently, the EEOC appears to have reinstated systemic investigation as a priority.[57] We discuss the systemic initiatives of the EEOC below. But we start our overall review with a detailed analysis of EEOC activities dealing with complaints of individuals, which still form the bulk of its work.

We first survey the volume of charges brought to the EEOC by individuals over the past few decades, by type of charge, and then focus on the resolution of these charges. In the next and major section, we examine the evidence on the EEOC's implementation of antidiscrimination law with respect to the most significant types of discrimination: disparate treatment discrimination, "reasonable accommodation" and religious discrimination, disparate impact discrimination, sexual harassment, and racial harassment. We then discuss recent EEOC initiatives to address systemic discrimination by using Commissioner's Charges.

Our analysis of antidiscrimination policy as pursued at the EEOC is based on information in the EEOC's compliance manual and other EEOC guidelines as well as on information from court cases in which the EEOC was involved. Records of some of the suits brought to trial by the EEOC (or with EEOC support) are publicly available and often present considerable information about the details of charges, the rebuttals by the defending employer, and the opinions of the judges. Unfortunately for our analysis, most cases that are accepted and brought by the EEOC end with a settlement or a "consent decree" in which the accused employer agrees to pay damages but denies any discriminatory behavior. The complete records of those cases are not publicly available. However, the agreement is often prominently advertised by the EEOC as though it was a victory for the EEOC, particularly if the size of the settlement is large. Although the EEOC description does not typically give many details apart from the size of the settlement, and it generally avoids mention of the defense that the employer offered, prominent cases are frequently covered in the press, which can present the employer's version of events. When available, we draw upon press accounts

We also draw on findings from prominent cases involving discrimination that are brought to trial with the direct participation or support of the EEOC. Such case histories give unique insights into the nature of employer activities that are viewed as discriminatory by the EEOC and punished by the courts. However, many of these cases involve changes in the definition of discrimination that were made subsequent to the passage of Title VII of the 1964 Civil Rights Act. These revisionist definitions of discrimination, a prime example of which is disparate impact, are at odds with the expressed intent of the Act as we have discussed above (chapter 2). Their contribution to any meaningful reduction in discrimination is therefore controversial. If the judgments or settlements merely cause a firm to employ workers that they do not believe are qualified, no lasting effect on the hiring, pay or promotion of women or minorities will be achieved. We argue that many judgments fit this conclusion.

Charges against Employers Brought by Individuals

We consider the types of charges brought by individuals under Title VII and their resolution by the EEOC.

Trends in Types of Discrimination Claimed and Resolution of Charges. In 2010 the Commission received about 73,000 charges of discrimination brought by individuals against private employers under Title VII (table 4-1). The most frequent allegations, as in prior years, concerned race (49 percent of the total) and sex (40 percent). Charges based on national origin and religion have been growing since 1992 but are still relatively small (16 percent of the total for national origin; 5 percent for religion). Charges dealing with sexual harassment have declined since their peak in 1998 but still account for 16 percent of the total. They are often filed by those who are simultaneously charging sex discrimination in employment. Discrimination charges made under the Pregnancy Discrimination Act now make up 8 percent of total charges. Pregnancy discrimination may also be combined with other charges filed by women.

Table 4-2 focuses on the outcomes of individual charges. The first line (as in table 4-1) shows the trend in the number of people filing charges each year under Title VII. The next line gives the total number of charges resolved during the year. "Resolutions" can include charges held over from prior years as well as charges transferred from Fair Employment Practice Agencies (state and local agencies with roles analogous to that of the EEOC). The following lines present those resolutions by type of outcome. "Settlements" and "Withdrawal with Benefits" refer to instances where the EEOC has negotiated a settlement between the employer and charging party without any court proceeding. Settlements in total—with or without withdrawal—fluctuate as a percentage of total resolutions. From a low of 7.3 percent in 1998 they rose to 17.4 percent of the resolutions in 2007 before slipping to 13.8 percent in 2010.

After undertaking an investigation, the EEOC determines whether a charge of discrimination has "No Reasonable Cause"—by far the most frequent outcome—or has a "Reasonable Cause." If no convincing evidence has been presented to support the validity of the charge, the charging party is issued a "right to sue" by the EEOC, meaning simply that the person is entitled to bring a private case to court. When the evidence of discrimination is deemed to have some degree of validity ("Reasonable Cause"), the EEOC holds conciliation discussions in an effort to reach a settlement between the employer and the charging employee. Sometimes conciliation is successful and the charge process ends with agreement on a settlement

TABLE 4-1

EEOC CHARGES RECEIVED UNDER TITLE VII BY TYPE OF DISCRIMINATION CLAIMED

	1992		1995		1998		2001		2004		2007		2008		2009		2010	
Total Charges	55,391		62,159		58,124		59,631		58,328		61,159		69,064		68,710		73,058	
	$N=$	$\%^{1)}$	$N=$	$\%^{1)}$	$N=$	$\%^{1)}$	$N=$	$\%^{1)}$	$N=$	$\%^{1)}$	$N=$	$\%^{1)}$	$N=$	$\%^{1)}$	$N=$	$\%^{1)}$	$N=$	$\%^{1)}$
Race	29,548	53.3	29,986	48.2	28,820	49.6	28,912	48.5	27,696	47.5	30,510	49.9	33,937	49.1	33,579	48.9	35,890	49.1
Sex	21,796	39.3	26,181	42.1	24,454	42.1	25,140	42.2	24,249	41.6	24,826	40.6	28,372	41.1	28,028	40.8	29,029	39.7
Pregnancy	3,385	6.1	4,191	6.7	4,219	7.3	4,287	7.2	4,887	8.4	5,587	9.1	6,285	9.1	6,196	9.0	6,119	8.4
Sexual Harassment	10,532	19.0	15,549	25.0	15,618	26.9	15,475	26.0	13,136	22.5	12,510	20.5	13,867	20.1	12,696	18.5	11,717	16.0
National Origin	7,434	13.4	7,035	11.3	6,778	11.7	8,025	13.5	8,361	14.3	9,396	15.4	10,601	15.3	11,134	16.2	11,304	15.5
Religion	1,388	2.5	1,581	2.5	1,786	3.1	2,127	3.6	2,466	4.2	2,880	4.7	3,273	4.7	3,386	4.9	3,790	5.2

1) The number of total charges reflects the number of individual charges of discrimination filed. Because individuals may file charges claiming multiple types of discrimination, sum of filings under separate types of discrimination often sums to more than the total.
SOURCE: The U.S. Equal Employment Opportunity Commission (EEOC). Data are compiled by the Office of Research, Information, and Planning from EEOC's Charge Data System—quarterly reconciled Data Summary Reports, and the national data base.

TABLE 4-2
EEOC Charges and Resolutions under Title VII

	1992		1998		2001		2004		2007		2008		2009		2010	
Charges Filed	55,391		58,124		59,631		58,328		61,159		69,064		68,710		73,058	
Resolutions[1]	47,014		60,888		54,549		51,355		53,631		58,104		64,304		77,644	
Type:	N=	%	N=	%	N=	%	N=	%	N=	%	N=	%	N=	%	N=	%
Settlements	3,261	6.9	2,657	4.4	4,493	8.2	5,365	10.4	6,423	12.0	6,416	11.0	6,292	9.8	7,024	9.0
Withdrawals w/Benefit	3,031	6.4	1,767	2.9	2,201	4.0	2,151	4.2	2,907	5.4	3,427	5.9	3,542	5.5	3,746	4.8
Administrative Closures	10,645	22.6	16,114	26.5	10,766	19.7	8,563	16.7	9,475	17.7	9,827	16.9	12,104	18.8	12,790	16.5
No Reasonable Cause	28,969	61.6	37,792	62.1	32,075	58.8	32,646	63.6	32,123	59.9	35,695	61.4	39,418	61.3	50,290	64.8
Reasonable Cause	1,108	2.4	2,558	4.2	5,014	9.2	2,630	5.1	2,703	5.0	2,739	4.7	2,948	4.6	3,794	4.9
Successful Conciliation	401	0.9	671	1.1	1,177	2.2	697	1.4	840	1.6	841	1.4	905	1.4	996	1.3
Unsuccessful Conciliation	707	1.5	1,887	3.1	3,837	7.0	1,933	3.8	1,863	3.5	1,898	3.3	2,043	3.2	2,798	3.6
Merit Resolution	7,400		6,982		11,708		10,146		12,033		12,582		12,782		14,564	
% of Total Resolutions	15.7		11.5		21.5		19.8		22.4		21.7		19.9		18.8	
Monetary Benefits[2] (in million of dollars)	52.5		78.0		141.1		128.6		220.0		201.4		214.4		229.8	

Settlements (Negotiated): Charges settled with benefits to the charging party as warranted by evidence of record. In such cases, EEOC and/or an FEPA is a party to the settlement agreement between the charging party and the respondent (an employer, union, or other entity covered by EEOC-enforced status).

Withdrawal with Benefits: Charge is withdrawn by charging party upon receipt of desired benefits. The withdrawal may take place after a settlement or after the respondent grants the appropriate benefit to the charging party.

Administrative Closure: Charge closed for administrative reasons, such as failure to locate a charging party, charging party refused to accept full relief, closed due to the outcome of related litigation, charging party requests withdrawal of a charge without receiving benefits or having resolved the issue, no statutory jurisdiction.

No Reasonable Cause: EEOC's determination of no reasonable cause to believe that discrimination occurred based upon evidence obtained in investigation. The charging party may exercise the right to bring private court action.

Reasonable Cause: EEOC's determination of reasonable cause to believe that discrimination occurred based upon evidence obtained in investigation. Reasonable cause determinations are generally followed by efforts to conciliate the discriminatory issues which gave rise to the initial charge.

(continued)

TABLE 4-2 (*continued*)

EEOC CHARGES AND RESOLUTIONS UNDER TITLE VII

Successful Conciliation: Charge with reasonable cause determination closed after successful conciliation. Successful conciliations result in substantial relief to the charging party and all others adversely affected by the discrimination.

Unsuccessful Conciliation: Charge with reasonable cause determination closed after efforts to conciliate the charge are unsuccessful. Pursuant to commission policy, the field office will close charge and review it for litigation consideration. Note: Because "reasonable cause" has been found, this is considered a merit solution.

Merit Resolution: Total of charges with outcomes favorable to charging parties and/or charges with meritorious allegations. These include settlements, withdrawals with benefits, successful conciliation, and unsuccessful conciliation.

[1] Resolutions include charges carried over from previous fiscal years, new charge receipts, and charges transferred to EEOC from Fair Employment Practice Agencies (FEPAs). Resolution of charges each year may therefore exceed or be lower than the number of charges filed during the same year.

[2] Does not include monetary benefits obtained through litigation.

SOURCE: Data are compiled by the Office of Research, Information, and Planning from EEOC's Charge Data System—quarterly reconciled data summary reports.

("Successful Conciliation"), but the majority of conciliations are classified as "Unsuccessful Conciliation." An unsuccessful conciliation can lead either to closing of the charge and issuance of a right to sue to the charging employee or to pursuit of the charge by the EEOC through litigation in the federal courts. The category of outcomes labeled as "Administrative Closures" covers an array of reasons (see full definition in table 4-1). Included in that group are persons who withdrew their charges with the EEOC and may have filed a private suit.

Three striking observations emerge in table 4-1. One is that the total number of charges brought under Title VII each year is tiny compared to the total number of female and minority workers in the labor force. About 62 million women of all races and ethnicity and 20 million male minorities were wage and salary workers in 2010. The nearly 73,000 charges that were brought under Title VII that year corresponds to much less than 1 percent of the total number of workers at risk of being affected by labor market discrimination. But the minuscule proportion of protected workers who file charges could mean *either* that many protected workers who experience employment discrimination do not step forward and bring charges to the EEOC or that discriminatory behavior by employers is relatively rare. Our findings in chapter 8 suggest that discriminatory behavior by employers is rare in today's labor market. But this not to say that discrimination has been abolished—a point made clear by several of the cases reviewed in this chapter.

The second observation is that a majority of total charges brought are resolved with an EEOC finding of "No Reasonable Cause" to believe discrimination had occurred: 64.8 percent in 2010. Thus a large majority of all the charges of discrimination brought against employers under Title VII are found to have no significant basis in fact after investigation by the staff of the EEOC.

The third observation is the small share of resolutions classified as "Merit Resolutions" (18.8 percent in 2010), i.e., those resolutions with a favorable outcome to the charging party. However, this statistic may overstate happy endings, since merit resolutions include charges that had an "Unsuccessful Conciliation" even though they were originally found to have a reasonable cause. The outcome is uncertain for this group. Some of the 2,798 unsuccessful conciliations may go to court if litigation is chosen, and in court the charging party may win or lose. Others may simply withdraw their case.

Combining those charges deemed to have "No Reasonable Cause" with those with unsuccessful conciliations brings the proportion of charges brought that yield nothing to the charging party up to about 65 percent. Many, perhaps most of those with administrative closures, will also receive nothing. But they, like those with unsuccessful conciliations, can and may bring suit against the employer, because under Title VII all employees have a "right to sue" their employers. But those who have won a "Reasonable Cause" judgment from the EEOC will likely have an advantage if they decide to sue privately.

Consent Decrees versus Court Resolutions. Few EEOC cases ever reach court. Yet those cases often provide useful information on the modus operandi of the EEOC as it pursues its objective of reducing discrimination.

Over the period 1992 to 2009, the number of charges filed each year found to have a reasonable cause averaged about 2,550. Of those, about 710, only about 28 percent, were resolved each year by successful conciliation, leaving about 1,840 that were unresolved. On average, during this period, the EEOC initiated about 230 court cases a year. Thus about 1,610, or 63 percent of the annual charges judged to have a reasonable cause, were neither resolved by a settlement nor taken to court by the EEOC within a year. Some may yet settle or go to court in a future year. But, as noted, the charging parties in this group who no longer expect assistance from the EEOC will be issued a "right to sue," which some may use to bring a private case against the employer they charged with discrimination. When no action is taken, the firm "wins" by default, although the costs it has incurred during the investigation are not reimbursed.

If the EEOC decides to bring a case to court, there are three possible outcomes. Two of these are comparatively rare. One of these is that the firm will win outright: i.e., the defendant wins either a summary judgment against EEOC on the merits of the case or wins in a jury trial, or the EEOC voluntarily accepts the court's offer to dismiss the charge without charging EEOC with any misconduct. A second possible, but also comparatively rare, outcome is that the EEOC will win a summary judgment or win at a trial, which means that the firm will not only have to pay damages to the individual or individuals, but it will have been convicted of having discriminated against members of a protected group. This will become part of the firm's public record in dealing with any future charges by the EEOC.

However, by far the most frequent outcome is a settlement or "consent decree" (CD). In such cases the charged firm, the EEOC, and the plaintiffs agree on the amount of compensation the firm will pay to the individuals or classes of individuals in the case. But the agreement terminates the case without the charged firm having been found guilty of committing any discriminatory act. For the years 2003 to 2005, between 75 percent and 80 percent of cases brought to court by the EEOC ended with a CD.

Why are settlements and CDs the dominant outcome? Unfortunately little can be assumed about the merits of cases that conclude with a settlement or a CD. An employer sued by the EEOC has much more to lose if it loses the case in a summary judgment or jury verdict than does the EEOC if it loses. The charging party anticipates a more certain monetary settlement with a CD than if he or she gambles in court, and is also spared the anxiety of a trial. All in all, the firm likely confronts much larger costs if it continues the battle in court than if it settles. In addition to direct legal costs, it faces indirect costs that could result from lost business due to the negative publicity of the trial and its possible negative effect on the morale of its workers. The longer the case drags on, the greater those costs. And if the outcome of a long battle should be a summary judgment or a guilty verdict, its business could be seriously harmed. Thus the firm is likely to accept the offer of a CD.

On the other side, the EEOC is also likely to offer a CD. Large monetary settlements are loudly touted by the EEOC as victories over discrimination. The general public is unlikely to be aware of the difference between a CD and losing or winning on the merits. On the other hand, if the firm turns out to be particularly stubborn and will not settle, a summary judgment or jury verdict that goes against the EEOC is not likely to be noticed by the public except in high-profile cases.

Given the pressures pointing to settlement, it is important to keep in mind that the acceptance of a settlement or a CD by the defending firm does not constitute proof of actual guilt.

Enforcement through Litigation by Type of Discrimination

Currently the EEOC recognizes five categories or types of discrimination that are covered by Title VII as amended by Congress, interpreted by the judiciary, and interpreted by the various EEOC Commissioners: disparate treatment discrimination, discrimination because of inadequate religious accommodation, disparate impact discrimination, sexual harassment, and racial harassment. We examine EEOC's enforcement procedures by drawing upon both its manuals and the results of court cases involving each type of discrimination. We will find that only one of the EEOC's targeted categories—disparate treatment—on balance might lead to a reduction in labor market discrimination. Other procedures, particularly the pursuit of disparate impact and systemic cases, are not likely to reduce labor market discrimination and may have a perverse effect on the progress of protected groups.

Disparate Treatment Discrimination. The EEOC Compliance Manual and other materials provide extensive guidance on analyzing charges of disparate treatment of individuals based on their race, sex, religion, and national origin. Title VII is said to be violated when any of these characteristics are "all or part of the motivation for an employment decision." This applies to many different kinds of employment decisions: hiring, compensation determinations, decisions about grooming and appearance policies, and promotion decisions.

The accepted tests for disparate treatment charges are based on *McDonnell Douglas Corp. v. Green* (411 U.S. 792, 1973), a Supreme Court case. The *McDonnell* decision stipulated a three-step process for adjudicating disparate treatment discrimination cases: first, the charging employee must present a prima facie case of discrimination; second, the employer must articulate a legitimate nondiscriminatory reason for the allegedly discriminatory action; and, finally, the charging employee must show that this alleged nondiscriminatory reason is not pretextual—that is, a device for hiding an underlying discriminatory reason.

The logical steps in *McDonnell* are not always simple to execute, as firms no longer dare to display signs declaring "no African Americans or women may apply." In the absence of overt evidence of an employer's discriminatory intentions it can be difficult to detect when a disparity in hiring, promotion, or pay in fact reflects illegal discrimination.

To establish a prima facie case, a minority complainant might show, for example, that he or she was qualified for a job or promotion and was turned down in favor of a comparable member of a nonprotected group. But what constitutes "comparability"? If the comparison is restricted to easily measured characteristics such as years of experience with the firm and educational attainment, it could miss the important aspects of a worker's performance that affect his or her value to the firm. The EEOC manual provides one such example.[58] In this example, Alex, a Hispanic male, has done well at a public relations firm and applies for a senior management job that has opened up. He is not selected and the position goes to Jennifer, a white female with somewhat less experience. He files a charge of national origin discrimination. The investigation, however, shows that Jennifer has displayed more creativity than Alex by developing new marketing tools and a new system for disseminating time-sensitive documents. Alex, on the other hand, is competent but not innovative, a skill needed for the new job.

In commenting on the example the EEOC says that, given Jennifer's observed strengths, minor differences in formal qualifications without any evidence of discriminatory behavior by the firm are not enough to conclude that the firm's nonpromotion of Alex was motivated by discrimination. But they add that additional evidence indicating that management was prejudiced, such as derogatory comments about the leadership potential of Hispanics or other disparaging remarks, would strengthen Alex's claim of discrimination.

To understand better how the EEOC interprets its mandate, we shall consider several examples of disparate treatment that have been addressed in court.

Disparate treatment in compensation. The need to find true comparators when performance differences cannot be evaluated merely by the number of years of experience and educational credentials is illustrated in *EEOC v. Kettering University* (No. 2-73901, E.D. Michigan, April 21, 2003). In this case, the EEOC alleged that Kettering University, an engineering college, paid the charging party, a female professor of communications, a lower base salary than comparable or even "less qualified" male professors. The case was settled with a payment of $55,000 to the charging party. No information was given about the comparable male professors other than their rank. However, the pay differential may reflect that engineering faculty at U.S. universities are typically among the highest paid faculty. If the supposedly comparable male professors were disproportionately in engineering, their higher pay may simply reflect differences in labor market demand for engineers and communications professors. Even if the male professors were also in communications, rank would not be a sufficient qualification to evaluate pay differences. One would need to know about the quantity and quality of publications, teaching evaluations, and other credentials that influence academic salaries. We cannot tell if the EEOC addressed a situation of true discrimination or simply raised the operating costs for Kettering University.

Disparate treatment in hiring decisions. Consider a hiring decision when a white male job candidate was preferred to a minority candidate. An employer might cite as a nondiscriminatory reason that the nonprotected individual had more qualifications (such as an MBA or other graduate degree). A successful argument that this reason is pretextual might cite evidence that the employer has recently hired nonprotected employees for the same or a very similar job who did not have an MBA or equivalent degree. If there is no evidence that the firm had ever hired a nonprotected individual who did not have an MBA, then the case may end in favor of the employer. However, the issue of disparate impact discrimination may then enter the case. The EEOC may argue that the minimum requirement of an MBA has an adverse impact on minorities and is not a business necessity. As we have stressed, the disparate impact criterion is in direct conflict with the original intention of Title VII. We discuss the problems associated with charges of disparate impact below.

Often the EEOC appears to proceed with a balanced approach in disparate treatment adjudication that follows the *McDonnell* decision as closely as possible and uses the available objective data. Often the EEOC finds "no reasonable cause" for the charge, as in the four cases referenced below, in which a right to sue was issued to a charging party who subsequently lost the case in court, reaffirming the opinion of the EEOC.[59]

And, of course, the EEOC also takes on cases that seem to present direct evidence of discrimination. In one such case involving racial discrimination (*EEOC v. EQW Temps Inc.*), an employment agency was shown to be servicing client requests for nonblack employees. In another case (*EEOC v. Milgard Manufacturing Inc.*), a plant manager ordered his personnel department not to hire African Americans because "black people are lazy and move too slowly."

When it comes to their methods regarding standard disparate treatment cases, the EEOC often appears to be reasonable and, in those instances, their judgments are likely to contribute to reducing labor market discrimination. However, this assessment applies to situations in which the type of disparate treatment charged involves issues that conform to what most people would consider to be serious discrimination addressed by Title VII. But the EEOC also pursues charges in which the concept of disparate treatment discrimination is stretched to cover situations that are at best problematic. We discuss several kinds of such situations below.

Disparate treatment in grooming policies. For many years a recurring type of sex discrimination charge involved men who complained to the EEOC that their job required short hair for men, while women faced no restriction regarding hair length. The men filing charges claimed they were forced to choose between their job and their long hair, while women faced no such Hobson's choice. The EEOC championed these men's cause despite unfavorable ruling from the courts. Eventually the EEOC was compelled by the courts to change their treatment of male long hair cases. The crowning blow to male hair cases was delivered in *Harper v. Blockbuster Entertainment Corp.* (U.S. Eleventh Circuit Court of Appeals, #97-4364, April 1999). In the words of the Appeals Court:

> The reasonableness of the plaintiffs' belief in this case is belied by the unanimity with which the courts have declared grooming policies like Blockbuster's non-discriminatory. Every circuit to have considered the issue has reached the same conclusion reached by this Court in the *Willingham* decision.

The circuit court pointed out that Title VII only prohibits disparate treatment based on a person's sex per se. It went on to say that requiring one sex to change a neutral characteristic like hair length does not constitute illegal discrimination, because the intent is not to deprive one sex of employment opportunities.

The EEOC long sought to maintain that disparate hair length rules were in violation of Title VII but, in the face of the unanimous position of the courts of appeal that have addressed the issue, the EEOC finally conceded that "successful litigation of male hair length cases would be virtually impossible." (U.S. EEOC 2006a, § 619.1). As the circuit court concluded,

"Accordingly, the EEOC ran up a white flag on the issue, advising its field offices to administratively close all sex discrimination charges dealing with male hair length."[60]

Disparate treatment of women in promotion decisions: the "glass ceiling." The idea of a glass ceiling as an important indicator of discrimination gained credence when Title VII of the 1991 Civil Rights Act created the Glass Ceiling Commission. As defined by the U.S. Department of Labor, the glass ceiling refers to "those artificial barriers based on attitudinal or organizational bias that prevent qualified individuals from advancing upward in their organization into management-level positions." The catchy term was originally inspired by statistics revealing the near absence of women in the highest management levels in the Fortune 500. It was popularized by a 1986 article in the *Wall Street Journal* (Hymowitz and Schellhardt 1986) and quickly captured the attention of the media and the public. Even today, few women occupy the highest rungs of business. Only 2–3 percent of the CEOs of the Fortune 500 companies are women (Catalyst 2011). When the group at the top is broadened to include all top corporate officers, the women's share increases, but only to about 16 percent. Yet, women make up close to half of the labor force.

These statistics are dramatic, but what do they mean? Are they indicative of serious gender discrimination? It is always difficult to determine whether an observed gap in the gender or racial composition of high-level offices reflects discrimination or simply a small pool of highly qualified women and minorities. The concept of a glass ceiling presupposes that firm management and even lower- and mid-rank employees hold negative stereotypes and that simply holding those stereotypes can be viewed as discrimination.

As we discuss in chapter 8, the lower representation of women in jobs that require a consuming commitment to work—and, in the case of CEOs, a lifetime commitment—can be explained by the fact that women assume a greater share of the responsibilities involved in child rearing than men. Those freely assumed responsibilities consume time and energy and often slow women's career progress.

The concept of the glass ceiling has introduced new opportunities for litigation. Over the past fifteen years the EEOC has moved forward with a number of glass ceiling cases and initiatives. We note a few below.

Wall Street has become a ripe target for disparate treatment cases that charge sex discrimination in hiring, pay, and promotion, sometimes punctuated with charges of sexual harassment. Pay is high—particularly in occupations such as trader, investment banker, and stockbroker—while the percentage of those jobs held by women is unusually low. In large securities firms the female percentage in 2003 was 15 percent among traders, 17 percent among investment bankers and 16 percent among brokers.[61] At first blush these statistics look like enough for a prima facie case against the Morgan Stanleys and Smith Barneys of this world.[62]

The 1996 so-called "boom-boom-room" case brought by Pamela Martens and other employees against Smith Barney became notorious. The lewd antics of male employees at one Smith Barney brokerage office were colorfully described in a popular book and in the media (Antilla 2002). The behavior in the one office was given as evidence of universal sexual harassment and gender discrimination against female brokers and financial assistants. The case settled, with an agreement to further pursue the charges of individual women in arbitration, a process that lasted a number of years.

The boom-boom room seems to have ushered in a wave of cases involving gender discrimination on Wall Street. The EEOC undertook a case against Morgan Stanley on its own initiative and scored a highly publicized $54 million settlement with Morgan Stanley in 2004. The case involved Allison Schieffelin, a bond salesperson who complained to the EEOC in 1998 that she had been denied pay and promotion because of her sex. She was awarded $12 million for wrongful termination, while $40 million was set aside for other professional women who had worked at Morgan Stanley since 1995 and were able to provide evidence that they too suffered discrimination. The case was set to go to trial but settled just before the trial was about to begin.

Because the case was settled, the public will never know all the details. But the general outline of the case was discussed widely in the press. Allison Schieffelin was one of the top earners in her unit within Morgan Stanley's Institutional Equity Division. She regularly earned around a million or more and was reported to have earned $1.35 million in 1998 (Ackman 2001). Her allegation of discrimination was based on the fact that she was not promoted to managing director of her unit when the post opened up. But promotion to management is not an entitlement, and surely there were some disappointed men. As it turned out, the job was given to another woman. Along the way, Ms. Schiefflin was fired after an altercation, supposedly with the woman who became her boss. She added a claim of retaliation for the firing.

Would the EEOC have won had the case gone to trial? We cannot know. The *Economist* magazine writing on the case thought the EEOC would have had a hard time proving discrimination, "given that she was making over $1 million at the time she was fired and the only other co-worker making more was another woman" (*Economist* 2004). Another op-ed article asked, "Did Allison Schiefflin's claims have any merit? From what we know they seem not to—but we will never really know for certain, since the case never made it to trial. Yet whatever the merits of this case, the law does not—and should not—guarantee against unsuccessful work experiences" (Jones and Osorio 2004). Why did Morgan Stanley settle? One factor that may have contributed was the possible move by the plaintiff to introduce accusations of bawdy behavior by male employees and allegations about men-only golf games and strip-club visits, which would have been embarrassing for executives at Morgan Stanley to defend in open court (Doran 2004). Given the potential for more legal fees and further negative publicity, Morgan Stanley may well have thought that $54 million was the cheaper alternative.

The EEOC has also reached settlements in "glass ceiling" suits involving a variety of industries. For example, in 2009 Outback Steakhouse agreed on a payment of $19 million to settle a class action suit alleging sex discrimination against thousands of women at hundreds of its restaurants nationwide. The alleged discrimination was that women hit a glass ceiling when they were denied kitchen management experience that was a requirement for promotion to management jobs in the restaurants. The EEOC does not report on the proportion of comparably situated men and women turned down for kitchen management jobs. Thus we cannot evaluate whether justice was served.

One thing that the EEOC's support for glass ceiling cases seems to have achieved is an onslaught of litigation, the most recent example being the effort to expand a sex discrimination case against Wal-Mart (*Dukes v. Wal-Mart*) into a giant class action suit involving as many as 1.5 million women and potentially billions in payments to the aggrieved parties.[63] The EEOC filed an amicus brief in support of the plaintiffs when the case was before the Ninth Circuit. To build the class action membership, lawyers for the plaintiffs developed a website to recruit current and former employees of Wal-Mart who believe they have been denied pay or promotion.[64] But in June 2011, the U.S. Supreme Court, in response to an appeal by Wal-Mart, denied the claim that the case met the standards of what constitutes a class under federal Rule of Procedure 23.[65] The judgment and its discussion of what properly qualifies as evidence of employer discrimination will likely raise the bar for individuals claiming discrimination and for plaintiffs trying to form a class action suit.

Disparate treatment based on bona fide occupational qualifications. Title VII also provided a narrow direct exception to nondiscrimination in the following provision: "Notwithstanding any other provision of this title—it shall not be an unlawful employment practice for an employer to hire and employ employees . . . on the basis of . . . religion, sex, or national origin in those certain instances where religion, sex, or national origin is a bona fide occupational qualification reasonably necessary to the normal operation of that particular business or enterprise."[66]

In other words the original Title VII not only provided that employers could specify minimal qualifications for prospective employees even when the protected workers scored lower or had fewer qualifications so long as the purpose was not "pretextual," it also allowed them to specify types of employment for which they were allowed to discriminate in favor of one sex, religious group, or national origin for specific types of employment. These are called bona fide occupational qualifications (BFOQ).

Many businesses and organizations find it necessary at times to employ people of one sex, a particular religion, or a particular national origin. The business necessity exemption for BFOQ is notably not extended to race. Some of these situations are unlikely to be challenged—employing a soprano to sing Tosca, a man to play Moses. It can be hard to judge when there is a legitimate BFOQ that justifies discrimination based on sex, religion, or national origin. Many situations have been highly controversial and were challenged by the EEOC and in the courts, which have tended to be skeptical of all BFOQ defenses. The situations cover a range of occupations and settings.

The EEOC will support a BFOQ defense in certain instances—a nursing home with all female residents that employs female nurses, and a prison that resembles Attica in the 1970s that employs only male guards.

However, in recent years the EEOC has frequently moved to prohibit businesses and organizations from pursuing justifiable modes of operation that appear necessary for them to achieve their legitimate business objectives. Among the EEOC's targets have been a seafood restaurant accused of employing only male waiters in formal dress to project an "elegant old world atmosphere," another restaurant that hired all-female waitstaff dressed in period costumes to provide an historical ambiance, and a women's prison that hires only female guards because of the privacy needs of women inmates. The EEOC manual actually rules that situations like those just described are violations of Title VII because they cannot be proven to be an absolute business necessity.[67]

How does the EEOC justify these decisions? We review some of the key cases, starting with one in which the EEOC appears to have been justified in challenging an employer's practice of hiring an all-female staff and before turning to consider several of the EEOC's later and more unreasonable interventions.

We begin with *Diaz v. Pan American World Airways Inc.*, in which Pan American Airlines sought to maintain its policy of employing only women as flight attendants, arguing that customer preferences required that they do so. The Fifth Circuit Court, however, stated that:

> . . . we do not feel that the fact that Pan Am's passengers prefer female stewardesses should alter our judgment. On this subject, EEOC guidelines state that a BFOQ ought not be based on the refusal to hire an individual because of the preferences of co-workers, the employer, clients or customers. . . . Indeed while we recognize that the public's expectation of finding one sex in a particular role may cause some initial difficulty, it would be totally anomalous if we were to allow the preferences and these prejudices the Act was meant to overcome. Thus we feel that customer preference may be taken into account only when it is based on the company's inability to perform the primary function or service it offers.[68]

The court affirmed the EEOC guidelines barring a BFOQ based on customer preferences and gave little weight to consideration of customers' supposed preferences. The court decreed Pam Am's business interests were restricted to the firm's inability to perform its primary function, namely flying customers to their destinations. However, the decision denying Pan Am a BFOQ exemption appears reasonable. It had little impact on Pan Am's business, because all airlines had to follow suit, and good substitutes for traveling by air are often unavailable, so it was unlikely to hurt Pan Am's business.

However, since the *Pan Am* decision, the EEOC sought to deny BFOQ exemptions to others with little regard to the possible adverse effect on the business or organization involved. The EEOC has not paid due attention to balancing the benefits and costs of heavy intrusion into how businesses and other organizations function.

The EEOC's initiative to bring gender neutrality to the waitstaff of fine dining establishments is a case in point. In the 1990s the EEOC became concerned about what it perceived to be the tradition of the industry to employ all-male waitstaff to emulate "the European fine dining restaurant model." Among those investigated were the "21" Club in New York, the Mansion on Turtle Creek in Dallas, and Pat O'Brien's Bar in New Orleans. One of the targeted restaurants, Joe's Stone Crab in Miami, became a famous case that ultimately went to the Supreme Court, where the EEOC prevailed (U.S. Supreme Court, No. 02-1384, *Joe's Stone Crab, Inc., Petitioner, v. EEOC*).

Recently, however, the EEOC has come full circle, charging a restaurant chain that employs only women as servers (dressed in period costumes to fit with an historical theme) with violating Title VII (*EEOC v. Lawry's Restaurants Inc., d/b/a Lawry's, and The Prime Rib, et al.* CV 06-1963 DDP (PLAX)). The words of EEOC regional attorney Anna Y. Park provide an insight into what the EEOC's views will be on almost any BFOQ: " . . . the practice of denying men the opportunity to work in the higher paying server jobs is blatant sex discrimination. An employer as large and sophisticated as Lawry's should certainly know better" (http.//www.lawmemo.com).

In these cases, the EEOC and the courts argue that the "essential service" does not include a "European fine dining experience" or a period atmosphere. It is rather the service of waiting on tables, and this can be done by females in a restaurant with an old world atmosphere and males wearing period costumes. Clearly the EEOC and the courts have gone beyond the *Pan Am* decision where one could argue that providing the essential service—transportation—can be reasonably provided with stewards as with stewardesses without seriously affecting the business of the defendant. But this is not the case with Joe's Stone Crab or Lawry's, which compete in a highly competitive industry and are trying to create a unique niche for themselves. Nor does it seem that they are having any significant impact on the employment opportunities of men and women in the restaurant business.

The case of Joe's Stone Crab is revealing in other ways. Although the EEOC argued that Joe's was intentionally recruiting men to invoke an image of a "European fine dining experience," Joe's argued that low representation of women on its waitstaff was the result of low turnover combined with the fact that few women ever applied. Joe's noted that the job might be less attractive to women because the formal presentation of food at the restaurant required the lifting and holding aloft of unusually heavy trays of stone crabs, and the restaurant was in a dilapidated neighborhood. No evidence of intentional discrimination was ever identified by the EEOC or the courts. Indeed, the owner and most of the management staff were women. The court, however, was persuaded by the testimony not of actual applicants but of women who said that they did not apply because "it was like [sic] common knowledge that they didn't hire women at the . . . ." (quoting a woman who worked as a wait person at another restaurant).[69] The court refused to consider actual application data on the grounds that it was tainted by reputation. The case therefore revolved around statistics based on data on the percentage of women among waitstaff in the Miami area (including servers at Denny's, cocktail waitresses at pubs, etc.).

The case of Joe's Stone Crab went on for years after settlement. After the settlement, the EEOC imposed and supervised requirements for recruiting. At one point the waitstaff at Joe's (which now included some women) started wearing black and yellow campaign-style buttons that said "JOE'S STAFF, I AM GOVERNMENT APPROVED." The EEOC obtained some of the offending buttons and gave them to the court, which determined this was an improper use of First Amendment rights, an indication of "management insensitivity to the serious issues in this case," and evidence of "its disdain for court-ordered remedial measures."[70] In this context we note that the Supreme Court has found that flag burning is protected by the First Amendment.

Although Joe's was not able to prevail in court, on other occasions the courts have been more sympathetic to restaurateurs' wishes about whom to hire as waitstaff. The Mansion on Turtle Creek, an upscale restaurant in Dallas, was also sued by the EEOC based on the observation that no women had been hired as waitstaff in more than eight years.[71] The Mansion's defense was similar to Joe's—no women were hired because no women with the relevant skills had applied (the wait jobs at both restaurants required considerable skill and experience). The court was convinced, however, by the statistics on the available applicant pool brought in *Mansion* and ruled in favor of the Mansion.[72] The decision was upheld on appeal.

We also note that the EEOC was reported to have had its eye on Hooters, widely known for hiring only shapely women as servers. After investigating their hiring practices for several years, however, the EEOC decided not to file suit. They evidently were convinced that, in the case of Hooters, shapely women were a BFOQ.

Controversy has also arisen over the employment of women guards at women's prisons. In one case, female inmates demanded that they be guarded only by female guards at night for privacy reasons. In this case the court ruled that it was not necessary to exclude male prison guards from nighttime cell block duty in order to protect the privacy rights of female inmates. The court noted:

> Resolution of privacy rights versus employment rights cases requires a careful inquiry as to whether the competing interests can be satisfactorily accommodated before deciding whether one interest must be vindicated to the detriment of the other.[73]

The court found that permitting the female inmates to cover their cell windows for short intervals at night, as was permitted during the day, and providing appropriate sleepwear would adequately protect their privacy interests.

The EEOC followed the principle of the court rulings in inmates' cases in assessing the practice of mental hospitals of using only male orderlies to supervise their male mental patients. Mental hospitals judged that female orderlies might upset their patients' fragile mental states. The EEOC ruled that this practice was "pretextual"—i.e., it was just a cover for prejudice against females. Since this was not a court case, the evidence on which the EEOC based its conclusion is not available.

Another problematic EEOC effort was directed against Abercrombie & Fitch, the well-known retailing chain. In this case, the EEOC accused Abercrombie & Fitch of engaging in "image discrimination": hiring only white, attractive young people with the "look" projected in their advertising.[74]

CBS investigated "The Look of Abercrombie & Fitch" in one of its *60 Minutes* programs. It noted how the store had thrown off its venerable image of old money and classic sportswear after bankruptcy and a buyout and transformed itself into the "clothier of choice" for the hip twenty-five-and-under crowd:

> Now, the provocative strategy aimed at teens and twenties has done wonders for Abercrombie's bottom line. And of course, the more parents are outraged, the bigger the sales. And now with more than 600 stores and annual revenues well over $1 billion, Abercrombie & Fitch has become just about the largest teen retailer on the block—and a mainstay of "Generation Y" couture, and even its music. But all that fair hair and skin has made them a juicy target. They're being taken to court, accused of racial discrimination in their hiring.

EEOC's General Counsel Eric Dreiband stated, "The retail industry and other industries need to know that businesses cannot discriminate against individuals under the auspice of a marketing strategy or a particular 'look.' Race and sex discrimination in employment are unlawful, and the EEOC will continue to aggressively pursue employers who choose to engage in such practices" (U.S. EEOC 2004b).

The EEOC claimed that its evidence showed that the store had turned down African Americans, Asians, and Hispanics for sales jobs. From the store's point of view, its hiring patterns could be defended as a business necessity. The EEOC disagreed. Faced with a long, drawn-out court case that would be expensive and undoubtedly bad for business, Abercrombie & Fitch settled. In its consent decree, Abercrombie & Fitch agreed to pay $50 million to resolve the EEOC lawsuit along with two private class actions filed against Abercrombie & Fitch: *Gonzalez, et al. v. Abercrombie, et al.* and *West v. Abercrombie, et al.*

The following details are given in the EEOC's press release:

The Consent Decree enjoins Abercrombie & Fitch from:

a. discriminating against applicants based upon race, color, national origin which includes African Americans, Asian Americans, and Latinos;

b. discriminating against women due to their sex; and

c. denying promotional opportunities to women and minorities.

Abercrombie & Fitch has also agreed to develop and implement hiring and recruiting procedures to ensure compliance under the Decree. Abercrombie & Fitch agreed to ensure that minorities and women are promoted into manager-in-training and manager positions without discrimination. A monitor will be hired to ensure Abercrombie's compliance with the terms of the Consent Decree, including reporting. Abercrombie & Fitch will hire a Vice President of Diversity and employ up to 25 diversity recruiters. Abercrombie & Fitch will devise new protocols for each of these areas. Abercrombie & Fitch will post a notice on an internal web site and at all stores which will be periodically distributed to employees. Additionally, Abercrombie & Fitch will provide training to all of its managers. Most importantly, Abercrombie & Fitch also agreed to ensure that its marketing materials will reflect diversity (U.S. EEOC 2004b).

At first blush this case may appear a more "reasonable" application of the disparate impact concept to the use of the BFOQ exception, closer to the Pan Am case than to the Joe's case. But consider the following critique of EEOC's behavior, supporting Abercrombie & Fitch's point of view:

A popular Los Angeles Thai restaurant features an all Thai, female waitressing staff. The restaurant, part of a chain, hires Thai women, some relatives of the owners, but many outside the founding and operating family circle. Meanwhile, Black Entertainment Television hires African American hosts, African American news anchors, and plays pre-dominantly all African American videos. . . . Yet . . . Abercrombie and Fitch (must) face government laws preventing it from determining how, for ill or for good, to best meet its perceived marketing niche. Never mind that customers, employees and prospective employees who feel "discriminated against" can refuse to patronize an establishment that refuses to hire those who "look like us." (Elder, 2003)

Similar views were expressed on the *60 Minutes* show mentioned above.

What can be made of the Abercrombie & Fitch saga? It appears that the successful Abercrombie & Fitch marketing campaign was associated with a reduction in their employment of nonwhites who did not fit with its marketing image. But has the EEOC brought a case against the BET network for employing too few whites, or the myriad ethnic restaurants who hire only their own ethnic group? Or what about the African American–owned clothing company FUBU, which stands for For Us By Us? One can only understand EEOC's behavior as pursuing the goal of raising the earnings of protected groups by almost never accepting the plea of "business necessity" from a white male business owner.

"Reasonable Accommodation" and Religious Discrimination. The Eleventh Circuit court decision on hair length made it clear that employers could impose different dress codes on men and women in order to accommodate its business needs. In the 1972 Amendments to Title VII, Congress expanded on its provision that it is unlawful for employers to discriminate on the basis of religion by stating that an employer must accommodate employee religious observance unless so doing would place an "undue hardship" on the employer.[75] Although the amendment was intended to clarify the responsibilities of employers when religion is involved, it did not come close to ending all debate. The definition of "undue hardship" has proven to be highly contentious. The definition of religion has also been liberalized to include any sincerely held belief, further complicating the concept of religious discrimination.

The reasoning of the courts and the EEOC is reflected in several recent cases. Taken as a whole, these cases suggest that the "reasonable accommodation" standard generally requires employers rather than employees to yield in cases of conflict.

"Reasonable accommodation" and employees' appearance. One of the most contested areas about what is required of employers in order to make

"reasonable accommodations" concerns questions about the degree to which employers may insist on a dress code.

A number of such cases involve conflicts over the appearances of Muslims. For example, A McDonald's franchise in rural Virginia discharged Muslim employees who wore beards for religious reasons, refusing to make an exception to its dress code that requires employees to be clean-shaven. The EEOC obtained a consent decree from McDonalds (as it had from other employers), not for refusing to hire Muslims because of their religion, but for refusing to allow them to wear beards on the job—a requirement imposed on all of their employees regardless of their religion, race, or national origin (*EEOC v. Russell Enters, L.L.C., d/b/a McDonalds* E.D.,Va, August 2005). The conflict between beards for religious reasons and the firm's idea of how their enterprise should be run is another recurring type of claim. (For example, the EEOC has recently charged the United Parcel Service with religious discrimination for refusing to hire a Rastafarian who refused to shave off his beard that he wore for religious reasons.)

But the most widely noted case involving a Muslim is *EEOC v. Alamo Rent-A-Car LLC* (No. CIV 02-01908-PHX-ROS). Judge Roslyn Silver of the Arizona Federal district court ruled that Alamo Car Rental committed "post-9/11 backlash discrimination" based on religion when it terminated the employment of Bilan Nur, a rental agent, for refusing to remove her hijab, or head scarf, while working at the counter during the Muslim holy month of Ramadan, in violation of Alamo's "Dress Smart Policy." According to Judge Silver's ruling: "It is undisputed that the accommodation Alamo offered Ms. Nur required her to remove her head covering during Ramadan when she served clients but still required her to serve clients, making it impossible for Ms. Nur to avoid removing her head covering at work." Accordingly, Alamo would have failed to provide Ms. Nur a "reasonable accommodation" for practicing her religion. (Actually, Ms. Nur was told she could wear her head scarf during Ramadan when she worked in the back office, but not when she worked at the counter where she would be interacting with customers, which evidently was necessary some of the time.)

The judge felt so strongly about the case that she took the unusual step of finding that the question of whether Alamo had violated the law was so clear that it did not need to be decided by a jury. In the subsequent trial, the jury was only asked to decide the amount of monetary damages to which Ms. Nur was entitled. The amount awarded was $287,000.

After the verdict, the EEOC attorney who tried the case said, "Bilan Nur is truly a remarkable woman. A refugee from war-torn Somalia when she came to this country as a young woman, Ms. Nur viewed America as the country that offered her hope, safety, and equality. With the jury's findings today, Ms. Nur has been reassured that, even after 9/11, Americans still believe in justice for all people. Ms. Nur and the EEOC are both very pleased with today's results. We hope this verdict sends a message to the community that the community will not accept religious intolerance in the workplace" (U.S. EEOC 2007b).

The emotion shown by the EEOC notwithstanding, the question remains whether this was a clear-cut case involving "religious intolerance." Alamo had employed Ms. Nur for a few years knowing that she was a Muslim. Ms. Nur had been told in the two years before 2001 that she could not wear the scarf during Ramadan and Alamo when working at the counter, and Alamo testified that she had complied.

Although the EEOC and Judge Silver believe Alamo should be punished for failing to make a reasonable accommodation, they did not say what that accommodation should be; nor did they spell out to what lengths the firm should go, and at what cost. At the start, the EEOC termed the case a "post 9/11 backlash"—a political statement that is surely inappropriate for a supposedly impartial government agency to make. The EEOC did not appear to consider that Alamo might fear customer backlash and suffer business losses if it allowed Ms. Nur to wear her head scarf to serve customers just after 9/11.

While many of the cases involve widely held faiths such as Islam, other cases involve the treatment of adherents of minority religions. One such case is *EEOC v. Red Robin Gourmet Burgers, Inc.* (No.C04-1291 JLR [W.D. Wash. Sept. 7, 2005]). Red Robin is a chain of casual dining restaurants throughout the country with a uniform and appearance code that prohibits servers from displaying tattoos and body piercing. One employee, a member of the Kemetic religion, said to be an ancient Egyptian faith, refused to wear any garment covering the special religious tattoos circling his wrists while serving food to customers on the grounds that covering the tattoos was a sin to his religion. He was fired for continuing to display his tattoos, and the EEOC concluded that Red Robin had violated the disparate treatment provision of Title VII.

This judgment would appear to clash with the Eleventh Circuit Court's ruling in the case dealing with men's long hair. Following the logic of the Eleventh Circuit, if a man is not being denied employment because he is a man but only because he has long hair, a practitioner of Kemet is not being denied employment because of his religion but only because of his display of tattoos. However, the 1972 amendments to the Civil Rights Act mandated only that firms should make a "reasonable accommodation" for religious practices in work situations, unless they can show that this accommodation would seriously affect their business. The EEOC asserted that Red Robin could allow the showing of the tattoos without seriously affecting its business. Red Robin believed that workers with visible tattoos conflict with the image of family values that its restaurants seek to project.

The court denied a request for a summary judgment ruling that, notwithstanding the employer's purported reliance on a company profile and customer study suggesting that it seeks to present a family-oriented and kid-friendly image, the company failed to demonstrate that allowing an employee to display religious tattoos was inconsistent with these goals. "Hypothetical hardships based on unproven assumptions typically fail to constitute undue hardship. . . . Red Robin must provide evidence of 'actual imposition on co-workers or disruption of the work routine' to demonstrate undue hardship."

The EEOC obtained a consent decree from Red Robin despite the seemingly weak link to religious discrimination. The charging party received a monetary award of $150,000 and Red Robin was ordered to provide managers with training on discrimination and harassment, to write reports on and to distribute discrimination policy materials as though it had been guilty of a straightforward disparate treatment discrimination case.

However, in contrast to the cases discussed above, in *Cloutier v. Costco Wholesale Corp.*, No. 04-1475 (1st Cir. 2004), the court was more sympathetic to the needs of employers to control how their employees appear to the public. In this case, Kimberly Cloutier, with the backing of the EEOC, alleged that her employer, Costco, had failed to offer her a reasonable accommodation to her religious practice as a member of the Church of Bodily Modification (CBM) which, according to the plaintiff, requires the open display of facial jewelry, including her eyebrow ring. According to the discussion in the court record, the CBM website, its primary mode for reaching its members, does not state that members' body modifications must be visible at all times. Cloutier's interpretation was that the ring must be displayed at all times and could not even be temporarily covered. The latter point was important because Costco had agreed that she could wear the ring if she covered it with a plastic retainer or bandage. She refused and her employment was terminated. The district court granted summary judgment for Costco, concluding that Costco had offered a reasonable accommodation by agreeing to reinstate her if she agreed to cover her ring while at work. The First Circuit Court affirmed the grant of summary judgment but did so on another basis. The First Circuit instead held that Costco "had no duty to accommodate Cloutier because it could not do so without undue hardship."

Cloutier was a sharp rebuttal to the EEOC and to the courts, which had been tightening the requirements for religious accommodation. But it may have set a precedent. In *Brown v. F. L. Roberts*, 419 F. Supp. 2d 7, 17 (D. Mass. 2006), the district court, stating it was bound to follow *Cloutier* as the law of the circuit, held no Title VII violation occurred when an employer transferred a lube technician whose Rastafarian religious beliefs prohibited him from shaving or cutting his hair to a location with limited customer contact because he could not comply with a new grooming policy. But the obviously unhappy court nevertheless observed in dicta: "If *Cloutier's* language approving employer prerogatives regarding 'public image' is read broadly, the implications for persons asserting claims for religious discrimination in the workplace may be grave. One has to wonder how often an employer will be inclined to cite this expansive language to terminate or restrict from customer contact, on image grounds, an employee wearing a yarmulke, a veil, or the mark on the forehead that denotes Ash Wednesday for many Catholics. More likely, and more ominously, considerations of 'public image' might persuade an employer to tolerate the religious practices of predominant groups, while arguing 'undue hardship' and 'image' in forbidding practices that are less widespread or well known."

These cases involving dress codes, the wearing of beards, and body marking and piercing feature concerns about the limits to which the government should go in determining how firms conduct their businesses. The reasonable accommodation decisions have been increasing the costs placed on employers. But will these decisions prove to be the best decisions for society as a whole? Should not workers with special religious requirements be expected themselves to seek employment where their religious practices may be more easily accommodated?

"Reasonable accommodation" and workers' schedules. Although the religious accomodation cases discussed above have concerned appearance in the workplace, other religious discrimination issues have also occassionally been addressed in court. One such case is *EEOC v. Aldi* (W.D. Pa. March 28, 2008), in which an employee said she could not work on Sundays after Aldi, a grocery shopping chain store, instituted a policy of staying open on Sundays and rotating cashiers so that they need not work every Sunday. The employee stated she was a Christian and could not accept any of her employer's accommodations, which included coming in after church on Sundays (she declined this accommodation because she did not belong to a church but stayed home watching services on television with her family on Sundays) and arranging with her co-workers to take her place on Sundays (she declined this accommodation because she thought it was a sin to induce anyone to work on Sunday). The court ruled against Aldi on the grounds that business hardship had not been adequately proven.

Disparate Impact Discrimination. With *Griggs v. Duke Power*, the Supreme Court dramatically broadened the definition of discrimination and the scope of antidiscrimination legislation to include disparate impact discrimination. The concept of disparate impact discrimination is one of the most controversial pillars of antidiscrimination law and of the EEOC enforcement program.

The EEOC Compliance Manual describes disparate impact discrimination as follows:[76]

> A finding of discrimination in the form of disparate impact does not depend on the existence of an unlawful motive.[77] Disparate impact analysis is aimed at removing barriers to EEO that are not necessarily intended or designed to discriminate—"practices that are fair in form, but discriminatory in operation"[78] in that they operate as "built-in headwinds for [a protected class] and are unrelated to measuring job capability."[79]

The statute exempts certain policies or practices from disparate impact challenges—most notably, seniority systems.[80] Otherwise, however, the disparate impact approach applies to all types of employment criteria, whether objective or subjective,[81] including recruitment practices, hiring or promotion criteria, layoff or termination criteria, appearance and grooming standards, education requirements, experience requirements, and employment tests.

How do the EEOC and the courts determine whether a firm is guilty of disparate impact discrimination? The proof needed to establish disparate impact discrimination has three parts:

1. *The prima facie case.* The plaintiff must first establish, usually by means of a statistical demonstration, that the employer utilizes a practice or policy that results in a significant disparate impact on a protected group.[82]

2. *Business necessity.* Once the plaintiff has established that a practice has a significant disparate impact, the employer has the burden of demonstrating that the practice is "job-related for the position in question and consistent with business necessity."[83]

3. *Finding an alternative practice with lesser adverse impact.* If the employer satisfies the burden of proving business necessity, the plaintiff may still prevail by showing that the employer has refused to adopt an alternative to the challenged practice that meets the business needs of the employer yet has a lesser disparate impact.[84]

Consider this simple example: A bank requires that all applicants for the job of investment counselor have an MBA degree. But a much smaller percentage of potential African American applicants have an MBA than white applicants. If it were found that the bank hired white males without an MBA, the bank's MBA requirement would be declared "pretextual" and the bank would be charged with disparate *treatment* discrimination. However, even if there were no evidence of pretextual discrimination, the bank could still be guilty of disparate *impact* discrimination if it could not show that it is a business necessity that investment counselors have an MBA. Moreover, demonstrating business necessity would still not be enough if it was shown that an alternative to an MBA, such as work experience, would meet the bank's needs for identifying qualified applicants.

A crucial part of the process is the analysis of the statistical evidence needed to establish disparate impact. The basic standard for measuring disparate impact is the "80 percent rule," formulated by the EEOC in 1978 in its Uniform Guidelines.[85] The 80 percent rule finds an employer practice to have an adverse impact if, as a result of that practice (e.g., a test or job requirement), members of a protected class are selected at a rate less than 80 percent of that of the nonprotected group. For example, if 50 percent of white applicants receive a passing score on a test, but only 30 percent of African Americans pass, the relevant ratio would be 30/50, or 60 percent, which would violate the 80 percent rule. Other methods have also been proposed and are considered in court cases. However, all of them are based on statistical differences in results and do not take account of genuine differences in the qualifications to be found among different groups of applicants for various types of jobs.[86]

The underlying assumption of disparate impact seems to be that applicants from all groups are equally likely to be qualified for job openings and so should be selected at rates proportional to their presence in the actual (or even the potential) applicant pool. The 80 percent rule presumably adjusts for chance differences in selection rates. With this line of reasoning, a racial or gender difference in selection rates based on differences in test scores or job requirements reflects a discriminatory roadblock to employment at a firm.

As we discussed in chapter 2, Title VII explicitly states that, without evidence of pretext, nothing in the title will prevent a firm from determining its own job requirements and screening devices. But the majority of judges in *Griggs* simply asserted that a hiring requirement, even without an intent to discriminate, could be illegal if it had a disparate impact on a protected class of workers. Although *Griggs* was narrowly focused on the legality of relatively straightforward job tests for moderate-skill jobs, it now encompasses a large number of screening practices that firms and institutions believe are useful in their hiring process. These practices can now be barred (and frequently are) unless the EEOC rules and the courts agree that the firm or organization has adequately demonstrated that its screening practice is a business necessity and no reasonable substitute for the practice is available. But determining business necessity can be a difficult and expensive procedure.

In the following discussion we examine a small sample of the many cases involving disparate impact and describe the reasoning used by the EEOC and the courts to determine whether the business necessity stated by the firm justifies the use of a job requirement or screening test that has an adverse impact on protected workers. The bulk of cases that are brought by the EEOC are concluded with a settlement or a consent decree; in those cases, only limited information about the evidence and issues is made available to the public. In fact, the information made available by the EEOC is likely to be one-sided reporting, since the EEOC is effectively the lawyer for the plaintiff and will view the situation from the perspective of its client. Cases that are tried in open court are available to the public, and so we report on those brought by private parties or the Department of Justice, in addition to cases determined by the EEOC, to get a full picture of the EEOC's reasoning.

Disparate impact in employment tests. One of the most important cases since *Griggs* involving tests for employment is *EEOC v. Ford Motor Co. and United and Automobile Workers of America* (S.D. Ohio June 16, 2005), a case involving the use of a written test to screen applicants for an apprenticeship program—an issue close to that raised in *Griggs* thirty-five years ago. The EEOC charged that the test had an adverse impact on African American applicants who were thereby denied entry to the skilled trades. The case was resolved with a settlement in which Ford agreed to pay $8.55 million to the plaintiffs. In its announcement of the settlement the EEOC described the details of the case, from which we extract the following:

> The settlement also provides that Ford will select 280 class members for apprentice positions. . . . The 13 charging parties will receive $30,000 each in monetary relief, and approximately 3,400 additional class members will receive $2,400 each, for a total recovery to the class of approximately $8.55 million. In addition, counsel for the private class will receive $1.1 million in fees and expenses for work through final approval of the settlement and $567,000 in fees and expenses for work to be performed in implementing and monitoring the settlement (U.S. EEOC 2005).

In addition, Ford could no longer determine its own selection test but had to accept one crafted by a third party. As the same EEOC announcement describes:

> The settlement provides that an industrial organizational psychologist selected by the parties will design and validate an apprenticeship selection instrument(s) consistent with the Uniform Guidelines on Employee Selection Procedures and professional standards within the field of industrial organizational psychology. If after reviewing the expert's validation report any party believes the proposed selection instrument(s) does not comply with applicable law or professional standards, the parties will attempt to resolve the dispute through a procedure established in the settlement agreement, with the court retaining jurisdiction to enforce the agreement if voluntary resolution efforts fail.

A number of questions are raised by this case and its settlement. First is its relation to *Griggs*. Cyrus Mehri, the prominent attorney who brought the private component of the Ford case on behalf of thirteen individuals (*Robinson v. Ford Motor Company*), quoted from *Griggs* in a statement on testing and the case: ". . . Under the Act, practices, procedures, or tests neutral on their face, and even neutral in intent, cannot be maintained if they operate to 'freeze' the status quo of prior discriminatory employment practices" (Mehri 2007). But the status quo in *Griggs*—African Americans seeking to gain employment a formerly segregated southern firm—can hardly be compared to the situation of minority employment in auto companies today. The only fact we are given is that black applicants who took the test passed at a much lower rate than white applicants.[87] No information is given about the proportion of African Americans among Ford employees overall, or in skilled trades in particular. Nor have we found any discussion of evidence that the rejected plaintiffs would have met Ford's standards for qualified apprentices under a fairer test.

As to the new test to be developed, will equal pass rates (or the 80 percent rule) show that the test is fair to both applicants and to Ford? The cost of having an employee fail to complete his apprenticeship is high (the four-year cost of training an apprentice was said to be $100,000). Surely Ford has a strong incentive to choose the most highly qualified applicants and to develop instruments that will enable them to make a successful choice. Will the team of industrial psychologists, lawyers, and EEOC staff know better how to do this than Ford?

The settlement pays $10,000 each to the thirteen named claimants in the case and $2,400 each to the 3,400 African American members of the class action who took the test (between 1997 and 2004) and were rejected. Would all of these applicants have passed an EEOC-approved test? Seemingly not, since the EEOC conducted an analysis to select individuals who would have been selected by a "fair procedure" and identified only 279 individuals in this "shortfall" group (Mehri 2007). Ford agreed to select this group for the next 279 apprenticeship positions. And, finally, one might ask whether there is any good evidence that Ford discriminated against African Americans in 2005.

Many issues in this case were replayed in other cases. Some of these cases suggest considerable ambivalence about the concept of disparate impact and the involvement of the courts in determining the validity of a test and the manner in which it is used.

In *Hands v. DaimlerChrysler Corp.* (282 F. Supp. 2d 645 (N.D. Ohio 2003), an employee charged that the company's use of an apprenticeship examination had a disparate impact on African Americans. The evidence presented was the fact that all but one employee accepted into the apprenticeship program was white. This case went to trial. But the court dismissed the claim, finding the evidence insufficient because the plaintiff did not demonstrate that the disparity in acceptances was the result of the employer's practices. Whether such evidence was produced in the Ford case is not known to the public.

Disparate impact cases can become extremely complicated when the use of a valid test conflicts with avoidance of a disparate impact charge. The case of *Biondo v. Chicago*[88] required two jury trials and an appellate decision to resolve. In *Biondo*, white applicants for the Chicago Fire Department (CFD) brought suit claiming they were denied promotion as a result of the method used by the CFD to avoid a charge involving the disparate impact of an examination on minorities who were less likely to score at high levels. Since choosing in rank-order fashion from a unified list would lead to the promotion of fewer minorities, the CFD drew up racially segregated lists and selected 29 percent from the minorities-only list. As a result white candidates were denied promotions that went to minority candidates with lower scores. In court the CFD argued that they had a compelling need to follow the EEOC Uniform Guidelines to avoid charges of discrimination.[89] The court, in a "scathing opinion," held that compliance with a government regulation—in this case the EEOC Guidelines—is not automatically a compelling interest.[90] If it was, said the court, "then racial quotas in public employment would be the norm." The lower court ruled in favor of the plaintiffs. On appeal, the Seventh Circuit also ruled in favor of the plaintiffs on the merits but found the damages awarded to be too generous and ordered a new trial on the calculation of monetary relief. But the second jury trial awarded even more money to the plaintiffs in view of the passage of time and the resulting loss of pension benefits.

In a recent and much publicized disparate impact case, *Ricci v. DeStefano* (June 29, 2009), the Supreme Court found the city of New Haven to be in violation of Title VII of the Civil Rights Act when it invalidated the results of a test for promotion taken by firefighters because no African American applicant had passed the test. The city claimed that its action was based on the fear that the African American firefighters would bring a disparate impact suit if the predominantly white group who passed the test were given the promotions.

The *Ricci* decision highlighted the glaring inconsistency that has prevailed between disparate impact and disparate treatment provisions of Title VII. Writing for the majority, Justice Kennedy concluded that the City of New Haven had engaged in "express, race-based decision-making" (i.e., disparate treatment discrimination) in violation of Title VII when it denied promotion to the white and Hispanic firemen solely on the basis of a racial disparity in results on its own validated test.

The Court's opinion in the *Ricci* case essentially states that discrimination in favor of one group to the detriment of another constitutes illegal discrimination. That, of course, would appear to be repudiation of *Griggs* as well as of the affirmative action practices by the OFCCP. Will Congress follow up the decision of the Supreme Court with a clarifying amendment to Title VII that disallows the use of disparate impact to establish guilt when evidence of discriminatory intent is not present?

The foregoing is not intended to imply that the use of tests as a pretext—the intentional discrimination prohibited by Title VII—no longer exists. We note one such case (*Sledge v. Goodyear Dunlop Tires N. Am. Ltd.* 275 F.3d 1014 (Eleventh Cir. 2001)) involving a large manufacturing company that repeatedly manipulated the administration and contents of a job-skill test to prevent a qualified African American applicant from taking the test. In view of the byzantine sequence of events, the appeals court held that a reasonable jury could find that the plaintiff was qualified for a maintenance mechanic position and that the written examinations developed over a six-month period were nothing more than a pretext for racial discrimination.

Another example of a case in which screening requirements were patently used as pretext involved a female police officer who was repeatedly turned down for promotion to sergeant (*Kielczynski v. Village of LaGrange*, 122 F. Supp. 2d 932 (N.D. Ill, 2000)). The promotion criteria involved written tests, an oral interview, and a series of subjective merit and efficiency ratings completed by police supervisors. In the trial the court discovered blatant inconsistency between the subjective merit and efficiency ratings given (very low) and the female officer's performance on the more objective written and oral exams (the highest of any test taker). It is always possible that a person who scores high on a cognitive test has personal traits that make him or her unsuitable for leadership. But other evidence was adduced to show that the merit and efficiency ratings were inconsistent with other written statements about Kielczynski's performance on the job. The court found clear evidence of pretext in the merit and efficiency ratings part of the selection process and ruled against the Village of LaGrange.

This case is quite different than disparate impact cases, such as the *Ricci* case and the case against the Ford Motor Company. Disparate impact attempts to compel an employer to disregard the results of a test if it would result in the hiring of fewer minorities or women. In the case of *Kielczynski v. Village of LaGrange*, the city refused to use the results of the test when its preferred male candidate did not do as well as the female candidate. That is straightforward discrimination.

Disparate impact based on conviction records. Sometime after *Griggs*, the EEOC recognized that the charge of disparate impact discrimination could be brought against an employer who refused to hire any worker who had a record of conviction for a crime. The EEOC holds the position that because

African American and Hispanic men have higher crime and conviction rates than white, non-Hispanic men, a policy of excluding from employment all individuals with conviction records has an adverse impact on the employment opportunities of African Americans and Hispanics.

The EEOC manual gives the following guidance to employers: "With respect to conviction records, the employer must show that it considered the following three factors: (1) the nature and gravity of the offense(s); (2) the time that has passed since the conviction and/or completion of the sentence; and (3) the nature of the job held or sought. A blanket exclusion of persons convicted of any crime thus would not be job-related and consistent with business necessity. Instead, the above factors must be applied to each circumstance. Generally, employers will be able to justify their decision when the conduct that was the basis of the conviction is related to the position, or if the conduct was particularly egregious" (U.S. EEOC 2006a, section 15).

The leading case on this issue is *Green v. Missouri Pacific Railroad Company*, Eighth Circuit, 1975 and 1977. In this case, the court, following the EEOC guidelines, held that the defendant's policy of absolute refusal of employment to any person who had been convicted of a crime other than a minor traffic offense had an adverse impact on black applicants (as evidenced by national data on convictions by race) and therefore must pass the business-necessity hurdle. The court, in strong terms, quickly swept away the idea that an absolute bar was a business necessity:

> Although the reasons [the employer] advances for its absolute bar can serve as relevant considerations in making individual hiring decisions, they in no way justify an absolute policy which sweeps so broadly. We cannot conceive of any business necessity that would automatically place every individual convicted of any offense, except a minor traffic offense, in the permanent ranks of the unemployed. This is particularly true for blacks who have suffered and still suffer from the burdens of discrimination in our society.[91]

Fulfilling the EEOC's requirements is surely a difficult task for any employer. Subsequent to *Green,* other cases clarified the types of statistics that could be used to determine if the conviction record bar would actually create a disparate impact in the firm's relevant labor market area.

The EEOC has extended the reasoning in *Green* to arrests and concludes that a blanket exclusion of persons from employment who have arrest records would have an adverse impact on African Americans and Hispanics because they are arrested disproportionately more than whites.[92] Recognizing that, unlike convictions, arrest records may not be reliable evidence of guilt, the EEOC requires an additional inquiry into the facts before an arrest record can be used in establishing business necessity. The commission also questions the propriety of using arrest information at all in the hiring process. Recently the EEOC has pursued disparate impact litigation involving firms that use information on the credit history as well as the criminal justice history of applicants, again citing the adverse impact of such information on the employment of African Americans and Hispanics.[93]

Note that *Green*, coming only a few years after *Griggs*, shows how rapidly the concept of disparate impact discrimination spread to cases that are unlikely to have been anticipated by the Supreme Court judges who gave us *Griggs*. The idea that a private firm would be required to justify all negative employment decisions concerning an individual with a conviction record, the seriousness of which is likely to be difficult to determine, is unlikely to have been contemplated by the judges who decided *Griggs*. In *Griggs* the case only concerned the use of job tests to screen workers. The judges were concerned that the tests could be manipulated by a racist employer to the disadvantage of black workers who could, in fact, perform equally well on the job.

The ruling in *Green* puts Title VII in a position of participating in social policy that was never considered part of the objectives of any title of the 1964 Act. Individuals who commit felonies are at a serious disadvantage when they attempt to reenter the labor market. A more appropriate way to improve the job opportunities of felons is to develop organizations that can aid their reentry into the workforce, for example, by providing references from prison and assurances to employers that they can discharge former inmates if they are not satisfactory employees.

Disparate impact because of height and weight requirements. Employers have established minimum height and weight standards in a variety of occupations: flight attendants; lifeguards; firemen; correctional officers;

and even production workers and lab aides in some industries. In most cases common sense suggests that such requirements are efficient screening devices for the jobs involved. The involvement of the EEOC arises because women, as well as male Hispanics and Asians, have heights and weights that are disproportionately outside the cutoff points, raising the possibility of adverse impact. As a result, the business and/or organizational necessity of these screening devices must be demonstrated.

The EEOC is skeptical of height and weight requirements and tends to view them as unjustifiable obstacles to the employment opportunities of women and especially the opportunities of women to obtain work such as in fire and police departments. An alternative to the use of measures of height and weight is to measure the attribute that is of concern—e.g., strength—by having applicants lift weights over barriers. Unfortunately such tests cannot get at the entire range of attributes that are encapsulated in height and weight cutoffs. For example, in a number of cases, police departments have argued that a policeman's size can be an important deterrent to crime. A short officer, even one who is equally strong as a taller officer, may not be as effective on the beat: for example, inmates might be less likely to attempt an escape if the officer guarding them is large and strong. In three cases (Accord Horace v. City of Pontiac, Sixth Circuit 1980; Vanguard Justice Society Inc. v. Hughes, District of Columbia Circuit Court, 1979; Blake v. City of Los Angeles, Ninth Circuit, 1979), the judges concluded that the assertions of the police about height and strength were self-serving and could not constitute a valid justification for the adverse impact.

The EEOC has appeared to accept results on weight-lifting tests as a valid screening requirement for certain jobs (and therefore a business necessity) even if women scored lower on these strength tests than men. For example, fire departments have been allowed to require that an applicant demonstrate the ability to carry a body of a particular weight up a flight of stairs. But in a recent case (EEOC v. Dial Corp., Eighth Circuit, #05-4183/4311, November 2006) the Eighth Circuit Court of Appeals upheld a lower court's verdict in a jury trial that Dial's use of a strength test at its meat packing plant created a disparate impact against women and therefore was illegal. Dial's test was intended to simulate the actual work at the plant, which involves carrying thirty-five pounds of sausage at a time and lifting and loading the sausage to heights between thirty and sixty inches above the floor. Dial maintained that the test was implemented as part of a plan to reduce injuries among the sausage packers, who had had a much higher injury rate than other employees in the plant. In the three years before the test was introduced, women made up 46 percent of the new hires. After the test was introduced, the proportion of women hired fell to 15 percent— seemingly the result of the lower percentage of women passing compared to men. (Initially about 40 percent of women passed the test compared to 97 percent of men, and the percentage of women who passed the test declined each year after that.)[94]

Based on these developments, the jury found Dial's behavior pretextual, motivated simply to avoid hiring many women, and the court concluded that Dial's use of a strength test had an "unlawful disparate impact on female applicants." Dial argued that overall safety improved after the introduction of the tests, but the jury did not accept the statistics presented by Dial. The court awarded more than $3 million to fifty-two rejected female applicants. This would appear to be an unfortunate development for the use of tests of physical strength because the use of tests, rather an absolute bar based on the applicant's height and weight, appears to be a good compromise. However, one analysis of *Dial* concluded that the case does not demonstrate that pre-employment physical testing is discriminatory against women across the board because the particular test used and the subjective manner in which it was scored made it indefensible.[95]

Debate over the appropriate fitness standard for police frequently is central to disparate impact charges concerning women. In *Lenning v. Southeastern Pennsylvania Transportation Authority*, the issue was the relevance of a physical fitness test that required an applicant to run one-and-a-half miles in twelve minutes. That standard was the recommendation of one expert hired by Southeastern Pennsylvania Transportation Authority. However, the pass rate for women was substantially lower than that for men (12 percent compared to 60 percent in one year), a disparate impact. The district court, however, found that the level of fitness as measured by the test was consistent with "business necessity." On appeal the court concluded that the district court had not evaluated the expert's judgment carefully enough and should have considered the minimum qualifications for performing the job. On remand, the district court's analysis examined the relation between a successful run time and performance on twelve job standards and found a high correlation. Those who failed the run test had only a 5–20 percent success rate compared to a 70–90 percent success rate for those who passed the run test. The appeals court this time concluded that the evidence validated the use of the running test. A minority on the appeals court provided a lengthy dissent, maintaining that not enough situations that police encounter were used to compare with the run test results.

Disparate impact due to language requirements at the worksite. Employers of individuals of foreign national origin sometimes require that they have certain levels of English proficiency in order to qualify for the job. The EEOC enters the picture when the question is raised whether an employer is engaging in national origin discrimination when taking an adverse employment action against an individual because of a foreign accent or use of a foreign language on the job. There are some situations in which a business must employ workers who can be readily understood by customers or fellow workers. In other situations more options may be available for dealing with the problem. The EEOC Compliance Manual gives an example of a concierge named Bill who works at a hotel where he is required to assist guests with directions and traveling arrangements.[96] Numerous people have complained that they cannot understand Bill because of his heavy Ghanaian accent. The hotel handles the situation by transferring Bill to a clerical position that does not require extensive communication. The EEOC concludes that "the transfer does not violate Title VII because Bill's accent materially interferes with his ability to perform the functions of the concierge position."[97] The solution seems reasonable.

Less reasonable is the EEOC's handling of an actual case brought against a medical research company in 2002. In *EEOC v. Innovative Medical Research*, "the Commission alleged that the medical research firm discriminated against applicants with foreign accents for Medical Recruiter and Interviewer positions. Individuals in those positions conduct telephone interviews of potential participants in medical research projects. Twenty-two applicants, including the Nigerian charging party, received a total of $200,000 in damages."[98] However, callers with a heavy accent could experience a high rate of turndowns for participation in medical projects simply because those called cannot understand what the interviewer is saying. Indeed, if the interviewer not only has an accent but does not adequately understand English, the information he conveys or records may be inaccurate. On its face, in this instance the ability to speak English clearly would seem to be a business necessity.

The EEOC, with mixed support from the courts, has taken a decidedly dim view of "English-only" rules and allows only the most narrowly drawn situations to qualify as a legitimate business necessity. The EEOC has adopted the standard that the English-only rule is justified by "business necessity" "if it is needed for an employer to operate safely or efficiently."[99] As an example of what it considers to be a fully justifiable situation, the EEOC cites an oil refinery with a rule requiring all employees to speak English during an emergency situation. English is also required of employees while working in laboratories and processing areas where there is the danger of fire or explosion. But the rule does not apply to casual conversations between employees in the laboratories or processing areas when they are *not* performing a job duty. The EEOC concludes that in this case, "The English-only rule does not violate Title VII because it is narrowly tailored to safety requirements."[100]

The EEOC has garnered large settlements in situations in which a firm broadly applied "English-only rules" to workers outside situations strictly concerned with safety. In *EEOC v. Watlow Batavia Inc.*, N.D. Ill., No. 99C1435 (0/1/00), the EEOC reached settlement of a case involving eight Hispanic workers of Watlow Batavia, Inc. who were either disciplined or fired for speaking Spanish in the workplace. The firm had barred communication in languages other than English during work hours, including breaks and lunch periods. Under the settlement, the employer was to pay a total of $192,500 (consent decree, 9/1/00).

In *EEOC v. Premier Operator Services Inc.*, N.D. Tex., No. 3:98-CV-198-BF (9/13/00) a federal magistrate judge ordered Premier to pay $710,000 in damages to thirteen Hispanic employees because the company's English-only policy "constitutes disparate treatment . . . based upon their national origin." The employees were initially hired by Premier, a long-distance telephone-operator service, because of their bilingual ability. But Premier had instituted an "English-only" policy during employee lunch periods and breaks, and Spanish-speaking employees had slipped into conversing in their native tongue during these periods. The business necessity justifications for the rule cited by management included the need to serve customers better by improving the English of their operators and to allow management—who did not speak Spanish—to better oversee the work of their employees. The magistrate's finding of discrimination was based on the fact that employees who refused to sign the Speak-English-Only policy were terminated.

The current status of English-only rules is somewhat confusing. It seems that a firm will not be challenged by the EEOC if it imposes English-only in situations in which there is a safety issue at a workplace. In most cases it would also seem that the courts would allow English-only rules if bilingual workers were at issue and the rule did not apply to nonwork time and locales. Workers who do not learn English clearly limit their own work opportunities because they are likely to be restricted to work in ethnic enclaves where the management speaks their language as do the customers. For this reason most immigrants in the United States do learn English. It would be counterproductive if the EEOC or the courts would require firms to adapt to workers speaking a foreign language rather than the other way around.

Sexual and Other Harassment. Sexual harassment is a later addition to the lexicon of cases that may be viewed as discrimination covered by Title VII. Indeed, Richard Epstein, a prominent legal expert, raises the question whether it is "a tort in disguise."[101] Rape, assault, intimidation, and other attacks on individuals in all spheres of life are clearly long-term parts of the common law. One difficulty in making sexual harassment a crime under Title VII is that such acts are not part of official firm policy, but are typically individual actions of firm personnel. The link of harassment to sex discrimination is credited to the highly persuasive book *Sexual Harassment of Working Women* by Catharine A. MacKinnon (MacKinnon 1979). The courts soon followed by making sexual harassment actionable under Title VII (Epstein 1992, 357). In its current guidelines, updated in 1990, the EEOC defines sexual harassment as:

> Unwelcome sexual advances, requests for sexual favors, and other verbal or physical conduct of a sexual nature . . . when
>
>   (1) submission to such conduct is made either explicitly or implicitly a term or condition of an individual's employment,
>
>   (2) submission to or rejection of such conduct by an individual is used as the basis for employment decisions affecting such individual, or

(3) such conduct has the purpose or effect of unreasonably interfering with an individual's work performance or creating an intimidating, hostile, or offensive working environment (U.S. EEOC 1990, 29CFR1604.11).[102]

The first two types of sexual harassment are referred to as "quid pro quo" harassment, since the individual's job situation is directly affected by agreeing or refusing to engage in particular sexual conduct. The third type of discrimination, usually referred to as "hostile environment" harassment, recognizes that even if a worker's employment status is not directly affected by any threats of retaliation, sexual behavior or a sexually charged atmosphere may make a job unendurable. Applying these broad definitions to actual cases, however, has proven to be highly problematic.

Quid pro quo harassment. Quid pro quo is usually the least contentious form of harassment to establish. A clear and direct example of the conditioning of employment on sexual favors comes from the relatively early case of *Barnes v. Costle.*[103] Paulette Barnes worked for the Environmental Protection Agency. Her supervisor, Douglas Costle, solicited a sexual relation and suggested that her cooperation would better her job position. When she refused, her position was abolished.

In one uncontroversial case (*EEOC v. Taco Bell*, No. 02-7634, E.D. Pa. July 23, 2003), a sixteen-year-old girl was raped by her male shift supervisor at a Taco Bell restaurant. The girl reported the sexual assault to the police and the supervisor pled guilty to a "corruption of minor" charge. Although the girl and her mother had informed the management of Taco Bell about the attack, it was only after learning about the supervisor's guilty plea that they terminated his employment. The EEOC brought suit, which was settled with a consent decree providing payment of $150,000 to the charging party.

In its 2005 lawsuit against Caesars Palace in Las Vegas the EEOC alleged that male supervisors forced Latina kitchen workers to perform sex with them in makeshift sex rooms and subjected them to various lewd sexual acts under threat of being fired.

Caesars Palace denied all of the charges (*EEOC v. Caesars Entertainment, Inc. et al.*, 2:05-CV-0427-LRH-PAL). The case was settled in 2007 with a consent decree under which Caesars Palace agreed to pay $850,000 to the employees identified by the EEOC as having been harassed or retaliated against.

Not all cases involving overt sex involve men harassing women. The EEOC confronts situations of women harassing men, women harassing women, and men harassing men. In one particularly nasty case of the quid pro quo variety, a male business owner exploited young Hispanic male warehouse workers by requiring that they submit to oral sex as a condition of employment (*EEOC v. Craftex Wholesale and Distributors, Inc., & Ashcroft Leasing LLC*) (S.D. Tex. May 20, 2004). The case was settled with a consent decree that provided payment of $190,000 and required extensive reporting and inspections.

Many, cases, however, are not as clear-cut as these examples. Over the years the courts have mulled over the complex issues that determine whether an employment complaint constitutes sexual harassment. We review some of the major decisions that illustrate the conflicts of interpretation.

We start with the Supreme Court's decision in *Meritor Savings Bank v. Vinson*, which addressed a number of these issues. Michelle Vinson testified that over a period of four years she had sexual relations with her supervisor. She had started out as a bank teller and was promoted several times, eventually becoming the assistant branch manager. She ended the relation after she started dating someone else and was fired the following year on grounds of abusing sick leave. Sidney Taylor, her supervisor, denied all charges. The lower (district) court denied any relief to the plaintiff, noting that if a relation had existed it was a voluntary one since she was not required to grant sexual favors as a condition of employment or promotion. Moreover, she had never filed a complaint, even though the employer had an antidiscrimination policy and an internal grievance procedure. Consequently the district court did not find the employer liable for the supervisor's actions.

The case went to the court of appeals where it was reversed and remanded. The appeals court found that the lower court had mistakenly tried the case as a quid pro quo when in fact it was more properly a situation of "hostile environment." It found, second, that Vinson's voluntary submission to the supervisor's sexual advances was not material to the charge of sexual harassment which stemmed from the hostile environment. Finally, it found that an employer is absolutely liable for sexual harassment committed by a supervisor, regardless of what the employer knew about the situation or could do to stop it.

The Supreme Court agreed with the appeals court that the case should be remanded and treated as a situation of hostile environment. The Court also agreed that whether the plaintiff's participation was voluntary was not relevant. Instead the proper question was whether the supervisor's advances were unwelcome. (Whether welcomeness is something that is readily, if ever, plainly discerned is surely debatable; yet the terminology has been used frequently in sexual harassment cases.) The Court also held that for harassment to violate Title VII it must be "sufficiently severe or pervasive to alter the conditions of the [the victim's] employment and create an abusive working environment." Unfortunately, what that standard should be in practice is bound to be subjective, varying both with the sensitivity of the victim and the standards of those who are asked to judge it. On the issue of employer liability the Supreme Court rejected the court of appeals' rule of automatic liability for the actions of supervisors, yet noted that failure to notify the employer does not necessarily insulate the employer from liability.

The Supreme Court revisited the issue of employer liability in the complicated 1998 case *Burlington Industries, Inc. v. Ellerth* (97-569) 123 F. 3d 490.[104] Kimberly Ellerth, the plaintiff, was a marketing assistant at Burlington Industries, where she worked with her immediate supervisor in a two-person office in Chicago. Her supervisor reported directly to Ted Slowik, the accused harasser, a mid-level manager located in New York. After a little more than a year of employment, Ellerth quit and shortly thereafter filed a charge of sexual harassment with the Illinois Department of Human Rights and the EEOC citing constructive discharge.

The Supreme Court summarized the case as follows:[105]

> Respondent Kimberly Ellerth quit her job after 15 months as a salesperson in one of petitioner Burlington Industries' many divisions, allegedly because she had been subjected to constant sexual harassment by one of her supervisors, Ted Slowik. Slowik was a mid-level manager who had authority to hire and promote employees, subject to higher approval, but was not considered a policy-maker. Against a background of repeated boorish and

offensive remarks and gestures allegedly made by Slowik, Ellerth places particular emphasis on three incidents where Slowik's comments could be construed as threats to deny her tangible job benefits.[106] Ellerth refused all of Slowik's advances, yet suffered no tangible retaliation and was, in fact, promoted once. Moreover, she never informed anyone in authority about Slowik's conduct, despite knowing Burlington had a policy against sexual harassment. In filing this lawsuit, Ellerth alleged Burlington engaged in sexual harassment and forced her constructive discharge, in violation of Title VII of the Civil Rights Act of 1964, 42 U.S.C. § 2000e *et seq.* The District Court granted Burlington summary judgment. The Seventh Circuit en banc reversed in a decision that produced eight separate opinions and no consensus for a controlling rationale. Among other things, those opinions focused on whether Ellerth's claim could be categorized as one of *quid pro quo* harassment, and on whether the standard for an employer's liability on such a claim should be vicarious liability or negligence.

On the issue of employer liability, six of the appeals court judges agreed that the proper standard for liability was vicarious liability, in which case Ellerth could recover damages even if Burlington was not negligent. Four of them gave as a reason that vicarious liability applies when quid pro quo was involved but defined quid pro quo to include a supervisor's threat to affect adversely the employee's job situation whether or not the threat was carried out. Judges Wood and Rovner would impose vicarious liability on employers for most claims of supervisor sexual harassment, even without a quid pro quo.

Chief Judge Posner, joined by Judge Manion, dissented, stating that Ellerth could not recover damages against Burlington despite having put forth a quid pro quo claim. Judge Posner would only apply vicarious liability to "acts that significantly alter the terms or conditions of employment" or "employer acts." An unfulfilled quid pro quo is a threat, not an act. Therefore, an employer can only be found liable for actual negligence, which, Posner found, Ellerth had not demonstrated. It should be noted that Burlington's policy against sexual harassment, in force throughout the time Ellerth was employed there, stated that "the company will not tolerate any form of sexual harassment in the workplace. . . . If you have any questions or problems, or if you feel you have been discriminated against, you are encouraged to talk to your supervisor or human resources representative or use the grievance procedure promptly." It is undisputed that Ellerth did not use the grievance procedure or complain to her direct supervisor.

This case was appealed to the Supreme Court. The Supreme Court came to the opinion of Judges Wood and Rovner. As the majority stated:

> Given the Court's explanation that the labels *quid pro quo* and hostile work environment are not controlling for employer-liability purposes, Ellerth should have an adequate opportunity on remand to prove she has a claim which would result in vicarious liability. Although she has not alleged she suffered a tangible employment action at Slowik's hands, which would deprive Burlington of the affirmative defense, this is not dispositive. In light of the Court's decision, Burlington is still subject to vicarious liability for Slowik's activity, but should have an opportunity to assert and prove the affirmative defense.

To reach this judgment the Court reasoned that there is no bright line between quid pro quo and hostile environment and both are applicable in Ellerth's case. "The fact that Ellerth did not invoke the remedies provided by Burlington's sexual harassment policy is not dispositive, as the Court held in *Meritor*." Moreover, "Burlington's liability for actions of its supervisor taken within the actual or apparent scope of his employment does not depend on whether someone else at the company knew or should have known that Slowik was abusing the authority he had been given. The common law of agency places the responsibility on the employer to monitor the supervisory employees to whom it has entrusted special powers, to ensure that those powers are not misused." Therefore, the Supreme Court seems to say, if the supervisor is a harasser, the employer is liable.

Justice Thomas, joined by Justice Scalia, dissented. They note that this case creates different liability standards for sexual and racial harassment.

> The Court today manufactures a rule that employers are vicariously liable if supervisors create a sexually hostile work environ-

ment, subject to an affirmative defense that the Court barely attempts to define. This rule applies even if the employer has a policy against sexual harassment, the employee knows about that policy, and the employee never informs anyone in a position of authority about the supervisor's conduct. As a result, employer liability under Title VII is judged by different standards depending upon whether a sexually or racially hostile work environment is alleged. The standard of employer liability should be the same in both instances: An employer should be liable if, and only if, the plaintiff proves that the employer was negligent in permitting the supervisor's conduct to occur.

In his dissent, Justice Thomas draws the distinction between the situation where the supervisor is acting as an agent of the employer and the situation in *Ellerth,* where he is not:

> When a supervisor inflicts an adverse employment consequence upon an employee who has rebuffed his advances, the supervisor exercises the specific authority granted to him by his company. His acts, therefore, are the company's acts and are properly chargeable to it. . . . The supervisor has been empowered by the company as a distinct class of agent to make economic decisions affecting other employees under his or her control. . . . If a supervisor creates a hostile work environment, however, he does not act for the employer. As the Court concedes, a supervisor's creation of a hostile work environment is neither within the scope of his employment, nor part of his apparent authority. . . . Indeed, a hostile work environment is antithetical to the interest of the employer. In such circumstances, an employer should be liable only if it has been negligent. That is, liability should attach only if the employer either knew, or in the exercise of reasonable care should have known, about the hostile work environment and failed to take remedial action.

Thomas deals with some of the implications of the majority opinion. With respect to the conflict with *Meritor* and its broader ramifications:

The Court's decision is also in considerable tension with our holding in *Meritor* that employers are not strictly liable for a supervisor's sexual harassment. . . . It provides shockingly little guidance about how employers can actually avoid vicarious liability. Instead, it issues only Delphic pronouncements and leaves the dirty work to the lower courts. . . . The Court's holding does guarantee one result: There will be more and more litigation to clarify applicable legal rules in an area in which both practitioners and the courts have long been begging for guidance. It thus truly boggles the mind that the Court can claim that its holding will affect "Congress' intention to promote conciliation rather than litigation in the Title VII context." . . . All in all, today's decision is an ironic result for a case that generated eight separate opinions in the Court of Appeals on a fundamental question, and in which we granted certiorari "to assist in defining the relevant standards of employer liability.

As Justice Thomas articulated, the standards for employer liability remain murky. So does the concept of vicarious liability and of behavior that constitutes illegal sexual harassment when a quid-pro-quo is not involved. Needless to say, this is an area where there is no bright line. But should an employer be held liable if the only allegation is that the supervisor created a hostile work environment unknown to the employer and involving no quid-pro-quo? Has the expansion of sexual harassment law improved employment opportunities for women? For women who fear sexual encounters it may provide assurance that the workplace is protected. But it may have negative effects on the firm's willingness to employ women when costly lawsuits are a possible outcome.

Hostile working environment. When liability hinges on whether the employer, knowingly or not, has allowed for a hostile environment, judgments are bound to be highly subjective. In *Rabidue v. Osceola Refining Co.* 805 Fed. 2d ser. 622 (Sixth Circuit 1986), the standard for a work environment to qualify as constituting harassment was one that would cause serious psychological harm. The court noted that "in some work environments, humor and language are rough-hewn and vulgar. Sexual jokes, sexual conversations, and girlie magazines may abound. Title VII was not meant to or can change this." The court also considered the sexual remarks and posters at issue to have a "de minimis" effect on the plaintiff's work environment "when considered in the context of a society that condones and publicly features and commercially exploits open displays of written and pictorial erotica at the newsstands, on prime-time television, at the cinema, and in other public places."

The EEOC believes, quite the contrary, that these factors are rarely relevant for setting standards for sexual harassment. In its 1990 *Policy Guidelines on Current Issues of Sexual Harassment*, the EEOC sides with the dissent in *Rabidue* stating that "a woman does not assume the risk of harassment by voluntarily entering an abusive, anti-female environment." "Title VII's precise purpose," the EEOC says, quoting the dissent, "is to prevent such behavior and attitudes from poisoning the work environment of classes protected under the Act" (U.S. EEOC 1990, section C.3).

This sentiment in the *Policy Guidelines on Current Issues of Sexual Harassment* was echoed by Justice O'Connor, writing the opinion for the Supreme Court in *Harris v. Forklift Systems, Inc.* (U.S. Sup. Ct.1993) ruling that a plaintiff may prevail in a suit "before the harassing conduct leads to a nervous breakdown." Charles Hardy, the owner of the company and the accused harasser, was characterized by the district court as a vulgar man. Did his behavior qualify as intolerable? Charles Hardy's conduct was viewed differently by other female employees at the same firm and by the trial court and the appeals court, both of which ruled against Teresa Harris, the plaintiff. The initial report of the referee noted that other female clerical employees described the ambiance at Forklift as a "joking work environment" and commented that Teresa Harris, as a manager, may have been more sensitive to Charles Hardy's behavior.[107] Teresa Harris resigned, as workers often do when they do not like the atmosphere at a firm for all sorts of reasons. One question raised by *Harris v. Forklift* and *Rabidue* is whether the role of the EEOC in enforcing Title VII is to change the social standards of firms that allow bawdy environments.

Clearly there are important unresolved issues concerning the evaluation of sexual harassment charges. The most difficult harassment situations to interpret involve no evidence of threats of job action but do involve varying degrees of sexual harassment. Some situations are obvious, such as physical coercion to engage in sex acts, and would be covered by the common law even if Title VII did not exist. Some situations involve requirements of employees to participate in lewd behavior that simply are not part of their job description. For instance, in *EEOC v. BlueGreen Corp.* (N.D. Tex. June 14, 2004), "a female sales representative was taken to a seamy club during a company-sponsored trip to Las Vegas and told to simulate oral sex with a kilt-wearing waiter after watching her boss engage in such conduct with a bikini-clad waitress. She refused and left the club. The EEOC settled her claim for 85,000 dollars."[108]

A much larger settlement was eventually awarded to three women employed by the Alaskan affiliate of the National Education Association who claimed to have been subjected to a sexually hostile work environment (*EEOC v. National Education Association and NEA-Alaska*, No. A01-0225-CV (JKS) (D) Alaska May 19, 2006). But in this case nothing sexual, in the usual sense of the word, actually occurred. The charge was that Thomas Harvey, the executive director, was a bully who subjected the women to verbal abuse and intimidation, including yelling at them and shaking his fist in their faces. The district court dismissed the case on the grounds that Harvey's behavior was not overtly sexual and therefore not unlawful sexual harassment. But the Ninth Circuit Court of Appeals reinstated the case, ruling that harassing conduct does not have to be motivated by lust or misogyny to be illegal sex discrimination. The Court noted that it made no difference that Harvey treated men in the same manner as women, because the issue was whether Harvey's conduct affected women more than it affected men. (When yelled at, the women shed tears; the men did not.)

Oddly, the Ninth Circuit presumed the validity of the stereotype that women have more delicate sensibilities than men. Many women are as capable of standing up to a bully as men. Many women and men might not want to work at a firm that employed such a person. But it seems unfair to hold Thomas Harvey's employer, the National Education Association, guilty of a violation of Title VII. Again, the EEOC, this time joined by a court, appears to be attempting to shape the workplace to its own tastes—in this instance making it more civil. The case was settled with an award to the three employees of $750,000.

Racial Harassment. In a racial harassment case (*EEOC v. Foster Wheeler Construction Inc., et al.,* U.S. District Court, N.D. Illinois, Eastern Division,

Nos 98 C 1601, 98 C 3217, March 28, 2002), the palpability of the hostile environment to African American construction workers was so severe that the district judge was moved to write:

> There can be no serious contention that the racial environment of the Robins construction site was not racially hostile. Despite the contentions of Local 597 the graffiti on the walls of the port-a-johns was vile, disgusting, and insulting. Only a visitor from another planet would fail to understand the ugliness of what was written and drawn on those walls.

EEOC won both compensatory and punitive damages for the affected workers in this case.

Systemic Discrimination. Ever since Congress in the 1972 amendments granted the EEOC the right to litigate and to bring pattern-or-practice suits there has been a tension among the succession of commissioners as to the proper use of their expanded powers in the enforcement of Title VII. As described in an EEOC history:

> The Commission has at different times encouraged pursuit of large, complex, time-intensive systemic investigations and lawsuits that involve mostly larger employers and significant numbers of potentially affected class members. At other times, the Commission has emphasized an individual victim approach, designed to remedy particularized fact-intensive wrongs affecting one or a few identifiable individual (U.S. EEOC 2000).

The two approaches to enforcement are radically different. The individual charge surely was the intended mode of enforcement under Title VII since it requires the EEOC to evaluate whether an intentional act of discrimination has occurred. A Commissioner's Charge can begin without a complaint from any individual and is usually based on a statistical imbalance between numbers of protected workers and the commission's standard of the appropriate distribution of protected workers.

Although the 1972 amendments allow Commissioner's Charges and pattern-or-practice suits, it might be thought that these new powers would be constrained by the original Title VII language disallowing the prospect of finding a firm guilty of violating Title VII in the absence of any evidence that individual(s) in the firm were subject to some form of discrimination. This follows from the fact, discussed at length in chapter 2, that Title VII explicitly prohibits the government from forcing a firm to hire protected groups in particular proportions, if it has not been found guilty of any discriminatory act. However, the EEOC has not constrained itself to pursue cases only when there was at least some evidence of discriminatory acts by employers against particular individuals.

In fact, in one of its earliest systemic cases (*EEOC v. Sears, Roebuck & Co.*, 628 F.Supp.1264 (N.D. Ill. 1986), the EEOC brought a charge that was based strictly on numbers without any evidence of a complaint by an individual. This case was based only on the low percentage of commissioned sales jobs held by women during the period 1973–80. However, the EEOC did not produce a single woman who had complained of discrimination. In this case the judges in both the district and appeals courts found for Sears, and the lack of a single complaining protected worker was an important reason for the judgments.[109]

Presumably, if the EEOC had prevailed in *Sears*, the anomalous situation would have arisen of the EEOC's using a law that prohibits affirmative action—the hiring of workers simply on the basis of proportional representation—to enforce affirmative action! However, the loss in *Sears* did not blunt the Commission's desire to fight systemic discrimination. Shortly after *Sears*, the EEOC succeeded in negotiating consent decrees against several very large companies, including General Electric, United Airlines, Illinois Central Railroad, and Bechtel Corporation.

What appears to distinguish the EEOC's systemic approach is a reliance on statistical evidence without waiting for a significant number of individual charges to be brought and resolved against the same firm. This was illustrated in a recent systemic charge brought against the Burger King chain (*EEOC v. Carrols Corp.*, 98-1772). The judges ruled against EEOC, finding that EEOC brought forth too few women who actually alleged Burger King tolerated sexual harassment to justify a charge that harassment was endemic throughout the chain's thousands of stores (0.4 percent of the women at Burger King complained). This does not seem like an unreasonable demand to make of EEOC. Moreover, only a third of the women cited on the complaint had ever complained to their supervisors. Clearly a firm with thousands of employees like Burger King is unfortunately likely to have a few employees whose behavior is reprehensible, but this in no way proves that the entire organization is shot through with harassers.[110]

After a number of years during which the use of systemic charges had ebbed, there has been a fresh emphasis on their use at the EEOC. A March 2006 report of the Systemic Task Force under the leadership of Commissioner Leslie Silverman examined the EEOC's systemic program and recommended new strategies for combating systemic discrimination. The report states that systemic discrimination should be a "top priority at EEOC" and discusses ways of promoting it. However, nowhere does the task force offer any explanation why the systemic approach is needed at this point in time (U.S. EEOC 2006c).

Expansion of enforcement that accepts numerical discrepancies as evidence for a wholesale investigation of a firm is a serious and unfortunate development. Like *Griggs* and the "reasonable accommodation" amendment for accommodating the religious beliefs of employees, it has brought about an EEOC that promotes affirmative action with quotas, a development never anticipated by the originators of Title VII.

A telling sign of what the EEOC may be planning is indicated by a recent short report entitled *Diversity in the Finance Industry* (U.S. EEOC 2006b), which contains a series of tables showing the percentages of protected groups in major occupational categories within each of the subcategories of the finance industry (banking, credit, securities, and insurance activities). After computing meaningless statistics of the odds of each racial-ethnic sex group becoming managers, professionals, and other positions, the report concludes with suggestions of where the industry needs to improve its hiring.

Conclusion

The EEOC is an agency that reviews tens of thousands of individual complaints to determine whether there is reasonable cause for believing each individual is a victim of discrimination. It follows up the cases where reasonable cause is found with a procedure that appears thorough and sensible. Yet, the fact that the EEOC chairman and commissioners are all presidential appointees and that the EEOC deals with such emotionally charged issues ensures that the EEOC will always bear some sort of political agenda.

The EEOC appears to administer many cases of disparate treatment in a sensible way and therefore likely acts as a deterrent to labor market discrimination. However, when it comes to other forms of discrimination, especially disparate impact as well as to cases involving reasonable accommodation of religious needs and sexual harassment, and when the EEOC expands its reach to systemic discrimination and class action suits, then the EEOC not only does not do much to reduce discrimination but has overall harmful effects. In such instances the EEOC imposes costs on firms that are not, by any reasonable definition, trying to use screening requirements or reasonable accommodation as "pretexts" for discriminating by race, gender, religion, or national origin. Thus no serious discrimination in the labor market has been reduced by these activities, and the costs of meeting reasonable accommodation standards or proving business necessity, plus legal costs, could be large (albeit difficult to measure).

In some instances the EEOC appears to be trying to foster social change rather than responding to serious charges of discrimination—for example, the *Green* case involving the use of disparate impact to force companies to consider individuals with a record of serious criminal activity. Ideological zeal would appear to be the motivation for the Commission's initiative to increase the employment of women on Wall Street and otherwise crack the proverbial glass ceiling. Despite a few highly publicized cases ending in settlements that included affirmative action to increase the proportion of females in jobs such as broker and trader, little has changed in the high-powered Wall Street firms.[111] Only a small proportion of women seek these jobs because they make unusual demands on time and energy that women with home responsibilities tend to avoid and require an attraction to risk-taking that women perhaps less typically feel. Yet the EEOC seems intent on pressuring employers to change their working conditions to serve what they believe to be the needs of women. In *Rabidue* the majority on the court noted that "in some work environments, humor and language are rough hewn and vulgar" but found that was not enough to qualify the environment as hostile to women in view of the standards prevalent in society today. But the EEOC sided with the dissent that seemed to believe that the more delicate sensibilities of women should be accommodated by the employer.

In the same spirit the Commission has recently taken on a new initiative called E-RACE, which stands for Eradicating Racism and Colorism from Employment. Presumably that was always the mission of the EEOC. But the EEOC's statement describing the initiative and explaining why it is needed suggests that the agency sees a world still drenched with racism. As the motivation for their initiative they cite dubious poll results concerning racism.[112] They also have a new focus on colorism—preferences for light-skinned over dark-skinned people within any race or ethnicity. The evidence they cite for their color alarm is flimsy. The five-year E-RACE plan notes that they will be expanding data collection for new systemic ventures and will be adding more "matched-pair testing," a method of testing for discrimination using actors to play job applicants. It is highly unreliable, as we will discuss in chapter 8. Such efforts can only detract from the important work assigned to the EEOC.

What lies ahead? The EEOC has tended to embrace disparate impact discrimination enthusiastically. It remains to be seen how it will respond to the recent *Ricci* case. *Ricci* seems to say that if the EEOC cannot prove that an employer's use of a particular screening device that adversely affects minorities is "pretextual"—i.e., used solely to exclude minorities—then the employer cannot be prosecuted for discrimination and barred from using the screening device. It also remains to be seen whether the reasoning in *Ricci* will extend beyond cases involving testing to other disparate impact situations such as the use of conviction and arrest records and height and weight restrictions. Will the EEOC attempt to prevent *Ricci* from becoming the possible fatal blow to its effort to pursue disparate impact cases? Of course, the EEOC does not act alone. There are significant checks and balances, and the courts and the views of the changing EEOC commissioners can either reinforce or restrain EEOC actions.

.

PART III

Analysis of Program Effects

5

Accounting for Changes in the Black–White Wage Gap

The passage of Title VII of the Civil Rights Act of 1964 ushered in a large national effort to end discrimination in the labor market. In previous chapters we examined the procedures and operations of the two major federal agencies charged with enforcement of antidiscrimination policy, the Office of Federal Contract Compliance Programs (OFCCP) and the Equal Employment Opportunity Commission (EEOC). This examination provided insight into the possible effectiveness of the agencies in actually reducing the amount of labor market discrimination in the economy. We now turn more directly to the key question: Have our civil rights policies and programs been effective in reducing discrimination? This is not an easy question to answer. Most analyses of the issue, including ours, start with the presumption that if federal policies have succeeded in reducing labor market discrimination, we should find increases in the relative earnings of minorities and women associated with the timing and intensity of program activities.

But federal policies are not imposed on a static world, and other forces are likely to be at work causing increases or decreases in the relative earnings of African Americans and whites, women and men. Among those other forces are changes in the relative skill levels of African Americans and whites and of women and men as well as structural changes in the economy that affect the demand for different skills.

This chapter broadly assesses program effects by relating changes in the timing of programmatic landmarks to changes in the relative earnings and employment of minority workers to white workers, taking account of contemporaneous changes in the relative skills of the workers compared and of economic and other forces affecting demand. In chapter 6 we undertake a parallel analysis of the gender gap.

The departure point for our analysis is the observable change over time in the wage gap between African Americans and whites. After adjusting for differences in skills and other factors that influence wages, we draw inferences of policy effects by comparing changes in the black–white wage gap during the period before and after the passage of the 1964 Civil Rights Act and before and after the implementation of specific enforcement tools. In the case of racial differentials we also examine the difference in those effects between the North and the South on the premise that the level of discrimination would have been much greater in the South, particularly before the passage of the 1964 Civil Rights Act, and, therefore, the potential effects of civil rights legislation would have been greater there as well.

Overview of Major Sources of Change in the Black–White Wage Gap

The long-term pattern in the relative economic status of African American men and women is depicted in figure 5-1, which shows the ratio of black men's earnings to white men's earnings and the ratio of black women's earnings to white women's earnings.[113] The "wage gap" as is customary refers to this ratio. Thus, a rise in the ratio indicates a decline in the wage gap; a decline in the ratio indicates a widening in the gap. The data span the period 1939–2010 and are measured as the median annual earnings of full-time year-round workers.[114] Significant landmarks in civil rights activity affecting labor markets are indicated with vertical lines. The lines divide the long stretch of time roughly into three subperiods:

1939–64: the pre–Title VII era: the wage gap between African Americans and whites narrows dramatically among both men and women;

1964–80: the immediate years following passage of Title VII: federal enforcement power grows; the black–white wage gap continues to narrow for both men and women;

1980–2010: federal enforcement is entrenched; court decisions and congressional action embellish the definition of discrimination and enhance benefits to potential victims of discrimination; the black–white wage gap stagnates among men and actually widens among women. Note

FIGURE 5-1
BLACK–WHITE WAGE RATIOS, 1939–2010

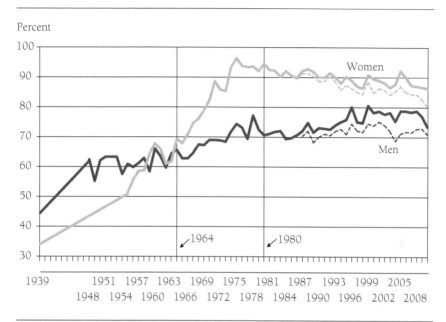

NOTE: Wages are defined as median annual earnings of full-time year-round workers. The dashed lines for 1987–2010 show earnings ratios for black workers relative to white non-Hispanic workers.
SOURCE: 1939 data are calculated from 1940 census microdata; 1948–1954, authors' estimates; 1955–2010, Current Population Survey, Annual Social and Economic Supplements, Historical Income Tables, Table P-38.

that the enlargement in the wage gap starting in the late 1990s is more pronounced when the comparison white group is defined as white non-Hispanic (the dashed lines in figure 5-1).

In examining the reasons for change in the racial wage gap after 1940 we consider several basic factors in addition to government antidiscrimination policy. Of particular importance are migration, educational attainment, school quality, and changes in the structure of wages by skill level. We start by discussing these overarching sources of change in the wage gap and then turn to analysis of the relative importance of these factors in each of the three periods along with the contribution of period-specific events such as World War II.

Migration. In the early part of the twentieth century, one important reason for low relative earnings among African Americans was their disproportionately heavy concentration in the South, where wages were low. In 1940 about three-quarters of African Americans lived in the South and two-thirds lived in nonmetropolitan areas, while close to three-quarters of whites lived outside the South and about two-thirds in metropolitan areas.[115] The potential gain to migration from the South to the North was enormous, particularly for unskilled African American workers. African American male high school dropouts aged 25–34 could earn 66 percent higher pay in the North than in the South. White southern men of the same age and schooling level could expect only half that gain.[116] Monetary gain was not the only benefit of migration. By moving North, African Americans left behind the harsh oppression of Jim Crow that pervaded social and economic conditions of life in the South.

Mass migration over the next two decades by African American men and women greatly reduced the fraction of African Americans living in the South from 77 percent in 1940 to 60 percent in 1960. In some southern states the outflow of young African Americans amounted to an exodus. Mississippi lost nearly half of its young black adults to out-migration, largely to northern states between 1940 and 1950 (Taeuber and Taeuber 1966).

As African Americans left the South they became more urban, moving to cities that offered wider job opportunities and higher pay. In 1940, blacks were less urbanized than whites primarily because a much larger proportion lived in the South, which was heavily rural. But within the South the same proportion—about one-third—of both blacks and whites lived in cities. Yet outside the South, blacks were more likely than whites to live in cities. Almost 90 percent of blacks outside the South lived in cities in 1940 compared to 64 percent of whites.

The proportion of the African American population living in metropolitan areas grew considerably between 1940 and 1960: from 45 percent to 65 percent nationwide. That increase is largely attributable to the great migration, as metropolitan areas continued to be the destination of African Americans moving to the North and West. Another contributing factor was the increased urbanization of the South, although by 1960 the South remained much less urbanized than regions outside the South.

On balance, the net loss of African American men in the South was 25 percent in each of the decades between 1940 and 1960, with an additional loss of 19 percent during the 1960s. But the days of southern out-migration ended by 1970. In fact the net flows began to reverse during the 1970s as African American migration to the South exceeded out-migration. More rapid economic growth in the South relative to areas outside the South narrowed the regional earnings differentials, and as a consequence the effect of geographic location on the level and trend in the wage gap became less important after 1970.

Educational Attainment. Education is important to the development of work-related skills and is therefore a stepping-stone to higher earnings. In the early decades of the twentieth century the African American population had limited access to education.[117] The vast majority of black workers counted in the 1940 census had grown up in the rural South, where school resources were meager. Large black–white differences in the length of the school term, in the number of students per teacher, and in the quality of teachers led to large racial disparities in both the quantity and quality of schooling. School resources for southern African American children began to improve after 1920, and over the next three decades racial differences in resources within the South narrowed significantly. Improvements in resources for extremely disadvantaged children will ultimately reduce the gap in educational attainment of adults, but only with a sufficient time lag. Thus, even though resources for black children improved after 1920, in 1940 a very large racial gap in educational attainment remained among older adults.

High school graduation is important for access to more skilled jobs and a college degree for access to professional and higher-level managerial employment. In 1940, among young men ages 25–29, only 11 percent of black men had completed high school compared to 39 percent of white men (table 5-1). After 1940 the proportion of young African American men who completed high school grew rapidly, reaching 40 percent in 1960, 74 percent in 1980, and 87 percent in 2000, where it has remained through 2009. As African American high school completion rates rose, the education gap with white men sharply narrowed. In 1940 the high school completion rate of young African American men was 27 percent of the completion rate of white men. In 1980 that ratio reached 85 percent and in 2009 it was 93 percent.[118] It should also be recognized that these statistics do not

TABLE 5-1
EDUCATIONAL ATTAINMENT OF MEN AND
WOMEN BY RACE AND AGE, 1940–2009

	Men				Women			
	% with 4 years HS or more		% with 4 years college or more		% with 4 years HS or more		% with 4 years college or more	
	White[1]	Black	White[1]	Black	White[1]	Black	White[1]	Black
Ages 25–29								
1940	38.9	10.6	7.5	1.5	43.4	13.6	5.3	1.7
1960	68.1	39.8	17.3	5.7	68.4	41.2	9.1	3.4
1980	87.3	74.4	26.3	11.9	86.7	76.8	21.8	12.1
1990	84.7	81.1	24.5	13.6	87.6	82.7	24.2	12.6
1995	91.0	85.5	27.6	14.5	92.7	85.1	28.3	14.5
2000	92.4	87.2	32.2	15.6	94.7	87.0	35.5	16.8
2009	93.5	87.0	32.6	17.0	94.8	89.2	41.9	22.4
Ages 25 and older								
1940	24.2	6.9	5.9	1.4	28.1	8.4	4.0	1.2
1960	46.0	21.4	11.6	3.9	48.8	23.9	6.6	3.5
1980	70.7	50.2	21.8	8.0	69.7	50.4	13.6	7.8
1990	78.9	65.0	25.4	11.8	78.6	65.8	18.8	11.4
1995	85.6	72.6	28.4	13.2	85.3	74.0	21.6	13.0
2000	88.1	77.7	30.7	15.3	88.1	77.8	25.3	16.6
2009	91.3	82.9	33.9	18.3	91.9	84.1	31.7	20.5

[1] Starting in 1995, whites are restricted to the white, non-Hispanic population.
SOURCE: 1940, Census of Population. 1959 to 2009, March Current Population Survey.

take into account differences in the quality of schools attended. At the high school level, attainment of a GED is counted as equivalent to receipt of a high school diploma, and black men (as well as women) are more likely to have a GED than whites.

It was rare to hold a college degree in 1940. Among those aged 25–29 only 1.5 percent of black men and 7.5 percent of white men were college graduates. College completion rates increased greatly between 1940 and 1980, rising to 12 percent for black men and to 26 percent for white men.[119] Although the college completion rate had increased considerably for young black men over the four-decade period, the differential with white men was still large, as the African American rate was only 45 percent of the white rate. Between 1980 and 1990 college completion rates declined somewhat for white men, and the increase for African American men slowed; these developments may have been a response to the sharp reduction in the college wage premium during the 1970s. As the monetary return to a college education once again increased, college completion rates likewise increased in the 1990s, particularly among white, non-Hispanics. College completion rates leveled off in the 2000s. In 2009, the absolute differential in college completion between blacks and whites was 15.6 percentage points—a larger gap than in 1990. Measured as a ratio, the gap changed little.

The growth in high school and college completion rates of African American women and white women followed a similar pattern but with some notable differences (table 5-1). In 1940, among 25–29-year-olds, 13.6 percent of black women had completed high school compared to 43 percent of white women. By 1980, 77 percent of black women had completed high school compared to 87 percent of white women. African American women increased their rate of high school completion by 10 percentage points between 1980 and 2000, compared to a gain of 8 percentage points for white, non-Hispanic women. By 2000, 95 percent of young white, non-Hispanic women had completed high school, and that rate has since been maintained. The high school completion rates of African American women continued to increase slowly, reaching 89 percent in 2009, further narrowing the gap with white women.

Although the pattern of change in high school completion is similar for women and men, the pattern is strikingly different when we consider college completion. Before 1980 white women were less likely to have a college education than white men, although college completion was about the same for women as for men among African Americans. But after 1980 both white and African American women greatly increased their rates of college attendance. In 2009, 42 percent of white, non-Hispanic women and 22 percent of African American women aged 25–29 had completed college, almost double the rates of 1980. However, a large racial gap among women remains. The black–white ratio of college completion rates among younger women was 53 percent in 2009, about the same as the ratio among young men.

In sum, African American men and women substantially narrowed the gap in high school completion with white men and women between 1940 and 1980 and came close to closing that gap by 2009. But large racial differences remain in college completion. At ages 25–29, both African American men and women are only about half as likely to have completed college as their white counterparts.

School Quality. The number of years of school completed is the most easily quantified measure of educational attainment. However, years of schooling alone do not adequately measure actual educational skills, particularly when the quality of schooling varies as it has between African Americans and whites. Several studies have linked relative improvements in the quality of schools attended by African Americans to increases in relative African American earnings (Welch 1973; Smith and Welch 1986; Card and Krueger 1992). School quality differences are inferred in these studies by comparisons of school resources provided to African American and white children.[120]

Achievement tests are a more direct measure of differences in educational skills. Holding grade levels constant, African Americans have been found to score significantly below whites on such tests.[121] The Armed Forces Qualification Test (AFQT) has been used by the armed services for many years to test individuals for military service. It is an achievement test of verbal and mathematical skills and reflects the quality and quantity of schooling received (as well as the effects of parents' education, since human capital is acquired in the home as well as in school).[122] AFQT scores are highly correlated with earnings for both African Americans and whites. Table 5-2 displays average percentile scores on the AFQT test by education level for two cohorts of men who took the test at ages 19–21, but in two different time periods: 1953–8 and 1980. The general level and pattern of scores within race and education cells are similar between the 1950s and 1980. However, at levels of schooling below the third year of high school, black–white differences in scores narrowed. At other levels of schooling, the score differential widened slightly. In both time periods the score differences grow larger as education increases.

Keep in mind that the differences shown are not just relevant for the late 1950s and 1980. As we show below, scores on the AFQT test taken

TABLE 5-2

MEAN AFQT PERCENTILE TEST SCORE OF MEN AGES 19–21
BY RACE AND EDUCATION

Years of school completed	1953–58		1980		Difference	
	Black	White	Black	White	1953–58	1980
Elementary						
5–6	7.7	15.4	4.5	7.3	7.7	2.8
7–8	12.4	28.1	9.4	14.9	15.7	5.5
High School						
1–2	19.1	40.4	14.0	30.4	21.3	16.4
3–4	32.2	57.2	19.4	46.5	25.0	27.1
College						
1–2	46.3	70.9	39.2	65.8	24.6	26.8
3–4	50.6	76.9	49.7	80.2	26.3	30.5

NOTE: Mean percentile scores on the Armed Forces Qualification Test (AFQT) for 1953–1958 are based on data obtained from a 50 percent sample (0.75 million men) of the records of all individuals called up for the draft or attempting to enlist between 1953 and 1958. Scores are reported for all tested, including those rejected. Scores for 1980 are based on the results of the AFQT administered by the Defense Department to a national sample of youth.
SOURCES: Data for 1953–58 are from D. O'Neill (1970). Data for 1980 are from National Longitudinal Survey of Youth, microdata files.

at ages 19–21 are strongly correlated with wages two decades later and therefore are relevant for explaining wages in 2000 for those reaching age 40 in the year 2000.

The racial differentials in AFQT scores are but one example of the worrisome and much-studied difference in performance of African Americans and whites on achievement tests. For example a black–white gap in SAT scores used for college entrance has persisted over the years. In 2008–9 the average score of whites on the verbal SAT was 99 points higher than that of African Americans, while the average score for whites on the mathematics SAT was 110 points higher than that of African Americans.

Changes in the Structure of Wages by Skill Level. The black–white wage gap has also been significantly affected by changes in the wage structure that relate to the monetary return to skill. A large literature has described and analyzed changes in the U.S. wage structure. Much of the focus has been on the widening in the wage structure that began around 1980 (e.g., Bound and Johnson 1992; Murphy and Katz 1992; Murphy and Welch 1992; Autor, Katz and Kearney 2008). In an article that set the stage for much subsequent analysis of wage differentials, economists Chinhui Juhn, Kevin M. Murphy, and Brooks Pierce (1991) first expounded the relation between the widening in the wage structure and the slowdown in black–white relative wage growth. Their basic idea is that when forces in the economy lead to an undersupply of skilled workers, the wages of more-educated workers increase relative to the wages of less-educated workers and therefore the wage structure widens.

Because black workers are less skilled than white workers as measured by educational attainment, a smaller proportion of blacks than of whites benefits from the increased spread in the wage distribution, and the black–white wage gap tends to widen. Conversely, in periods when the supply of skilled workers has overshot demand, wage compression results and the pay of skilled workers declines relative to that of the less skilled. In such situations, the black–white wage gap is likely to narrow. The two periods of wage compression that fall within our analysis are the 1940s and the 1970s. Expansion in the wage distribution and rising returns to skill have been a feature of recent years starting around 1980 and also occurred, but to a lesser extent, during the period 1950–70.

The change in inequality of the wage distribution in two periods is often identified by examining the change in the wage "premium" for a college education, measured by the change in the ratio of the hourly wage of college graduates to the hourly wage of high school graduates. Our own estimates of the change in educational wage premiums for black and white men and women are shown in table 5-3 for the years 1940–2010.

The change in inequality is also measured by comparing the ratio of the wage at the 90th percentile of the wage distribution to that of the wage at the 50th percentile and the ratio of the wage at the 50th with the wage at the 10th. Table 5-4 displays our estimates of those percentile ratios for the period 1979–2009.

Both the change in the college wage premium and the comparison of the wage gap between different percentiles of the wage distribution track changes in the reward to higher levels of skill. Consistent with the

TABLE 5-3

CHANGES IN WAGE DIFFERENTIALS BY EDUCATION: 1940–2010,
WAGE RATIOS OF COLLEGE GRADUATES TO HIGH SCHOOL GRADUATES;
HIGH SCHOOL GRADUATES TO HIGH SCHOOL DROPOUTS

	Census *					CPS				
	1940	1950	1960	1970	1980	1979	1989	1999	2009	2010
Men										
College/HS										
White	1.42	1.23	1.32	1.45	1.28	1.32	1.56	1.74	1.80	1.84
Black	1.44	1.21	1.27	1.46	1.29	1.40	1.47	1.69	1.68	1.70
HS/Dropout										
White	1.10	1.05	1.07	1.09	1.10	1.14	1.16	1.26	1.25	1.30
Black	1.12	1.06	1.07	1.12	1.13	1.13	1.16	1.23	1.29	1.19
Women										
College/HS										
White	1.64	1.38	1.54	1.65	1.47	1.38	1.59	1.75	1.75	1.81
Black	2.12	1.54	1.76	1.89	1.56	1.47	1.68	1.78	1.75	1.77
HS/Dropout										
White	1.13	1.13	1.14	1.16	1.14	1.17	1.24	1.32	1.28	1.32
Black	1.27	1.33	1.27	1.22	1.18	1.20	1.26	1.28	1.31	1.27

*NOTE: The census reports earnings for the prior calendar year. So 1940 earnings are for 1939. etc.
SOURCES: 1940–1980 hourly wages were calculated from the decennial censuses, Public Use Microdata Set (PUMS). The hourly wage is calculated by dividing annual wage and salary earnings by the
product of hours worked per week and weeks worked per year. The data are restricted to those who
worked full-time and 26 weeks or more during the year. Hourly wages are reported more directly in
the Current Population Survey Outgoing Rotation Groups (CPS ORG). Monthly reports are averaged
for the year. College graduates include those with postgraduate degrees.

discussion above, tables 5-3 and 5-4 show that the wage premium for high
levels of skill rose sharply during the 1980s, and continued to increase but
at a diminished rate during the 1990s and early 2000s.

Although the widening of the wage distribution in recent years has
received the most attention, periods of wage compression have also
occurred, first in the 1940s and again in the 1970s when there was a particularly sharp decline in the college premium (see table 5-3 and see Goldin
and Margo 1992; Margo 1995; Maloney 1994).

TABLE 5-4

TRENDS IN WAGE INEQUALITY: CHANGES IN HOURLY WAGE RATIOS
BETWEEN DIFFERENT PERCENTILES OF THE WAGE DISTRIBUTION
(90TH/50TH; 50TH/10TH; 90TH/10TH)

						Change in ratio		
		1979	1989	1999	2009	1979–89	1989–99	1999–2009
	Percentage wage ratio							
Men								
White	90/50	1.67	1.83	1.97	2.14	0.16	0.14	0.17
	50/10	1.80	1.91	1.86	1.94	0.11	−0.05	0.08
	90/10	3.00	3.62	3.66	4.15	0.62	0.04	0.49
Black	90/50	1.67	1.80	1.90	2.03	0.13	0.10	0.13
	50/10	1.85	1.78	1.71	1.70	−0.07	−0.07	−0.01
	90/10	3.08	3.20	3.26	3.47	0.12	0.06	0.21
Women								
White	90/50	1.66	1.85	1.99	2.02	0.19	0.14	0.03
	50/10	1.63	1.78	1.79	1.79	0.15	0.01	0.00
	90/10	2.71	3.30	3.57	3.61	0.59	0.27	0.04
Black	90/50	1.76	1.95	2.03	1.96	0.19	0.08	−0.07
	50/10	1.53	1.82	1.70	1.68	0.29	−0.12	−0.02
	90/10	2.71	3.55	3.44	3.30	0.84	−0.11	−0.14

NOTE: Hourly wages are for men and women ages 25–54 who worked full-time.
SOURCE: CPS ORG, microdata annual average.

We now turn to a more detailed discussion of changes in the black–white wage ratios within the three periods identified above and to the particular factors that appear to explain them.

1940–60: The Decline in the Black–White Wage Gap before Title VII

The period before passage of Title VII provides an opportunity to focus on the forces affecting the black–white earnings gap in the absence of significant government antidiscrimination policies.[123]

TABLE 5-5
BLACK–WHITE WAGE RATIOS BY SEX, AGE,
EDUCATION, AND REGION, 1940–60

	Men				Women			
	1940	1950	1960	Percent-age point change 1940–60	1940	1950	1960	Percent-age point change 1940–60
Ages 25–54	44.9	63.8	61.2	16.3	40.5	58.9	66.4	25.9
25–34	47.0	67.8	63.8	16.8	41.0	63.6	70.1	29.1
35–44	44.2	63.3	60.9	16.7	39.8	59.6	68.5	28.7
45–54	44.0	59.5	58.9	14.9	39.6	51.1	60.0	20.4
By Education								
0–8	48.5	66.8	67.3	18.8	44.7	57.8	61.4	16.7
9–11	54.6	71.8	68.5	13.9	47.9	66.0	68.4	20.5
12	55.6	71.8	68.1	12.5	53.2	76.9	75.6	22.4
13–15	50.2	66.1	66.5	16.3	56.7	73.1	80.0	23.3
16+	54.7	71.0	66.0	11.3	63.3	86.5	86.3	23.0
By Region								
Non-South	63.0	75.0	71.7	8.7	59.1	72.0	78.0	18.9
South	42.1	56.9	55.0	12.9	34.9	51.4	58.8	23.9

NOTE: Wages of men are weekly wages. Wages of women are hourly wages. Wages calculated from the decennial censuses, Public Use Microdata Set (PUMS) 1940–1960. The wage sample is restricted to those who worked full-time and 26 weeks or more during the year. Earnings refer to the prior calendar year.

Changes in Wage and Occupational Differentials. It is apparent that African Americans made large relative gains in earnings in this early period, particularly during the 1940s, which saw the largest relative economic gains for black men and women of any single decade. In 1940, black male workers earned a weekly wage that was only 45 percent as much as the weekly wage of a white male worker; by 1950, that wage ratio had increased to 64 percent (table 5-5). African American women made comparable gains over the 1940s as their hourly wage as a percentage of the hourly wage of white women rose from 41 percent to 59 percent.[124] In the 1950s there was a small erosion of those relative gains among men, although the wages

FIGURE 5-2

TRENDS IN REAL HOURLY EARNINGS FROM 1940–80
OF MEN AND WOMEN BY RACE AND EDUCATION

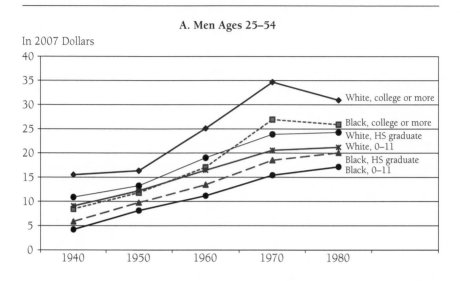

A. Men Ages 25–54

In 2007 Dollars

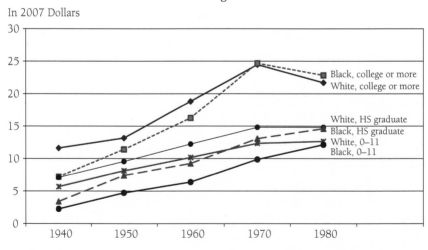

B. Women Ages 25–54

In 2007 Dollars

NOTE: Hourly wages were calculated from the decennial censuses, Public Use Microdata Set (PUMS) 1940–1980. Earnings in the census refer to the prior calendar year. We include wage and salary earnings only and restrict the data to those who worked 35 hours a week or more and more than 26 weeks during the year. We also exclude active military and students.

of black women continued to advance relative to those of white women. In absolute terms, however, the 1950s were a time of considerable growth in real wages for all workers, a point that is clearly demonstrated in figure 5-2.[125] By contrast, during the 1970s wage growth slowed and actually turned negative for college graduates; however, because the slowdown was more pronounced for whites, black–white wage ratios rose for African Americans generally, as noted above.

Despite the small reversal in the 1950s, over the two-decade period 1940–60, the black–white wage ratio increased at all ages and education levels and in both the North and the South (table 5-5). Some groups, however, gained more than others. The black–white wage ratio for men aged 25–54 increased by 16 percentage points. The increase for African American women was even larger, as the female black–white wage ratio rose by 26 percentage points. The relative wage gains made by both African American men and women tended to be somewhat larger among younger workers and larger for women within the South than within the North. Among African American men, the relative gains were also greatest for workers with eight or fewer years of schooling, who, in 1940, accounted for 80 percent of African American men. The pattern was reversed for African American women, whose relative gains were largest at the high school and college levels.

Occupation is another measure of economic status and provides insight into the route through which African American economic advancement was achieved. Consistent with their relatively low earnings, the occupational mix of African American men and women was relatively more concentrated in low-skill and low-paying jobs in 1940. About 77 percent of African American men worked as farmers and farm laborers and as non-farm laborers and service workers, compared to 36 percent of white men (table 5-6). Not surprisingly, the pattern is reversed at the skilled end of the occupational distribution, where white men were much more likely to be in white-collar jobs than African American men. While 15 percent of white men were managers or professionals and 14 percent were in clerical or sales jobs, fewer than 6 percent of African American men were in any white-collar job. African American men were better represented in the blue-collar industrial jobs at the operative level, which employed 12 percent of black men and 18.5 percent of white men. Only 5 percent of black men compared to 17 percent of white men held the more elite craft positions.

TABLE 5-6

OCCUPATIONAL DISTRIBUTIONS OF BLACK AND WHITE MEN AND WOMEN, 1940–80 (PERCENTAGE DISTRIBUTIONS)

	Men						Women					
	1940		1960		1980		1940		1960		1980	
	White	Black[1]	White	Black[1]	White	Black	White	Black[1]	White	Black[1]	White	Black
Professional and Managerial	15.0	3.4	22.7	6.4	28.0	13.7	23.7	5.5	20.1	8.8	25.5	19.9
Clerical and Sales	13.6	2.3	15.0	7.1	16.4	13.3	32.0	2.0	42.8	11.0	44.2	31.9
Craft Workers	16.9	5.0	21.6	11.1	21.4	15.5	1.5	0.5	1.4	0.8	2.3	2.3
Operatives	18.5	12.0	20.8	25.7	16.0	25.8	18.7	8.1	17.9	14.8	8.8	13.2
Laborers and Service	17.0	41.1	11.8	37.7	13.9	28.4	14.5	11.6	13.1	24.8	17.4	27.2
Private Household	—	—	—	—	—	—	7.9	58.4	3.2	37.7	0.8	5.0
Farmers and Farm Laborers	19.2	36.2	8.1	12.1	4.3	3.4	1.7	14.0	1.5	3.7	1.0	0.5
Total[2]	100.2	100.0	100.1	100.1	100.0	100.1	100.0	100.1	100.0	101.6	100.0	100.0

[1] Before 1970, nonwhite was the racial designation, but most nonwhites were black. The proportion of nonwhites classified as black or African American has been declining as Asians and other nonwhite groups have increased their share of the population.
[2] The distributions may not sum to 100 due to rounding.
SOURCE: The data for 1940–1980 were derived from decennial censuses.

Between 1940 and 1960 the proportion of African American men working in farm jobs declined by two-thirds as they moved into operative jobs in manufacturing as well as into the skilled crafts and clerical and sales jobs. Overall, the occupations of blacks and whites became more similar between 1940 and 1960. Thomas Maloney (1994) estimates an index of occupational dissimilarity comparing African American and white male workers in nonfarm employment and finds that the index declined from 47.1 in 1940 to 39.9 in 1960, with the bulk of the decline occurring between 1940 and 1950.[126]

In 1940 the occupational distributions of African American and white women were even more dramatically different than those of African American and white men (table 5-6). Close to 60 percent of black women were employed as domestic servants and another 14 percent as farmers or farm laborers. By contrast, only 8 percent of white women were domestic servants and fewer than 2 percent were employed on farms. White women were mainly employed as white-collar workers (much more so than white men). About 24 percent were in professional or managerial jobs and 32 percent in clerical or sales.[127] Only a small proportion of black women were employed in those fields (5.5 percent in professional or managerial and 2 percent in clerical or sales).

African American women significantly improved their occupational status between 1940 and 1960. The proportion working as domestic servants declined by 35 percent and the proportion in farming fell by almost 75 percent as African Americans increased their representation in service and operative jobs. Although the proportion of black women working in clerical and sales jobs increased from 2 percent to 11 percent between 1940 and 1960, they still were much less likely than white women to hold those jobs. Cunningham and Zalokar (1992) estimate indexes of occupational dissimilarity between black and white female workers.[128] They find a decline in the index from 64 percent in 1940 to 52 percent in 1960. The comparison of African American and white women, however, is influenced by changes in the labor force participation of women and changes in the composition of the female labor force.[129]

A combination of factors contributed to the large gains made by African Americans in relative earnings and occupational level in the years between 1940 and 1960. The migration of blacks out of the rural South and the rise in their relative education were the key changes that enhanced their productivity and helped to narrow the skill gap. In addition, a significant change occurred in the structure of wages that favored workers with less education. World War II played a dominant role in shaping the labor market of the 1940s, as it generated a huge demand for labor while at the same time drawing large numbers of workers into the armed forces. The resulting tight civilian labor markets undoubtedly facilitated the hiring of minorities. Another by-product of the war may have been a decline in racial prejudice, as whites in the armed services worked more closely with African Americans (even though units remained segregated). We review the possible contribution of these forces to the narrowing of the black–white wage ratio in the pre-1960 period.

Accounting for the Reduction in the Racial Wage Gap from 1940 to 1960. Several studies have estimated the sources of convergence in the black–white wage gap between 1940 and 1960. Such studies are difficult to conduct, in part because only some of the likely sources of change can be measured adequately and in part because of analytic difficulties with the basic econometric procedure. In their study of the economic progress of African American men between 1940 and 1980, the U.S. Commission on Civil Rights (1986) addressed the simplest version of the question: to what extent can measured changes in years of school completed and the geographic location of African Americans and whites explain the observed change in the wage gap?[130] For those aged 25–34 it found that the narrowing of the racial difference in years of school completed and the massive shift of African American men from the South to the North could account for close to half of the convergence in wages between 1940 and 1960. The commission noted that the contribution of education was likely underestimated because the quality of schooling had undoubtedly improved more for African Americans than for whites, although it did not include an empirical estimate of the effect.

Other studies have conducted analyses of the convergence of African American and white wages that take into account the effect of relative improvement in the quality of schooling and changes in the wage structure. Robert Margo (1995) and Thomas Maloney (1994) analyze the convergence in the black–white wage gap among men before 1960—Margo for the years

1940–50 and Maloney for the period 1940–60. Both economists include as potential causal factors the impact of the wage compression of the 1940s as well as black–white convergence in the quality of schooling.

Margo finds that an inclusive list of factors, including the contribution of traditional variables such as education and migration plus occupational upgrading as well as the effect of wage compression and adjustment for the quality of education, can explain 83 percent of the narrowing in the black–white wage gap among men between 1940 and 1950. Maloney follows a similar procedure for analyzing both the large increase in the relative wage of African American men between 1940 and 1950 and the smaller reduction in the ratio from 1950 to 1960. He finds both that wage compression played a strong role in the narrowing of the wage gap in the 1940s and that the subsequent widening in the wage structure in the 1950s accounted for the small widening in the wage gap in that decade.

During the 1940s and 1950s many economic and social changes occurred that cannot be precisely tied to changes in the black–white wage gap but may yet have had an impact on relative improvements in the economic situation of African Americans. World War II helped to generate strong economic growth that drove the unemployment rate below 2 percent. The strong demand for labor in the face of the large withdrawal of young men to serve as troops undoubtedly put pressure on some employers who might otherwise have been deterred by social mores or by their own prejudice from employing African American workers.

The armed forces, however, remained segregated throughout the war. Racist attitudes followed both white soldiers and officers into the armed forces. Segregated housing and training camps were unfair. They were also inefficient: it was difficult to assemble a balanced fighting unit made up solely of African American men because of the limited proportion of skilled black manpower to combine with the unskilled. Reflecting their inferior opportunities for education in the South, the vast majority of African American recruits scored in the lowest categories of the Army General Classification Test (AGCT); indeed, about one-third of African American recruits were illiterate, while few scored in the highest categories from which engineering, chemical, and other skilled manpower could be selected.[131]

African American soldiers were largely confined to service rather than to combat units and were disproportionately assigned to the Army. Few served abroad. But with the press of wartime needs and manpower shortages, some African American troops were eventually trained and served in ground combat units and fighter squadrons. Toward the end of the war a few of the African American units achieved success in combat. The 332nd Fighter Group was decorated with the Distinguished Unit Citation (the highest unit citation) for its roundtrip air attack on Berlin. By March 1945, this fighter group had flown 1,578 combat missions and had destroyed 111 enemy aircraft in the air and numerous other enemy targets. Individual officers and men in the group had received many commendations, including eight Purple Hearts.

The commingling of African American and white soldiers eroded some of the prejudice against African Americans. As one battalion commander reported to the commanding officer of the 309th Infantry Division, "When men undergo the same privations, face the same dangers before an impartial enemy, there can be no segregation. My men eat, play, work, and sleep together as a company of men with no regard to color."[132] White soldiers participating in the experimental integration projects may well have emerged with more tolerant attitudes that smoothed the way for President Truman's 1948 executive order that ended segregation in the armed forces.[133]

Another sign that prejudice was beginning to erode after World War II was the entry of African Americans into Major League Baseball, starting with the dramatic hiring of Jackie Robinson by the Brooklyn Dodgers in 1947. Segregation had been the official policy of professional baseball. The hiring of Jackie Robinson to play with the Brooklyn Dodgers, a white major league team, initially stirred some protest among white players. But Robinson's outstanding performance in the game quieted the opposition and led to the recruitment of many other African American players by white major league teams.[134]

The extent to which prejudice in white America changed during the 1940s and 1950s is difficult to quantify. Clearly the trappings of Jim Crow did not wither away, suggesting that it had the support of a majority of the southern white population. Yet some opinion polls suggest slow but steady improvements in southern attitudes toward the integration of schools, buses and streetcars, and residential neighborhoods between the early forties and 1963.[135] Those polls also indicate that the level of prejudice in the North in the early 1940s was much lower than in the South (though still rather high) and declined considerably over the 1950s and early 1960s.[136]

The more liberal attitudes in the North help explain why states in the North and West passed fair employment practices legislation starting in the late 1940s and continuing through the 1950s and 1960s, while no southern states joined them.[137] Did the actions of state fair employment practices commissions contribute to the narrowing of the African American–white wage gap during the 1940s and 1950s? We doubt that they had a large effect because the increase in the male African American–white wage ratio was larger in the South than in the North during this period at all educational levels, though the picture was more mixed for women (see tables 5-8 and 5-9).

1960–80: The Black–White Wage Gap
Continues to Decline Post–Title VII

The period before 1960 was largely devoid of significant federal laws or programs combating labor market discrimination. If the 1964 Civil Rights Act and the OFCCP and the EEOC were effective at reducing labor market discrimination, we might expect to see more rapid relative progress for African Americans after 1964. However, because the economic and social forces causing the relative gains before 1960 may have been more powerful than those in the post-1960s period, it may be difficult to measure the additional impact of the Civil Rights Act and of the subsequent development of federal antidiscrimination activities on labor market discrimination.

The black–white wage ratio continued to rise after 1960 (figure 5-1, table 5-7). African American women continued to narrow the wage gap with white women at a particularly impressive pace. Between 1960 and 1980 the black–white wage ratio for women ages 25–54 rose from 66 percent to almost 96 percent—a gain in the ratio of 29 percentage points, even exceeding the 26 percentage point gain between 1940 and 1960. That gain is partly explained by the relative gain in black women's completion of high school and college. African American women with a college education earned as much as or more than white women with a college education by 1970 and almost as much at the high school diploma level in 1980. In the South, African American women on the whole earned 93 percent as much as white women in 1980, up from 59 percent in 1960; outside the South, African American women earned 1 percentage point more than white women, up from 78 percent in 1960.

TABLE 5-7

BLACK–WHITE WAGE RATIOS FOR MEN AND WOMEN BY EDUCATION AND REGION, 1940–2000 (AGES 25–54)

	Men					Percentage point change			Women					Percentage point change		
	1940	1960	1970	1980	2000	1940–60	1960–80	1980–2000	1940	1960	1970	1980	2000	1940–60	1960–80	1980–2000
Ages 25–54	44.9	61.2	66.1	74.9	76.1	16.3	13.7	1.2	40.5	66.4	82.8	95.8	90.1	25.9	29.4	–5.7
By Education																
9–11	54.6	68.5	72.5	77.0	84.9	13.9	8.5	7.9	47.9	68.4	83.6	95.3	101.0	20.5	26.9	5.7
12	55.6	68.1	74.6	79.3	81.9	12.5	11.2	2.6	53.2	75.6	88.4	98.3	95.4	22.4	22.7	–2.9
13–15	50.2	66.5	73.3	80.7	81.7	16.3	14.2	1.0	56.7	80.0	92.5	100.5	94.8	23.3	20.5	–5.7
16+	54.7	66.0	74.4	80.5	81.4	11.3	14.5	0.9	63.3	86.3	101.2	104.9	96.3	23.0	18.6	–8.6
By Region																
Non-South	63.0	71.7	73.4	80.9	80.5	8.7	9.2	–0.4	59.1	78.0	89.9	101.4	96.3	18.9	23.4	–5.1
South	42.1	55.0	59.9	71.0	75.1	12.9	16.0	4.1	34.9	58.8	76.9	93.0	88.6	23.9	34.2	–4.4

NOTE: Male wage ratios are based on weekly wages. Female wage ratios are based on hourly wages. Wages were calculated from the decennial censuses, Public Use Microdata Set (PUMS) 1940–2000. The wage sample is restricted to those who worked 26 weeks or more during the year and excludes active military and students.

The wage gap also continued to narrow among men, but the relative gains attained by African American men were not as large as those made by African American women. Comparing the period 1940–60 with 1960–80 we find that among men the percentage point increase in the black–white wage ratio was larger between 1940 and 1960 overall, as well as within most education levels (table 5-7). The male black–white wage ratio in the South increased 3 percentage points more between 1960 and 1980 than it did between 1940 and 1960, although outside the South the gain in the two periods was about the same.

Migration out of the South had contributed significantly to the narrowing of the black–white wage gap between 1940 and 1960. The flow of migration in that two-decade period sharply reduced the proportion of African Americans living in the South, where wages were substantially lower than outside the South. But after 1960, migration out of the South began to wane and the wage differential between the South and outside the South narrowed as economic growth increased relative wages in the South. Between 1960 and 1980, migration played a much smaller role in reducing the black–white wage gap.

Some of the key factors that contributed to the reduction in the black–white wage gap in the years before 1960, such as continued narrowing in the black–white gap in years of school completed, also contributed to the relative wage gains by African Americans between 1960 and 1980. Studies of the narrowing in the black–white wage gap find that improvements in the quality of schools attended by African Americans, partly as a result of desegregation after the *Brown* decision, narrowed the difference in school quality, and that in turn narrowed the racial difference in the monetary return from an additional year of schooling. James Smith and Finis Welch's comprehensive analysis of the gain in earnings of African American and white men associated with an additional year of schooling found that the income gain from an additional year of schooling was 5 percent greater for white men than African American men in 1940 and that difference declined to 3 percent in 1960 (Smith and Welch 1989).[138] The black–white differential declined even more rapidly after 1960, and by 1980 the monetary return from an additional year of schooling was actually 1 percent lower for white men than for African American men. Other studies have found evidence of a similar pattern of change in the return to schooling (U.S. Commission on Civil Rights 1986).

What accounts for the growing racial equality in the pecuniary gain from an additional year of schooling? Smith and Welch suggest that the relative reward of schooling improved because the quality of schooling of African Americans was catching up to that of whites. Racial differences in parental education, income, and other family background factors are also likely to affect how much children gain from an additional year in school. Relative improvements in those areas also may have helped to account for the convergence in returns to schooling.

John Donohue and James Heckman (1991) find that assigning a plausible role to improvements in school quality and their effects would still leave a large unexplained rise in the black–white wage ratios after 1960. They point to the passage of the Civil Rights Act in 1964 and the assumed decline in discrimination as the better explanation for the increasing relative return to education by African American workers.

Can federal antidiscrimination policies account for all of the unexplained residual? As noted, statistical accounting for the contribution of migration and education to the decline in the racial wage gap in the period before 1960 also left a large unexplained component. As discussed above, the unexplained portion has been shown to be partly or even largely attributable to the change in the wage structure. The wage compression in the 1940s greatly benefited unskilled labor and was a major reason why the 1940s produced the largest relative wage gain for African American workers of any decade.

Less attention has been paid to the role of structural changes in wages that occurred between 1960 and 1980. The changes in the 1960s were quite different from those in the 1970s. The 1960s marked a continuation of the rapid growth in real wages of the 1950s and of a robust college premium (figure 5-2 and table 5-3). However, the 1970s was a decade of wage compression: there was a sharp decline in real wage growth at all levels of education and especially steep declines at the college level. Over the decade 1970–80, the average wage of white male college graduates declined by 3.7 percent and the average wage of white female college graduates declined by 2.8 percent. At lower levels of schooling, wage rates increased, albeit quite feebly. The black–white wage ratio increased for men and women in part because they were less likely to be college graduates and therefore avoided the sharpest wage reduction and, in part, because within each category of educational attainment, the wages of African Americans either fell less or grew a little more.

In addition to improvements in relative educational attainment, relative quality of schooling, and changes in the wage structure, the intervention of the federal government directly following the passage of the Civil Rights Act also contributed to the narrowing of the black–white wage gap, particularly in the South. With the enactment of Title VII, all Jim Crow activities in the South that imposed segregation of African American workers or barred African Americans from certain types of employment, along with the racially biased policies openly practiced by firms, became illegal and subject to prosecution by the Department of Justice. Because much of the impetus for the Act was the blatant discriminatory treatment of African Americans in the South, the initial activities of the Department of Justice were focused on that region. Southern employers who might have wanted to employ black workers but feared the retribution of the Ku Klux Klan before the Civil Rights Act was passed were now being required by the federal government to do just that. It is difficult to find measures of change in behavior that would capture the effects of the Civil Rights Act because they were so broad. But one indicator of a positive impact of Title VII on labor market discrimination would be the observation that relative wage gains of African Americans following passage of the Act were greater in the South than in the non-South.

Another reason for expecting a somewhat greater effect from the passage of the Civil Rights Act in the South is that a number of states outside the South had already passed antidiscrimination legislation. Starting in 1945 a number of northern and western states passed fair employment practices acts (FEPAs) that outlawed racial discrimination in employment practices and established commissions for enforcement. Six states passed FEPAs between 1945 and 1949; seven more did so in the 1950s; and even more did so in the 1960s (Neumark and Stock 2001). In an analysis of the effect of FEPA commissions on relative earnings and unemployment, William Landes (1968) found that the earnings of African Americans in 1959 relative to those of whites were about 5 percent higher in FEPA states than in non-FEPA states. (Landes also found that the relative unemployment of blacks relative to that of whites was higher in FEPA states.)[139] David Neumark and Wendy Stock (2001) examined a more complex menu of outcomes and found a positive effect of FEPA on black women's wages but no effect for black men. The presence of FEPAs outside the South presumably would have been a factor spurring more rapid relative gains for African Americans in the North than in the South in the 1940s and 1950s, although in fact we observed larger gains in the South.

Although the FEPAs had some positive effects outside the South, the passage of the 1964 Civil Rights Act brought a much more significant change to the South. Indeed the growth in relative wages of African Americans between the mid-1960s and the mid-1970s appears to be greater in the South than outside the South. John Donohue and James Heckman (1991) disaggregate annual time series data from the U.S. Census Bureau's Current Population Survey by region and find that it is largely the southern region that accounts for the rise in the black–white earnings ratio for men between 1965 and 1975. Detailed accounts of particular industries and states also testify to some of the radical changes in employer practices regarding the treatment of African Americans that followed on the heels of the Civil Rights Act. The change in southern textile manufacturing has been well documented (Heckman and Payner 1989; Wright 1999). The textile industry had been almost all white in the South for a century, but the proportion of African American employees jumped to 15 percent in the mid-1960s and continued to rise thereafter (Wright 1999).

Table 5-8 shows these trends in more detail. Between 1960 and 1980 the black–white weekly wage ratio for men ages 25–54 rose by 16 percentage points in the South and by 9 percentage points outside the South. The comparison varies by education. The gain was twice as large in the South as outside the South for those with fewer than twelve years of schooling. But for college graduates the gain was larger outside the South than in the South, and, outside the South, college graduates had larger gains than those with fewer years of schooling.

Considering the 1960s and 1970s separately, we find that in both decades the total gains are larger in the South than outside the South. Within each region and at the same level of schooling, black–white wage ratios rose more in the South than outside the South, except at the college level, where the ratio increased by 9 percent between 1960 and 1970, the largest decade gain in any region/education category. Although the greater relative gains made by African American men in the South than outside the South in the 1960s supports the view that passage of Title VII was an important catalyst

TABLE 5-8

MALE BLACK–WHITE WEEKLY WAGE RATIOS IN THE SOUTH AND THE NON-SOUTH BY EDUCATION:
1940–2000, AGES 25–54

	Black–White ratios (%)					Percentage point change				
	1940	1960	1970	1980	2000	1940–60	1960–80	1960–70	1970–80	1980–2000
South										
Total[1]	42.1	55.0	59.9	71.0	75.1	12.9	16.0	4.9	11.1	4.1
0–11	50.8	63.4	69.1	76.7	85.4	12.7	13.3	5.7	7.6	8.7
12	46.4	60.1	68.4	76.5	80.8	13.7	16.4	8.3	8.1	4.3
16+	52.2	64.9	69.0	76.3	80.1	12.7*	11.4	4.1	7.3	3.8
Non-South										
Total[1]	63.0	71.7	73.4	80.9	80.5	8.7	9.2	1.7	7.5	-0.4
0–11	68.1	79.1	80.9	85.5	95.6	11.0	6.4	1.8	4.6	10.1
12	64.7	73.9	79.5	84.4	86.8	9.2	10.5	5.6	4.9	2.4
16+	62.1*	69.5	78.9	84.6	84.1	7.4	15.1	9.4	5.7	-0.5

[1] The total includes those with 13–15 years of schooling.

*Between 50 and 100 observations for black men.

NOTE: Estimates are calculated from public use files of the 1940–2000 decennial censuses and refer to wage and salary workers who worked full-time and 26 or more weeks during the year.

for rapid gains for African American workers, note that table 5-8 also shows larger gains in the South than outside the South during the period 1940–60, when the state-level FEPAs were active only in states outside the South. However, the size of the difference between North and South in the relative African American gain was clearly larger in the period 1960–80.

The pattern of change just described for men also applies to women, as shown in table 5-9. But the rise in the black–white wage ratio was much larger for women than for men in every region/educational attainment category in all of the decades through the 1970s. One major reason for the strong relative gains of African American women during that period is their early acquisition of an important form of human capital, namely work experience. One of the ways that human capital is acquired is through years of continuous labor market experience (Mincer 1962, 1974). Differences in work experience play a major role in explaining differences in wage rates among women and between women and men (Mincer and Polachek 1974, 1985; O'Neill 1985, 2003).

We can infer something about the evolving differences in work experience between African American and white women from data on labor force participation. In the past, African American women were much more likely than white women to work outside the home (figure 5-3). In 1954, 53 percent of African American women and only 37 percent of white women were in the labor force. What explains that difference? Married women have always been less likely to work outside the home than single women, and, among married women, labor force participation has tended to be inversely related to the husband's income.[140] Higher marriage rates and higher-income husbands contributed to the lower labor force rates of white women compared to African American women. When the labor force participation rates of white women began to increase sharply as they did starting in the late 1960s, many white women with relatively little work experience entered the labor force. This reduced the work experience of the average employed white woman in the 1960s and into the 1970s (Goldin 1989, 1990; O'Neill 1985; Smith and Ward 1989).

Those inferences from labor force participation data are supported by measures of lifetime work experience of African American and white women reported in longitudinal surveys. These surveys show that African American women had already acquired significantly greater amounts of

TABLE 5-9

FEMALE BLACK–WHITE HOURLY WAGE RATIOS IN THE SOUTH AND THE NON-SOUTH BY EDUCATION: 1940–2000, AGES 25–54

	Black–White ratios (%)					Percentage point change				
	1940	1960	1970	1980	2000	1940–60	1960–80	1960–70	1970–80	1980–2000
South										
Total[1]	31.7	58.8	76.9	93.0	88.6	27.1	34.2	18.1	16.1	-4.4
0–11	37.7	55.4	73.6	93.5	101.0	17.7	38.1	18.1	19.9	7.5
12	43.8	63.7	79.6	92.3	92.1	19.9	28.6	15.9	12.7	-0.2
16+	64.8*	92.3	101.2	105.4	95.5	27.5*	13.1	8.9	4.2	-9.9
Non-South										
Total[1]	53.1	78.0	89.9	101.4	96.3	24.9	23.4	11.9	11.5	-5.1
0–11	59.6	81.6	91.4	102.4	112.2	22.0	20.8	9.8	11.0	9.8
12	55.8	83.5	94.4	105.6	104.4	27.7	22.1	10.9	11.2	-1.2
16+	ns	85.2	107.7	108.1	101.4	ns	22.9	22.5	0.4	-6.7

[1] The total includes those with 13–15 years of schooling.
*Between 50 and 100 observations for black men. ns indicates fewer than 50 persons.
NOTE: Estimates are based on public use files of the 1940–2000 decennial censuses and refer to wage and salary workers who worked full-time and 26 or more weeks during the year.

FIGURE 5-3

FEMALE LABOR FORCE PARTICIPATION RATES
BY RACE: 1954–2010 (AGES 25–54)

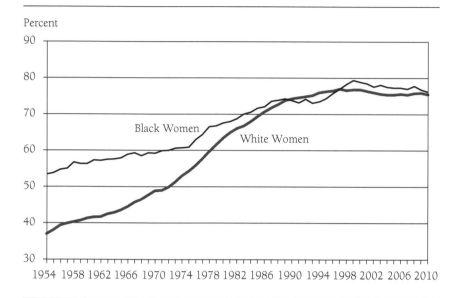

SOURCE: Bureau of Labor Statistics (http://www.bls.gov/data/home.htm). Prior to 1972, the black population includes other nonwhites.

work experience than white women by the 1960s and 1970s (O'Neill and Hill 1992). The work experience differential narrowed as white women increased their labor force participation and employment continuity during the 1980s and was erased by 1988.

The change over the years in the work experience of white women relative to that of African American women is bound to have affected the change in the black–white wage ratio and likely accounts for much of the apparent surge in the relative wages of African American women during the 1970s when white women with little experience were entering the labor market. The exaggerated slowdown in African American women's relative wages starting in the 1980s coincided with a period during which white women's work experience was catching up with that of African American women. In table 5-10 we conduct a demonstration that makes the point. We estimate the black–white wage ratio of African American women to

TABLE 5-10

THE CHANGE IN THE HOURLY WAGE RATIO BETWEEN
BLACK WOMEN AND WHITE WOMEN AND BLACK WOMEN AND WHITE MEN,
1960–80 AND 1979–2009

	Census		CPS ORG		Percentage point change	
	1960	1980	1979	2009	1960–80	1979–2009
Full-time workers ages 25–54						
Black Women/ White Women (%)	66.4	95.7	93.4	82.4	29.3	–11.1
Black Women/ White Men (%)	43.2	60.9	60.3	65.3	17.7	5.0
0-11/9-11*						
Black Women/ White Women (%)	62.6	95.9	91.4	86.0	33.3	–5.4
Black Women/ White Men (%)	38.8	57.3	56.7	65.0	18.5	8.3
HS grad.						
Black Women/ White Women (%)	75.6	98.6	95.0	88.8	23.0	–6.2
Black Women/ White Men (%)	48.6	60.2	61.4	69.1	11.6	7.7
College or more						
Black Women/ White Women (%)	86.3	105.2	101.6	89.0	18.9	–12.6
Black Women/ White Men (%)	64.8	73.8	68.3	67.4	9.0	–0.9

*ORG uses years of schooling 9-11.
NOTE: For census data, hourly wages were estimated from the decennial censuses, Public Use Microdata Set (PUMS) 1940–1980. Earnings in the census refer to the prior calendar year. For CPS ORG data, average hourly wage earnings are more directly reported for full-time wage and salary workers. Data for whites in the ORG are white non-Hispanics.

white *men*, a group with relatively stable work experience. The comparison is shown for three educational levels. Because white men are the highest earners, that wage ratio is obviously much lower than the ratio comparing African American women with white women, also shown in table 5-10. But it is striking that the swings in African American women's relative wages are much less exaggerated when their comparators are white men than when they are white women. Thus when African American women are compared with white women, the increase in the racial wage ratio between 1960 and 1980 is huge: 29 percentage points; when the comparison over the same years is with white men, the increase for African American women is much lower: merely 18 percentage points. Conversely, during the period 1979–2009, the wage ratio comparing African American women with white women falls sharply by 11 percentage points, but when the comparison is African American women with white men the ratio rises by 5 percentage points. The 5 percentage point rise is still a slowdown from the much larger increases between 1960 and 1980, but paints a different picture than the 11 percentage point decline shown in the traditional comparison of African American women with white women.

We have emphasized that passage of Title VII of the 1964 Civil Rights Act undoubtedly had a positive effect on the economic status of African Americans, although a precise measure cannot be assigned. More unsettled is the extent to which the observed gains in earnings can be attributed to the activities of the EEOC and the OFCCP. A number of economists have examined the effect of federal civil rights policies on the racial wage gap using more formal econometric models, and those who have studied the issue have conflicting views. Richard Freeman (1973) conducted the first systematic analysis that examined the link between federal civil rights activity and the rise in the relative earnings of African American men. Using time-series analysis, Freeman concluded that the government did in fact have a strong positive effect on the outcome even after controlling for business cycles, overall economic growth, and educational differences. Freeman measured civil rights activity by cumulative EEOC expenditures per nonwhite worker. Butler and Heckman (1977) countered that Freeman's results were contaminated by the selection effect of labor force dropouts on relative wages. Coincidental with the timing of the Civil Rights Act, the relative labor force participation of African American men to white men had declined (see figure 5-4 for all men ages 25–54 by race and figure 5-5, which also disaggregates by education) and the decline was greatest for less educated workers, who are likely to have had lower wages.[141] This dropout effect therefore could account for the relative increase in the average African American wage of those remaining in the labor force.

Charles Brown (1984) modified Freeman's analysis by statistically accounting for the selection effect of labor force dropouts and measuring civil rights activity with a time trend instead of EEOC expenditures. He concluded that the adjustment for selection reduced the effect measured by Freeman but only by about half.[142]

FIGURE 5-4

MALE LABOR FORCE PARTICIPATION RATES BY RACE:
1954–2010 (AGES 25–54)

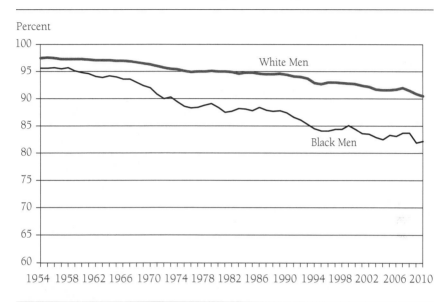

SOURCE: Bureau of Labor Statistics (http://www.bls.gov/data/home.htm). Prior to 1972, the black population includes other nonwhites.

Neither the Freeman nor the Brown study can be taken as conclusive. One problem is that both attribute all of the unexplained growth in relative African American wages to government antidiscrimination activity. Yet they could only measure a limited number of explanatory factors and omitted factors might have accounted for some or even most of the unexplained growth. A serious limitation of both studies is the time period covered by the analysis. Because annual data for time series do not start until 1948, their analysis excludes the years in the 1940s when the black–white wage ratio was rising more rapidly than in the 1960s. The comparison years that influenced their findings of a post-1964 effect are based mainly on the 1950s and early 1960s, when the relative wages of African Americans were declining or changing erratically.

A number of studies have examined more specifically the possible effects of the OFCCP on the relative economic status of African American

FIGURE 5-5

PERCENT OF MEN WHO WORKED AT SOME TIME DURING THE YEAR, BY RACE AND EDUCATION: 1967–2009

A. High School Graduate or Less

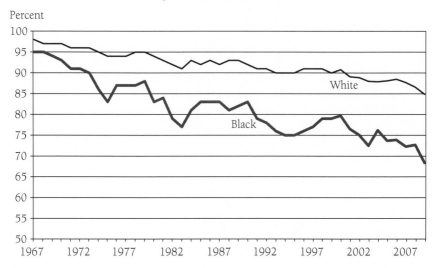

B. One or More Years of College

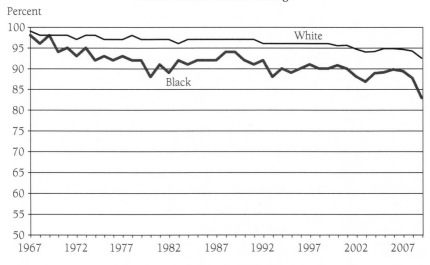

SOURCE: Calculated from CPS microdata for civilian adults, ages 25–54.

workers (e.g., Ashenfelter and Heckman 1976; Goldstein and Smith 1976; Leonard 1984, 1985). These studies typically compare changes in employment trends of minority and white workers in firms with federal contracts with other firms in the same industry who do not hold federal contracts. Because firms with federal contracts face loss of the contract if they fail to comply with the affirmative action requirements of the OFCCP, the presumption is that they should show more favorable outcomes for minority workers than non-contractor firms. Thus a finding that federal contractors increased their share of black workers at a faster rate than non-contractors is taken as evidence that the OFCCP has benefited African Americans.

Most studies of the effects of the OFCCP find a positive effect on the relative employment of blacks in firms holding federal contracts. However, the results are sensitive to model specification and differences in statistical methodologies have produced divergent estimates, sometimes from the same investigator.[143] The studies cover different time periods within the years 1966–80.[144]

Although studies generally find that federal contractors significantly increased the representation of African Americans in their workforce after 1965, that positive effect on employment shares did not translate into sustained wage gains for African Americans. Smith and Welch (1989) find a sharp rise in the relative earnings of young black male college graduates between the years 1967–8 and 1971(from 76 percent to 101 percent), which they attribute to an increase in the demand for black workers by OFCCP-covered firms spurred by the need to meet affirmative action requirements. But they also find that the surge was a "wage bubble" that eroded after a few years. The wage effect described was smaller for older workers and for those with less education. As shown in figure 5-1, the male black–white wage ratio for all full-time year-round workers increased from about 63 percent in 1966 to 72–74 percent in 1974–75 and then declined to a level of 70 percent by 1980. As noted above, the female black–white wage ratio increased even more sharply between 1966 and 1975, when it reached 96 percent, but has declined steadily since then. In chapter 7 we estimate the relative wage effects of affirmative action at the OFCCP and find no effect.

Some studies have examined the effects of EEOC on the relative economic status of African American workers. As described in chapter 4, the

EEOC was created by the 1964 Civil Rights Act but not given substantial resources and independent enforcement powers until additional legislation was passed in 1972. The Equal Employment Opportunity Act (EEOA) of 1972 granted the EEOC the right to initiate law suits against employers. The 1972 Act also extended coverage of Title VII to employers with 15–25 employees who had previously been exempt. The Act went into effect in 1973 and primarily affected small firms in several southern states, since most states by that time had passed FEPAs that extended coverage to small firms. Chay (1998) finds large relative wage gains and increases in employment share after 1972 for unskilled African Americans in the impacted sector, which he attributes to the 1972 coverage extension.

The EEOC and the OFCCP gained power and resources in the late 1970s. However, a long period of stagnation in the relative wages of African Americans began during the last years of the Carter administration when the OFCCP was greatly strengthened and consolidated.

After 1980: Stagnation in the Black–White Wage Gap

It is evident that black–white wage ratios for both women and men rose significantly from 1939 to the 1964 passage of the Civil Rights Act, and again from 1964 to the mid-1970s (figure 5-1). Over this long period, the wage ratio among men increased from 45 percent in 1939 to 66 percent in 1964 and to 74 percent in 1975, while the black–white ratio among women rose even more dramatically, from 34 percent in 1939 to 69 percent in 1964 and to 96 percent—near parity—in 1975. But after the late 1970s the rise in the black/white wage ratio slowed sharply for both men and women. The apparent rise in the ratio starting in the late 1980s is largely the result of a demographic change among white workers, as Hispanic immigrants with relatively low wages became an increasingly large percentage of the white population. The male wage ratio comparing African Americans to non-Hispanic whites (shown by the lighter and lower line in figure 5-1) rose only slightly in the 1990s and has since declined. Among women the wage ratio comparing African Americans to non-Hispanic whites began to decline in the late 1980s and has continued to erode. Thus a slowdown in the rise in relative African American earnings set in just before 1980 for women and men and has continued through to 2010.

The dramatic nature of the slowdown can also be seen when we examine wage rates using decennial census data measured at twenty-year intervals starting in 1940 (table 5-7). For the country as a whole, the black–white wage ratio for 25–54 year old men increased by 16 percentage points between 1940 and 1960 and by 14 percentage points between 1960 and 1980. But between 1980 and 2000 the ratio barely changed. The relative gains made by African American women were even larger from 1940 to 1960 and 1960 to 1980, but from 1980 to 2000 the black–white wage ratio for women ages 25–54 *declined* by 6 percentage points.

The pattern of change in the black–white wage ratio by education level between 1980 and 2000 appears roughly similar for women and men in that the slowdown is more pronounced for college graduates than for those at lower education levels. By region we find that the slowdown is more pronounced outside the South than in the South. Among men, the black–white ratio actually increased by 4 percentage points in the South between 1980 and 2000. The female black–white ratio, however, declined by 4 percentage points in the South and declined by 5 percentage points outside the South.

The most likely explanation for the large decline in the black–white wage ratio among women is the relative upgrading in the skills of white women who have increased their educational attainment and work attachment over the past two decades. As indicated in table 5-1 (for those ages 25–29), the proportion of white women graduating from college increased from 22 percent in 1980 to 36 percent in 2000 (when we consider white, non-Hispanic women, which is the more appropriate comparison). At the same time the proportion of African American women completing college rose from 12 percent in 1980 to 17 percent in 2000. With respect to work experience, black women in earlier decades were more likely to work continuously than white women. However, white women greatly increased their lifetime work experience and narrowed that gap with African American women during the 1980s.[145]

The reversal in the long-term trend in the black–white wage gap after 1980 was dramatic. It was most pronounced at higher education levels, affecting about 90 percent of African Americans with at least a high school diploma. At the lowest levels of education, the modest positive trends between 1960 and 1980 continued through 2009.

A number of economists have attributed the lack of any significant change in the black–white wage gap after 1980 to structural changes in the economy which led to an increase in the wage premium for skill (Juhn, Murphy, and Pierce 1991). As shown above in table 5-3, the wage premium for college graduates soared between 1979 and 2010. As shown in figure 5-6, the increase in male wage dispersion between 1979 and 1992 was the result of an actual decline in the real wages of men with less than a college education, combined with a moderate rise in the wages of college graduates. The wage decline for less educated men was in large part tied to a decline in demand for blue-collar workers in manufacturing and other production industries. Between 1992 and 2010 the wages of men with less than a college education stabilized, while the wages of college graduates rose ever more steeply as the Internet age created a demand for highly educated workers. African American men have less schooling than whites, primarily because of their lower rates of college completion. And as discussed, within each education level their educational attainment as measured by test scores is also lower (table 5-2). The relative increase in the demand for skilled labor would have the side effect of widening both the aggregate wage gap and, to a lesser extent, the gap within age-education specific cells.

As shown in table 5-7, and briefly noted above, the pattern of change in the male black–white wage ratio differs significantly by education and somewhat by age between 1980 and 2000. Since the AFQT gap is smallest at the less-than-high-school level and tends to widen with higher education levels, the observed pattern of trends in the wage ratio is consistent with a labor market in which premiums for skill are rising, which we know tends to increase the racial wage gap especially at higher education levels.

In chapter 8 we analyze in detail the sources of the black–white wage gap in 2000 and in 2008. The data indicate that little if any of the recent gap in earnings between African American and white workers is likely to be due to labor market discrimination. A major implication of this finding is that the emphasis of antidiscrimination policy is misguided. The skill differences that are the source of the black–white pay gap are not likely to be addressed by eliminating skill tests for hiring or by instituting quotas for minorities.

FIGURE 5-6

TRENDS IN REAL HOURLY EARNINGS FROM 1979 TO 2010
OF MEN AND WOMEN BY RACE AND EDUCATION

A. Men Ages 25–54

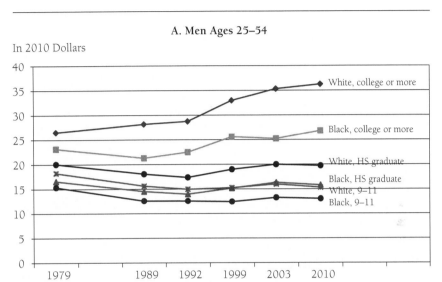

B. Women Ages 25–54

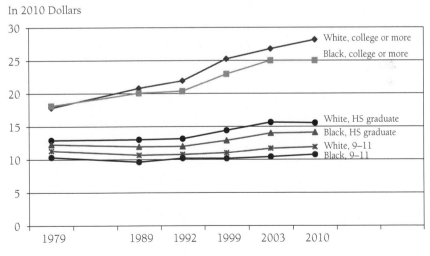

NOTE: Average hourly wage for full-time workers are estimated from CPS Outgoing Rotation Group (ORG) microdata files. Data for whites refer to white non-Hispanics.

6

Accounting for Changes in the Gender Wage Gap

The pattern of change in the gender gap in wages is strikingly different from the pattern of change in the black–white wage gap displayed in figure 5-1. As shown in figure 6-1, the most commonly cited measure of the gender pay gap, the female–male ratio of median annual earnings of full-time, year-round workers, declined from 65 percent in 1955 to about 59 percent in 1961. It remained there throughout most of the 1960s and 1970s, despite the enactment of Title VII, the establishment of the Equal Employment Opportunity Commission (EEOC) and the Office of Federal Contract Compliance Programs (OFCCP), and the rise in the feminist movement. The stagnation of the gender gap in those years was a puzzle to economists and a call to action of women's rights groups, which issued the famous button bearing the slogan "59 cents out of every dollar." The gender pay gap began to narrow in the early 1980s, and the female–male ratio of median annual earnings of full-time workers rose to 72 percent in 1990. After remaining at that level through about 1995 it rose again until it stabilized in a narrow range between 77 percent and 78 percent during the years 2005–10.

The size of the gender wage gap, however, differs depending on how it is measured. An alternative measure using the average hourly wage is also shown in figure 6-1.[146] In all years the hourly wage ratio is higher, and therefore the gap is smaller, than the gap based on annual earnings of full-time year-round workers. That difference occurs primarily because men who work full-time work about 8–10 percent more hours per week than full-time women, and the annual measure does not adjust for differences in hours of full-time workers. But the pattern of change is similar—the hourly wage ratio rose from 66 percent in 1979 to between 81 and 83 percent in the years 2005–10.

FIGURE 6-1

THE GENDER GAP: FEMALE–MALE WAGE RATIOS (1955–2010)

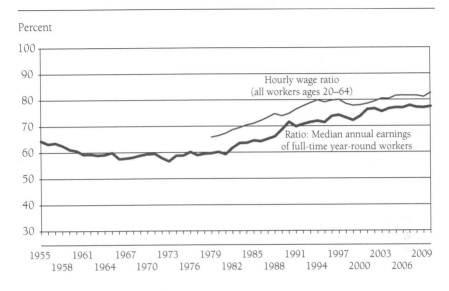

SOURCE: Hourly wage: annual average monthly hourly earnings calculated from Outgoing Rotation Groups (ORG). Median annual earnings: U.S. Bureau of the Census, Current Population Survey (CPS), Annual Social and Economic Supplements, Historical Income Tables, table P-38. The data for 1955–1959 refer to median annual income of full-time year-round workers instead of median annual earnings.

The shrinking of the gender gap after 1980 was a puzzle to many observers and cast further doubt on the power of federal antidiscrimination policies to influence the gender pay gap. Indeed, the administration of Ronald Reagan appeared to be unenthusiastic about the practices of the federal antidiscrimination agencies. A 1982 article in the *New York Times* commented, "Across the spectrum of civil rights enforcement, from public school desegregation to job discrimination to the rights of handicapped people, the administration has repudiated some key policies of past Democratic and Republican Administrations" (Taylor 1982).

If increased pressure from federal civil rights enforcement was not a major cause of the narrowing in the gender pay gap in the 1980s, then what was? Economic research provides a compelling explanation for both the stagnation of the female–male wage gap in the 1960s and 1970s and its significant narrowing during the 1980s and thereafter. In brief, the main source of the gender wage gap has always been a gender difference in work-related skills, most importantly those skills acquired through years of experience in the labor market. Ironically, as the percentage of women in the labor force grew during the 1960s and 1970s, the accumulated work experience of the average woman in the labor force declined, widening the differential in experience with men and consequently widening the wage gap. By the 1980s the gender difference in accumulated lifetime work experience began to narrow and provided the impetus for the narrowing of the pay gap in the 1980s. Women increasingly expected to have a career, which led to investments in education and career training that enhanced women's earnings and helped to narrow the wage gap with men.

Although civil rights enforcement does not appear to be correlated with changes in the wage gap, it is nonetheless possible that a reduction in the extent of societal prejudice toward women was an additional catalyst that improved women's labor market opportunities and encouraged work-related investments. We evaluate below various explanations for the change in the gender gap.

Skill Differentials between Women and Men

Earnings are linked to productivity, and productivity is enhanced by investments in education and in formal and informal training on the job. We discuss the trends in gender differences in education and work experience below. We start with lifetime work experience, which has been a fundamental reason for the wage gap.

Work Experience. Experience in the workforce, gained through years of both informal and formal on-the-job training, is a vital ingredient in building skills that influence earnings. Differences between men and women in work-related skills have been shown to stem primarily from gender differences in labor market participation. These have been shaped by differences in the roles of men and women in the family. The past century has witnessed a revolution in women's economic role; but not so long ago that role was sharply differentiated from men's.[147] Men had primary responsibility for the family's financial support, while women assumed primary responsibility

FIGURE 6-2
LABOR FORCE PARTICIPATION RATES BY SEX:
1948–2010 (AGES 25–54)

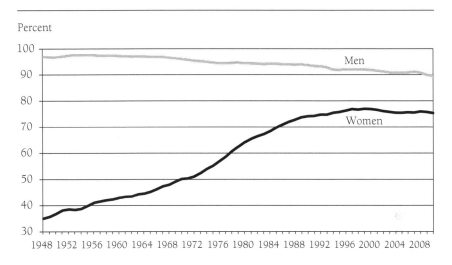

Percent

SOURCE: Bureau of Labor Statistics (http://www.bls.gov/data/home.htm), annual averages of CPS monthly data.

for childcare and the work involved in running a home. Housework and the care of children constituted a demanding full-time job. In 1900, 20 percent of all women but only 5.6 percent of married women were in the labor force; and the full-time homemaker is reported to have worked 84 hours a week in the home.[148]

Over the course of the twentieth century the division of labor in the family became less sharply delineated as women, particularly married women with children, shifted more of their time to the labor market. Initially the change was slow. Between 1900 and 1940 the percentage of women in the labor force rose modestly—from 20 percent to 25 percent. But starting with World War II, the movement of women into paid work outside the home rapidly accelerated. As shown in figure 6-2, the labor force participation rate of women ages 25–54 was 35 percent in 1948, rose to 50 percent in 1970 and to 75 percent in 1992, and has remained at about that level to the present. By contrast, 97 percent of men were in the labor force in 1948. That rate declined somewhat starting in 1970 and reached 89 percent in 2010. Largely because of the dramatic rise in women's labor force participation, the gender difference in market work participation has narrowed considerably. Nonetheless, a significant gender gap in work experience remains.

Marital status has always been an important source of differences in labor force participation among women. Women who have never married and widowed, divorced, or separated women have always had higher rates of participation than married women. By 1950, the nonmarried groups had reached levels of participation not far below those of today (table 6-1). Indeed, single women who never married had levels of participation close to those of men. The increase in women's labor force participation in the post–World War II period was mainly due to a shift in the work participation of married women. The first to respond were older married women beyond the usual childbearing years. But in the period after 1960, there was a sharp upturn in the labor force participation of younger, married women.

What caused the dramatic shift in women's work, especially that of married women, from home to market? The substantial postwar rise in the wage rate was undoubtedly one factor (Mincer, 1962; O'Neill 1981; Smith and Ward 1989). That change was facilitated by the greater demand for women's skills occasioned by the rapid expansion of employment in the service sector, which offered jobs that were more complementary to women's skills than the production jobs that had dominated the economy in earlier years. Such jobs also provided greater opportunities for part-time work and so enabled women to combined paid work with household responsibilities. On the supply side, technology contributed by reducing the amount of time and energy required to do domestic chores with the increasing availability of such items as affordable refrigerators, dishwashers, washers, and dryers. The development of "the pill" has also been cited as a factor enabling women better to control fertility to dovetail with patterns of work (Goldin and Katz 2002).

Liberalization of attitudes about married women's employment outside the home also may have contributed to the rise in work participation. Public opinion surveys taken over the years show considerable disapproval of married women's working in years past (less than 25 percent approved during the 1930s) and they show a rise to majority approval over time (Oppenheimer 1970). Of course, opinions themselves may simply reflect the

Table 6-1

Percent of Women in the Labor Force by Marital Status and Age

	Ages 16 and older[1]	Ages 25–34	Ages 35–44
Single, Never Married			
1940	48.1	84.4	80.7
1950	50.5	84.6	83.6
1960	44.1	79.9	79.7
1970	56.8	81.4	78.6
1980	64.4	83.3	76.9
1990	66.7	80.9	80.8
2000	68.9	83.9	80.9
2010	63.3	81.3	78.2
Married, Husband Present			
1940	14.7	19.4	16.5
1950	23.8	23.8	28.5
1960	30.5	27.7	36.2
1970	40.5	38.8	46.8
1980	49.8	58.8	61.8
1990	58.4	69.6	74.0
2000	61.1	70.3	74.8
2010	61.0	68.8	72.8
Widowed, Divorced, or Separated			
1940	32.0	66.7	61.3
1950	36.0	62.3	65.4
1960	37.1	55.5	67.4
1970	40.3	64.6	68.8
1980	43.6	76.5	77.1
1990	47.2	77.0	82.1
2000	49.0	83.1	82.9
2010	48.8	77.7	80.7

[1] 14 years and over through 1960; 16 years old and over thereafter.

Source: 1940 data are from Census Bureau; 1950–1960 are from Economic Report to the President: Annual Report of the Council of Economic Advisers, p. 92, 1973; 1970–2010 are from U.S. Census Bureau, Statistical Abstract of the United States: 2012, table 597.

changed behavior stemming from changed economic conditions. Indeed attitudes toward women and work during the 1930s were undoubtedly influenced by the Depression, and the jump in approval found in polls of the 1940s may well reflect the labor shortages of a wartime economy. Nonetheless, the attitudes of the majority can have significant effects on policy even if others do not share their views. For example, starting in the late 1920s and continuing through the 1930s, a majority of public school systems in the United States banned the hiring of married women or required that women resign their jobs when they married (Goldin 1990). However, the practice began to disappear in the late 1940s and ended in the 1950s.

In observing the huge increase in women's labor force participation between 1950 and 1980, one is prompted to ask why the gender wage gap failed to change throughout that period. The chief answer is that skills are based on accumulated work experience acquired over a lifetime. Labor force participation is simply the percentage of all women in the labor force at a point in time and conveys nothing about lifetime work experience. Most men are in the labor force continuously from the time they leave school or reach working age. Consequently, as they age they automatically accumulate more work experience. But a standard pattern for women for many years was to remain at home during years when young children were present. Women began to enter the labor force in large numbers in the 1960s and 1970s once their children were grown. But the rapid entry of inexperienced women is not likely to increase the average lifetime experience level of all employed women, which would either remain the same if the new entrants were similar to incumbents or would decline if the experience of new entrants was below the level of incumbents.

Figure 6-3 illustrates the situation. It traces the lifetime changes in labor force participation made by cohorts of women born at different times, the earliest cohort consisting of women born during the years 1886–95. Figure 6-3 therefore simulates the actual work history of women followed longitudinally. The figure demonstrates the point that the forces in the economy that induced women to work in the postwar period had a much stronger effect on women beyond the childbearing ages.

The labor force participation rate of the earliest cohort is shown when they were in their early twenties—a period that for many women predated marriage and childbearing. But their work participation declined at ages

FIGURE 6-3

LABOR FORCE PARTICIPATION RATES OVER A WORKING LIFE OF COHORTS
OF WOMEN BORN IN SELECTED TIME INTERVALS, 1886 TO 1965

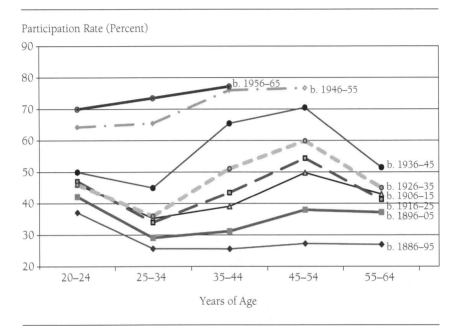

Participation Rate (Percent)

NOTE: Cohorts reach each age interval according to the midpoint of their birth years. Thus, the cohort born during 1886–95 reached ages 25–34 in 1920 and ages 55–64 in 1950; the cohort born 1916–25 reached ages 25–34 in 1950 and ages 45–54 in 1970.
SOURCE: The data are from Easterlin (1978, Appendix Table 3) and from the Bureau of Labor Statistics.

25–34, when most women were responsible for childcare and housework. This was an era when family size was larger than today and modern household equipment was not yet available. As this cohort grew older, their labor force participation essentially remained at the level reached at ages 25–34, forming an L-shaped pattern. But beginning with the 1896–1905 cohort, the L-shape became more U-shaped. Following the initial decline from their early twenties to ages 25–34, women's labor force participation began to rise as they reached the ages when children are likely to be at school or no longer at home and household responsibilities lessened. Family size was smaller in those years, as fertility had declined during the 1920s and even more so in the Depression years of the 1930s.

TABLE 6-2
PROPORTION OF YEARS WORKED SINCE AGE 18
BY EMPLOYED WHITE WOMEN[a]

Age	1967	1972/73	1977/78	1982/83	1988	1993	1998	2003
25–29	—	0.669	0.760	—	0.763			
30–34	0.645	—	0.689	0.744	—	0.773		
35–39	0.610	0.612	—	0.672	0.722		0.770	
40–44	0.594	0.600	0.638	—	0.675			0.787

[a] White includes Asians and other nonblack races.
NOTE: A year is counted as a work year if the woman worked at least 26 weeks.
SOURCE: The data are based on microdata files of the National Longitudinal Survey (NLS) for Mature Women (1967); for Young Women (1968); for Youth (NLSY79).

The pattern of decline in labor force participation as women reached ages 25–34 continued for the next three cohorts, influenced by the resumption of high fertility as the post–World War II baby boom got underway. However, those cohorts joined the labor force in ever larger numbers as they reached their thirties and forties and the pattern showed an ever steeper rise. The post–baby boom cohort born in the years 1936–45 had sharply lower fertility than their mothers.[149] Their labor force participation rates still declined as this cohort reached ages 25–34, but by not nearly as much as that of the generations who went before them. Moreover, the rise in their participation was steeper as they reached the ages when childcare responsibilities lessened. At ages 45–54, 71 percent of the women in this cohort were in the labor force.

The two most recent cohorts shown, those born 1946–55 and 1956–65, exhibit a significant break from the past, as their labor force participation did not decline as they reached ages 25–34. More than three-quarters of these women were in the labor force when they reached their thirties and forties, and it is likely that a large proportion of them will have accumulated more years of continuous work experience than the women who went before them.

The best way to measure years of work experience of employed women, however, is with actual longitudinal data. Table 6-2 shows the proportion of years worked since age 18 by women observed at different ages and time periods. The measures are based on longitudinal data from different cohorts of the National Longitudinal Surveys (NLS) sponsored by the Bureau of Labor Statistics. The table suggests that between the late 1960s and early 1970s there was little, if any, change in the proportion of lifetime years worked by women. However, between the 1970s and the 1990s accumulated work experience increased considerably. For example, women ages 35–39 in 1972–3 had worked for 61 percent of the years since they were age 18, while women who were ages 35–39 in 1998 had worked for 77 percent of the years since age 18. Thus women have been narrowing the difference with men in lifetime work experience and, as we show below, that is a major reason for the narrowing of the gender wage gap.

Education. Education, like experience acquired on the job, is an important element of skills that affect earnings. The size of the gender difference in education, however, varies by labor force status. Because most men are in the labor force continuously, the education level of all men is likely to be about the same as that of men of the same age who are wage earners. And that is what we observe for the group ages 25–54 over the period 1940–2000 (table 6-3).[150] But, as discussed above, the labor force participation rate of women has increased dramatically over time. Because the educational composition of women in and out of the labor force has changed as the proportion in the labor force has increased, we compare the educational attainment of men and women separately for those in the workforce and for all persons.

Among all persons, women were somewhat more likely than men to be high school graduates in almost all of the years 1940–2000. Men, however, were more likely to be college graduates throughout the period 1940–90, with very large differences prevailing between 1960 and 1990, after which time women moved to equality with men as men's college completion rates stalled.

But when the comparison is restricted to workers, we find that the female labor force has been highly selective of high school and college graduates throughout the period 1940–2000. As a result, women workers were significantly more likely to be high school graduates between 1940 and 1960 and continued to be in all years thereafter, though to a lesser extent. In 1940 and 1950, women workers were somewhat more likely than men to have graduated from college, but that advantage slipped as men's college completion rates increased rapidly between 1950 and 1980. Between 1950

TABLE 6-3

EDUCATIONAL ATTAINMENT OF MEN AND WOMEN:
PERCENT OF ALL PERSONS AND OF WORKERS COMPLETING HIGH SCHOOL
OR MORE AND COLLEGE OR MORE (AGES 25–54), 1940–2000

| | All Persons | | | | | |
| | Men | | Women | | Difference (M – F) | |
	HS grad or more	College grad or more	HS grad or more	College grad or more	HS grad or more	College grad or more
1940	25.8	6.2	29.8	4.3	–4.0	1.9
1950	39.8	8.0	43.1	5.8	–3.3	2.3
1960	47.9	11.6	51.3	6.7	–3.4	4.9
1970	62.2	16.4	63.4	9.4	–1.2	7.0
1980	78.7	25.6	78.6	17.3	0.1	8.3
1990	81.5	25.2	82.9	21.2	–1.4	4.0
2000	82.8	26.6	85.7	26.5	–2.9	0.1

| | Wage and Salary Workers | | | | | |
| | Men | | Women | | Difference (M – F) | |
	HS grad or more	College grad or more	HS grad or more	College grad or more	HS grad or more	College grad or more
1940	26.8	6.1	39.1	7.9	–12.3	–1.8
1950	39.7	8.5	49.2	9.5	–9.5	–1.0
1960	48.8	11.7	53.4	8.7	–4.6	3.0
1970	63.6	16.8	66.3	11.7	–2.7	5.1
1980	80.7	26.6	83.4	20.8	–2.7	5.8
1990	83.9	26.6	87.4	24.1	–3.5	2.5
2000	84.9	27.9	89.4	28.7	–4.5	–0.8

NOTE: Estimates are based on public use files of the 1940–2000 decennial censuses excluding members of the armed forces.

and 1960, the percentage of female wage earners who were college graduates actually declined as the composition of the female labor force shifted to include a larger proportion of older married women with less education. The decline in the female–male earnings ratio in the 1950s is likely to be partly explained by the relative rise of men's educational level at that time.

The college completion rates of female wage earners rose relatively more rapidly after 1980, and women regained a slight advantage over male wage earners in college completion rates in 2000, a trend that is also consistent with the rise in the wage ratio after 1980.[151]

The recent advance of women in higher education is truly eye-popping. Over the past four decades women have greatly increased their share of advanced degrees. At the bachelor's degree level the share awarded to women rose from 42 percent in 1972 to 57 percent in 2009 (table 6-4). Over the same period women's share of master's degrees rose from 21 percent to 60 percent, and their share of doctoral degrees rose from 16 percent to 52 percent.

Although the level of formal schooling is important, the subject matter of schooling also has an important effect on earnings. The very large gender differences in field of degree that prevailed in 1972 have diminished, although there are still significant gender differences. As table 6-4 shows, women dominated some fields, such as education and library science, in 1972 and they continue to do so. But women have also increased their representation in several formerly male-dominated fields. Women were awarded only about 7.6 percent of Ph.Ds. in economics and in physical sciences in 1972. But in 2009 they took about one-third of the Ph.Ds. in these fields. In other fields such as engineering, computer science, as well as finance and banking, women have made inroads but remain a small minority. However, in the biological and biomedical sciences, women's share of degrees at all levels rose sharply, bringing them to parity or better with men.

As recently as 1980 only a small proportion of professional degrees were granted to women (table 6-5). In 2009 women earned close to half of the degrees awarded in medicine, law, and dentistry. The gains made in higher paying professional and other fields help to account for the relative rise in women's earnings in the last thirty years. However, the most recent changes in degrees awarded are unlikely to influence the overall gender gap immediately. Because earnings tend to increase sharply with age in many highly skilled fields, these changes in field of degree are likely to affect earnings in future years.

Women's increased investment in schooling may be related to the increasing expectation of future work reported by successive cohorts of young women interviewed by the NLS. In 1968, a majority of young

TABLE 6-4

WOMEN'S SHARE OF BACHELOR'S, MASTER'S, AND DOCTOR'S DEGREES IN SELECTED FIELD OF STUDY: 1972–2009

	Bachelor's Degrees % female				Master's Degrees % female				Doctor's Degrees % female			
	1972	1978	1995	2009	1972	1978	1995	2009	1972	1978	1995	2009
All Fields	42.0	47.1	54.6	57.2	20.8	48.3	55.1	60.4	15.8	26.4	39.4	52.3
Business Fields	9.5	27.1	48.0	48.9	4.0	16.9	37.0	45.4	2.2	8.3	27.3	38.7
Finance, Banking and Fin. Supp. Serv.	n.a.	18.7	32.7	32.7	n.a.	16.8	28.1	33.1	n.a.	3.1	7.1	26.0
Education	74.1	72.5	75.8	79.2	57.4	67.7	76.5	77.4	23.6	39.1	62.0	67.3
Library Science	93.3	88.5	96.0	89.7	79.9	80.0	79.2	81.0	43.8	35.8	63.6	60.0
Computer/Information Sciences	13.7	25.7	28.4	17.8	12.1	18.7	26.1	27.1	7.2	7.7	18.2	22.4
Engineering	1.1	6.7	15.6	16.5	1.7	5.3	16.3	22.5	0.6	2.3	11.9	21.7
English Language and Literature	60.0	57.1	65.7	67.6	57.7	61.7	64.8	67.6	29.1	39.1	57.4	63.5
Social Sciences and History	36.3	40.5	46.8	49.4	28.2	33.1	44.7	50.1	14.7	24.3	37.7	44.4
Economics	11.7	24.9	30.7	29.5	12.8	19.8	31.1	38.0	7.6	11.3	24.8	33.8
Sociology	56.8	63.4	67.6	69.8	38.7	45.5	62.0	66.5	21.4	37.2	52.6	60.4
Psychology	46.3	58.8	72.9	77.2	38.4	52.0	72.0	79.5	24.8	37.3	62.6	73.0
Physical Sciences	15.1	21.3	34.8	40.8	14.3	16.9	30.2	39.3	6.6	10.0	23.5	32.3
Biological and Biomedical Sciences	29.5	38.4	52.3	59.2	33.0	35.4	51.8	57.6	17.0	24.1	40.3	52.7

NOTE: Aggregations by field of study derived from the Classification of Instructional Programs developed by the National Center for Education Statistics.
SOURCE: For 1971–72: Statistical Abstract of the United States 1975, U.S. Department of Commerce, Bureau of the Census; for 1977–78, 1994–95 and 2008–9: Digest of Education Statistics 1980, 1997 and 2010 editions, U.S. Department of Education, National Center for Education Statistics.

TABLE 6-5

PERCENT OF FIRST-PROFESSIONAL DEGREES EARNED BY WOMEN IN DENTISTRY, MEDICINE, AND LAW: SELECTED YEARS, 1949–50 THROUGH 2008–9

	% female		
	Dentistry (D.D.S. or D.M.D.)	Medicine (M.D.)	Law (LL.B. or J.D.)
1949–50	0.7	10.4	—
1959–60	0.8	5.5	2.5
1969–70	0.9	8.4	5.4
1979–80	13.3	23.4	30.2
1989–90	30.9	34.2	42.2
1999–2000	40.1	42.7	45.9
2008–2009	46.4	48.9	45.8

— Not available.
SOURCE: U.S. Department of Education, National Center for Education Statistics, Earned Degrees Conferred, 1949–50 through 1959–60; Higher Education General Information Survey (HEGIS), "Degrees and Other Formal Awards Conferred" surveys, 1969–70 through 1979–80; 1989–90 Integrated Postsecondary Education Data System (IPEDS), "Completions Survey" (IPEDS-C:87-99); and 2008–9: Digest of Education Statistics 2010 Edition, Table 291.

women ages 14–24 reported that they expected to be homemakers when they reached age 35; only 28 percent expected to be in the labor force. Yet those expectations were not met. When this group actually reached age 35 in the 1980s, more than 70 percent of them were in the labor force. Perhaps observing the experiences of their older sisters, recent NLS cohorts are more correctly anticipating a career. In 1982, 75 percent of women ages 14–21 indicated they would be working at age 35, a percentage close to the actual attained. Although nowadays most women work, it is nonetheless still the case that women, particularly those who marry and have children, are less likely than men to work full-time or to work continuously from the time of leaving school.

Why the Gender Gap Narrowed after 1980

In brief, the main source of the gender wage gap has always been a gender difference in work-related skills, most importantly those skills acquired through years of experience in the labor market. Ironically, as the percentage of women in the labor force grew during the 1960s and 1970s, the accumulated work experience of the average woman in the labor force declined, widening the differential in experience with men and consequently widening the wage gap. But by the 1980s the gender difference in accumulated lifetime work experience began to narrow and that was the big impetus for the narrowing of the pay gap in the 1980s. As women began spending more and more of their time in the labor force, their expectations of a career in the labor market led to changes in women's preparation for a career through educational and occupational investments that enhance earnings and also help to narrow the wage gap with men.

Empirical studies using longitudinal work experience data have found that the narrowing in gender differences in cumulative work experience and schooling can explain much of the narrowing of the wage gap in the 1980s. O'Neill and Polachek (1993) attribute one-third to one-half of the narrowing to those basic factors.[152] Other factors contributing to the narrowing include a relative increase for women in the wage gain from additional work experience and education. The skill level of women's occupations also increased relative to men's and further contributed to the wage convergence. The decline in wages of blue-collar workers was another factor that served to narrow the wage gap, because few women were blue-collar workers (11 percent in 1983) compared to men (42 percent in 1983). (Ironically, despite the urging of the women's movement and the efforts of the OFCCP and the EEOC to move women into construction and other male-dominated blue-collar jobs, women resisted, and their occupational choices proved advantageous.)

Conclusion

There is no apparent relation between the passage of the 1964 Civil Rights Act and women's gains in labor force participation or earnings. Nor does civil rights enforcement appear to be correlated with broad changes in the gender wage gap. Nonetheless it is possible that the spotlight placed on civil rights contributed to a reduction in the extent of societal discrimination toward women which in turn improved women's labor market opportunities and encouraged women to make work-related investments. Attitudes about women's role in society have changed dramatically over the past century. It would be a difficult task to identify the contribution of all the possible factors affecting that change, as they range from changes in the economy, fertility patterns, longevity, and in mores concerning marriage and much more. The civil rights movement may have played a role, but its precise contribution cannot be measured. Moreover the measured changes in the relative skills of women and men provide a compelling explanation for the early increase in the wage gap, the long period of stagnation in the wage gap in the face of both the passage of Title VII and the subsequent activities of the EEOC and the OFCCP, and the sharp narrowing of the gap that began in the early 1980s.

7

Effects of Affirmative Action on the Economic Status of African American and Women Workers

In the last two chapters, we began to assess the impact of federal antidiscrimination policies by examining changes over time in the black–white wage gap and the gender wage gap and relating those changes to developments in the implementation of civil rights policies. We found that little of the large growth in the earnings of African Americans relative to the earnings of whites since 1940 could be attributed to federal antidiscrimination activities. Except for the gains that immediately followed the passage of Title VII of the 1964 Civil Rights Act and its significant effect on discriminatory employment practices, particularly in the South, most of the growth in the relative wages of African Americans either occurred before a federal policy existed (1940–60) or could be attributed to factors unrelated to federal enforcement activities, such as relative gains in education and migration of blacks from the low-wage South to the urban North where wage rates were higher. Changes in the gender gap over time were even more remote from changes in civil rights policy as the gender gap first began to narrow after 1980.

In chapters 5 and 6 we inferred the effectiveness of federal enforcement by comparing the timing of the implementation of civil rights policies with changes in wage gaps. However, we were not able to directly link changes in the wage gaps to a measure of change in the degree of enforcement activity at the EEOC or the OFCCP. In this chapter we present an analysis that allows for a more direct link between policy measures and economic outcomes.

The OFCCP presents an opportunity for conducting such an analysis because its enforcement activities cover a specific sector of the economy, namely firms with federal contracts. We can therefore evaluate the effectiveness of the OFCCP by comparing the relative standing of minorities and women in federal contractor firms with their relative standing in a plausible control group, non-contractor firms. Moreover, data are available to make the distinction because the EEOC requires that each firm over which it has jurisdiction submit an EEO-1 form every year indicating federal contractor status along with the number of employees in each of nine occupational categories, classified by minority status and sex. The EEO-1 forms are used by the OFCCP as the basis for monitoring the affirmative action efforts of federal contractors.

The OFCCP has unique clout over federal contractors with its ultimate threat of contract cancellation and debarment from future federal contracts. Because violations are usually based on failure to employ minorities and women in proportion to their "availability," usually defined by their presence in the labor market, one would expect to find larger increases in the employment of protected groups in contractor than in non-contractor firms. In addition, one might expect increases in the relative occupational status of earnings of protected groups. Those indicators, therefore, can be considered to be measures of the "output" of the OFCCP.

Data from EEO-1 forms are the basis for much of this analysis. Up to 1980 researchers could gain access to EEO forms to compare changes in employment of minorities and women in contractor and non-contractor firms. After 1980 that access was denied, presumably because of the privacy concerns of firms, especially as litigation became more common. We use data for the period 1970–80 reported in an article by James P. Smith and Finis Welch (1984), who processed EEO-1 forms for their own analysis. For the year 2000 we use data on federal contractor employment reported in a handbook assembled by the Equal Employment Advisory Council (EEAC 2002). We combine data from the EEAC handbook with data from the microdata files of the 2000 Census, as described below.

As noted in chapter 5, a number of studies have used the data from EEO-1 forms to estimate the effects of the OFCCP's contract compliance program on economic outcomes of minorities. Although they use different methodologies and cover different time periods, they all generally conclude that the agency had a positive effect on the relative employment of African Americans in firms with federal contracts compared to non-contractor firms, although the magnitude of the effect varies considerably from study to study. We start with effects on relative employment.

The patterns displayed in table 7-1 are consistent with the results of these studies. Using data from Smith and Welch (1984, table 6) we report the percentage of all workers employed by firms required to file EEO-1 reports, as well as the percent employed by federal contractors and the percent employed by non-contractors over the period 1966–80. The data are reported separately by sex and by race. It is apparent that roughly half of both black men and of white men were employed in EEO-1 reporting firms in 1966: 53 percent of white men and 48 percent of black men. But after 1966 the percentage of black men in covered employment rose sharply, reaching 60.2 percent in 1970 and close to 65 percent in 1974, after which time it declined to 62 percent in 1980. Over the same period the fraction of white men in covered employment declined somewhat to 49 percent in 1980. Among women the racial difference in employment by EEO-1 firms is even more striking. The fraction of all black women employed by EEO-1 reporting firms increased from 48 percent in 1966 to 74 percent in 1974, compared to a high point of only 50 percent for white women in the early 1970s, falling to 47 percent in 1980.

Unfortunately, data for 1966 could not be obtained separately by federal contractor status. However, during the period 1970–80 it is apparent that the relative employment increases in covered employment made by black men largely stemmed from their increasing presence in the federal contractor sector. The percentage of black men employed by non-contractors even declined somewhat after 1970. It is black women, however, who registered the largest increase in employment by federal contractors of any group over the years 1970–80, while their employment by non-contractors declined. In 1980 almost half of all black women workers were employed by federal contractors. White women by contrast were the least likely to work for federal contractors over the years 1970–80.

One puzzle raised by the patterns shown in table 7-1, a puzzle noted by Smith and Welch, is that the largest shift of black men into covered employment occurred between 1966 and 1970, when the OFCC was a small decentralized agency with a minimal budget and staff, and the EEOC was similarly limited (Smith and Welch 1984, table 2). The OFCC only reached its full powers in the late 1970s, when it was consolidated into a single

TABLE 7-1

PERCENT OF WORKERS EMPLOYED IN EEO-1 REPORTING FIRMS
BY FEDERAL CONTRACTOR STATUS AND RACE AND SEX OF WORKER

	White men					Black men				
	1966	1970	1974	1978	1980	1966	1970	1974	1978	1980
Percent of All Workers										
In EEO-1 Firms	52.7	53.5	52.4	49.3	48.5	48.4	60.2	64.5	63.3	61.5
In Federal Contractor Firms	—	39.2	38.9	37.4	36.2	—	41.5	46.0	47.0	44.7
In Noncontractor Firms	—	14.3	13.6	11.9	12.2	—	18.7	18.0	16.3	16.8

	White women					Black women				
	1966	1970	1974	1978	1980	1966	1970	1974	1978	1980
Percent of All Workers										
In EEO-1 Firms	47.5	50.2	50.2	48.1	46.9	48.2	63.5	74.0	71.4	74.9
In Federal Contractor Firms	—	28.1	28.9	29.4	29.5	—	34.6	43.6	45.6	48.7
In Noncontractor Firms	—	22.1	21.4	18.7	17.4	—	28.9	30.5	25.7	26.6

NOTE: Data are from Smith and Welch, Affirmative Action and Labor Markets, *Journal of Labor Economics* 2 (1984): 269–302, table 6.

agency—the OFCCP. The EEOC gained the power to litigate in 1972, and its budget expanded in the middle to late 1970s. In light of these budgetary patterns it is surprising that the large shift into contractor employment should occur during the years when the agencies were at their weakest. However, with the heightened emphasis on civil rights, firms with federal contracts may have anticipated a strengthening of enforcement, especially when the filing of EEO-1 forms became a requirement for compliance.

Although a shift in the employment of protected workers from non-contractors to contractors may be a necessary condition for OFCCP to have any effect on wage rates or the quality of occupational distributions, it is clearly not sufficient. We turn now to investigate changes in other measures of the economic status of protected workers. We first examine the occupational distributions of blacks and whites, women and men, in contractor and non-contractor firms and the changes in those distributions over time to determine whether improvement in the occupational status of blacks and women was greater in contractor firms than in non-contractor firms. We then use regression analysis to estimate the effect of coverage by federal contractors on the relative wages of blacks and women.

Effects of the OFCCP on Occupational Upgrading

We examine the extent to which the occupational mix of protected workers was upgraded between 1970 and 1980 and how that upgrading differed between federal contractor and non-contractor firms. Table 7-2 shows the percentage of African American and white men and women who were employed as officials and managers and professional and technical workers in contractor firms as well as in non-contractor firms in 1970 and 1980. These four occupations—the top tier—are those with the highest pay, on average. We again use data tabulated from EEO-1 forms by Smith and Welch (1984).

In 1970, 5.8 percent of black men and 30.5 percent of white men employed by federal contractors were in the top tier, a black–white ratio of 0.19 (see table 7-2). By 1980 this ratio had grown to 0.34 as the percentage of black workers in the top tier grew at a faster rate than that of whites. However the same set of calculations for employees in non-contractor firms over the period 1970–80 yields almost the same pattern, a ratio that rises from 0.20 to 0.34.

TABLE 7-2

RELATIVE OCCUPATIONAL ADVANCEMENT OF PROTECTED WORKERS
IN FEDERAL CONTRACTOR AND NON-CONTRACTOR FIRMS (1970–1980)

I. Comparing Black and White Occupational Gains by Sex:	% Officials, Managers, Professional or Technical				Ratio of black % to white %		Percentage point change in ratio (1970–80)
	1970		1980				
	White	Black	White	Black	1970	1980	
Men							
Federal Contractor Employees	30.5	5.8	33.9	11.6	0.19	0.34	0.15
Nonfederal Contractor Employees	24.5	5.0	29.9	10.2	0.20	0.34	0.14
Women							
Federal Contractor Employees	10.3	6.7	17.2	10.7	0.65	0.62	−0.03
Nonfederal Contractor Employees	15.7	9.0	24.5	13.4	0.57	0.55	−0.03

II. Comparing Female and Male Occupational Gains by Race:	% Officials, Managers, Professional or Technical				Ratio of women's % to men's %		Percentage point change in ratio (1970–80)
	1970		1980				
	Men	Women	Men	Women	1970	1980	
White							
Federal Contractor Employees	30.5	10.3	33.9	17.2	0.34	0.51	0.17
Nonfederal Contractor Employees	24.5	15.7	29.9	24.5	0.64	0.82	0.18
Black							
Federal Contractor Employees	5.8	6.7	11.6	10.7	1.16	0.92	−0.23
Nonfederal Contractor Employees	5.0	9.0	10.2	13.4	1.80	1.31	−0.49

NOTE: Data are derived from Smith and Welch, "Affirmative Action and Labor Markets," *Journal of Labor Economics* 2 (1984): 269–302, table A3 and table A4.

Table 7-2 shows the same calculations for black and white women. In 1970, 6.7 percent of black women and 10.3 percent of white women working for federal contractors were in the top tier occupations. Both black and white women advanced into the top tier between 1970 and 1980, but white women advanced more rapidly. Thus in 1980 the black–white ratio of relative employment in top-tier occupations in federal contractor firms declined somewhat among women—from 0.65 to 0.62. The same ratio calculated for women in non-contractor firms also declined by about the same amount—from 0.57 to 0.55.

Table 7-2 also displays the same set of calculations comparing occupational changes of women and men, separately by race. White women were less likely than white men to be in the top occupational categories in both 1970 and 1980 but more likely in both years to be in those occupations if they worked for non-contractor firms. However, women moved ahead more rapidly than men in both contractor and non-contractor firms over the decade. In contrast, black women were more likely than black men to be in the top occupations in both 1970 and 1980 though their advantage declined somewhat over the decade.

In sum, in all of the group comparisons shown in Table 7-2, the relative occupational gains (and a few losses) were about the same in both the contractor and non-contractor sectors, suggesting that the OFCCP's affirmative action activities had no special effect on the relative occupational upgrading of black workers, both male and female, or female workers, both black and white. It is difficult to extend the occupational analysis beyond 1980 because parallel data are no longer available for contractor and non-contractor firms. We were able to make an estimate for men for the year 2000 using the occupational distribution of employees of contractor firms obtained from the Equal Employment Advisory Council (EEAC) handbook (2002).[153] We utilized the same methodology just described for 1970–80 but compared the changes in ratios between all employees of federal contractors with the ratio changes shown by all employees as reported in the 2000 Census. Since the occupational distribution of all employees is a weighted average of the occupational distributions of contractor employees and non-contractor employees, we can infer the size of the ratio change once we know the size of the change for the contractor distributions and the total distribution—i.e., if the ratio increased by more among all employees than among employees of contractors, then it must have increased by more in the non-contractor sector than in the contractor sector, given the rules of simple averages.

We find that among contractor employees the ratio hardly changed, remaining at 0.34 as both African Americans and whites increased their representation in the top two categories slightly. But among all employees the ratio increased from 0.40 to 0.57 as African Americans increased their representation in the two categories much more than did whites. This implies that the relative occupational gains of black employees in non-contractor firms were much greater than the gains of minority employees of contractor firms. In sum, there is no evidence in this comparison that OFCCP activities had a positive effect on the relative economic status of African Americans as reflected in occupational upgrading.

Effects of the OFCCP on Relative Wages

One might infer from the above occupational comparisons that the OFCCP was unlikely to have had a positive impact on the relative economic position of African American workers because occupational status is positively related to earnings. However, the absence of any impact of federal contractor status on the relative occupational status of African American workers is not conclusive proof that the OFCCP had no effect on the relative earnings of African Americans. OFCCP enforcement activities could have led to upgrading within the broad categories that we examined or to increases in relative wages within occupational categories.

A direct analysis of the effect of the OFCCP on economic well-being would require data comparing the relative wage rates of protected workers in contractor and non-contractor firms. Unfortunately no such data appear to be available. The EEO-1 system that produces the data for contractor firms does not include any information on wages; datasets that provide information on wages and worker characteristics do not provide information on whether or not the employer is a federal contractor. Moreover, privacy considerations prohibit the merging of data on contractor status from EEO-1 forms with other data from census surveys or Social Security Administration records that would provide wage and other information about the worker. As an alternative to direct matching we have simulated a wage comparison between workers in contractor and non-contractor firms, using a methodology that allows us to infer this comparison by combining information from the EEO-1 data with census data.

The basic approach is to estimate wage equations using the microdata files of the 2000 Census as our source of information on the wage rate of each individual and a set of explanatory variables that measure various work-related characteristics that influence wages, such as age, education, and industry. The key explanatory variable, however, is an additional variable measuring the probability that a worker's employer is a federal contractor, in which case his wage is susceptible to influence by the OFCCP. We have two alternative ways of measuring the employer intensity variable. For the first method we use the EEAC handbook (2002) to identify the number of workers in the federal contractor sector who are employed in eleven categories of industry and in the four geographic regions of the United States. We then have forty-four unique industry-region categories. We use the 2000 Census to obtain data on all workers (contractor and non-contractor) in the same forty-four industry-region categories. The ratio of the number of contractor employees to all workers is an estimate of the probability of working for a federal contractor for all those within a unique industry-region group.

For the second method we estimated the ratio of federal contractor employment in a Metropolitan Statistical Area (MSA), based on data from the EEAC handbook, to total employment in the same MSA, using data from the 2000 Census. This ratio was calculated for each MSA, and it is assumed that all individuals who reported to the 2000 Census that they worked in a particular MSA faced the same probability of being employed by a contractor firm. Because the EEAC used the MSA boundaries in the 1990 Census, not the 2000 Census, it was necessary to use a crosswalk developed by the Bureau of Labor statistics to adjust the MSA data. We omitted from this analysis MSAs that radically changed boundaries between 1990 and 2000, which reduced the set of MSA units for analysis.

Specifically, our analyses are based on multiple regressions in which the dependent variable is the logarithm of the wage rate. The data sample, drawn from the 2000 Census, includes either all workers (for the industry-region regression) or, for the MSA regression, workers living in MSAs for which we could reliably estimate the contractor probability variable. The analysis assumes that the partial regression coefficient of the variable measuring the probability of working for a contractor is an estimate of the differential in the average log wage between contractor and non-contractor workers in our sample (holding constant the other determinants of an individual's wage level). Therefore, it is an estimate of the net effect of OFCCP activities on worker earnings. Separate regressions were conducted for black men, white men, black women, and white women so that we could independently estimate the effect of the OFCCP on the wage rates of different groups.[154]

Results from Regression Analysis. The basic model regresses a measure of the individual's log wage rate (W) on the probability of employment in a contractor firm (C/T) controlling for other determinants of variation in (W)—age of the individual (A) and years of school completed (E). In regression specification 1, C/T is measured as the percent of all workers in contractor firms in an individual's industry/region. In regression 2, C/T is measured as the ratio of contractor to total employment in each individual's MSA.

$$\text{Thus: } W_i = a + b_1(C/T) + b_2(A_i) + b_3(E_i) + b_4(R) + b_5(I),$$

where the subscript (i) is the racial, sex group of the individuals in the regression. Regression model 1 omits region (R) and industry (I) from the set of explanatory variables.

The independent variable most important for our purposes is C/T, the contractor employment share (in percent), which is the estimate of the likelihood of working for a federal contractor. If the OFCCP affects the relative earnings of protected groups, then it is expected that the coefficient of C/T will be positive for black men and women and white women and insignificant or perhaps negative for white men.

The main results are summarized in table 7-3, and the full regression results are given in appendix tables 7A-1 and 7A-2. Results are provided for the two regression specifications. As noted, regression 1 uses a person's specific industry-region combination to measure the C/T variable and the other uses the person's residence in a particular MSA.

Working for a federal contractor appears to be generally associated with higher pay for workers as the coefficients of the C/T variable are positive for all four race-sex groups and for both regression models, indicating

TABLE 7-3

DOES EMPLOYMENT IN THE FEDERAL CONTRACTOR SECTOR
INCREASE THE WAGE RATE OF PROTECTED GROUPS?
RESULTS FROM REGRESSION ANALYSIS (2000)

Regression 1.   Effect on the hourly wage of a 1 percentage point increase in
the federal contractor share of employment in a worker's specific industry/region area:

Black Men	0.3 percent	Black Women	0.2 percent
White Men	0.4 percent	White Women	0.5 percent

Regression 2.   Effect on the hourly wage of a 1 percentage point increase in
the federal contractor share of employment in a worker's MSA:

Black Men	0.5 percent	Black Women	0.5 percent
White Men	1.3 percent	White Women	1.4 percent

NOTE: Two types of wage regressions were conducted, each using a different method for measuring federal contractor intensity. The first regression defines contractor intensity as the proportion of employment by federal contractors in a specific industry/region. The second regression estimates contractor intensity as employment by federal contractors in an MSA as a proportion of all employment in an MSA. Both sets of regressions control for age (and age squared) and education. All of the wage coefficients are statistically significant at the 1% level. See text for discussion and appendix table 7-1A and table 7-2A for detailed regression results.
SOURCE: Federal contractor employment data are from the *Equal Employment Advisory Council Handbook* (2002). All other data are based on the 2000 Census of population microdata files.

that hourly pay within a region and industry, or MSA, tends to be higher when the intensity of OFCCP activity is greater. The most striking finding is that the partial regression coefficients of the C/T variable (the probability of working for a contractor) are larger for white men and women than for African American men and women. The differences are small in regression 1 but quite large in regression 2.[155]

This finding suggests that any effect that OFCCP may be having on raising the relative economic status of African Americans is swamped by the fact that government contractors, in the same industry and region, pay workers of the same schooling level more than non-contractor firms. This could be due to a provision of the Davis-Bacon Act mandating that firms with federal contracts pay the prevailing union wage in their labor market area. The results of the industry-region and MSA cross-sectional analyses provide no support for the view that the OFCCP has increased the relative wages of protected workers.

APPENDIX TABLE 7A-1

REGRESSION I: INDUSTRY/REGION CROSS-SECTIONAL MODEL:
DEPENDENT VARIABLE—LOG HOURLY RATE OF PAY IN 2000, BY SEX AND RACE

| | Male | | | | Female | | | |
| | Black | | White | | Black | | White | |
Independent Variables	Coef.	t-stat	Coef.	t-stat	Coef.	t-stat	Coef.	t-stat
(Age − 18)	0.039	56.09	0.050	221.20	0.003	52.55	0.035	156.73
(Age − 18)^2	−0.001	−39.21	−0.001	−172.63	−0.000	−37.55	−0.001	−122.56
Education								
H.S. Degree	0.182	24.37	0.172	56.62	0.191	25.81	0.185	53.35
Some College	0.328	39.91	0.304	93.50	0.373	48.22	0.365	101.53
College Grad.	0.591	58.67	0.606	178.76	0.692	76.49	0.684	181.79
College Grad. +	0.767	57.35	0.800	204.09	0.929	82.50	0.889	208.79
Contractor Employment Share in Industry/Region (in percent)*	0.003	21.61	0.004	76.44	0.002	15.69	0.005	72.71
Adj. R-Square	0.2337		0.3008		0.2577		0.2825	
Dependent Mean (Log Hourly Wage)	2.523		2.758		2.413		2.487	
Sample Size	42,537		412,290		50,666		354,601	

*The partial regression coefficient for this variable is the change in the log wage for a 1 percentage point change in the share.
SOURCE: Federal contractor employment data are from the *Equal Employment Advisory Council Handbook* (2002). All other data are based on the 2000 Census of population microdata files.

APPENDIX TABLE 7A-2

REGRESSION II: MSA CROSS-SECTIONAL MODEL:
DEPENDENT VARIABLE—LOG HOURLY RATE OF PAY IN 2000, BY SEX AND RACE

| | Male | | | | Female | | | |
| | Black | | White | | Black | | White | |
Independent Variables	Coef.	t-stat	Coef.	t-stat	Coef.	t-stat	Coef.	t-stat
(Age − 18)	0.038	40.97	0.051	150.42	0.034	40.40	0.035	107.59
(Age − 18)^2	−0.001	−29.73	−0.001	−117.87	−0.001	−29.90	−0.001	−85.89
Region								
Northeast	0.070	6.26	0.088	24.33	0.111	11.85	0.130	36.90
South	−0.047	−4.95	−0.045	−13.34	−0.043	−5.37	0.006	1.89
West	0.056	4.35	0.058	15.85	0.077	6.79	0.116	32.16
Education								
H.S Degree	0.162	15.28	0.166	35.63	0.189	18.74	0.160	30.60
Some College	0.286	24.90	0.295	59.60	0.342	32.66	0.319	58.66
College Grad.	0.535	39.50	0.575	112.15	0.633	53.22	0.607	108.29
College Grad. +	0.704	40.47	0.769	132.28	0.864	60.70	0.804	128.99
Industry								
Manufacturing								
Non-Durable	0.039	1.82	0.042	6.31	−0.051	−1.34	0.034	3.16
Durable	0.034	1.81	0.012	2.29	−0.001	−0.03	0.057	5.42
Machinery	0.049	1.91	0.067	10.13	0.019	0.47	0.103	8.91

Transport, Utilities, etc.	0.049	2.88	-0.009	-1.65	0.082	2.26	0.099	9.20
Communications	0.127	5.69	0.085	11.79	0.083	2.27	0.132	12.49
Wholesale Trade	-0.059	-2.59	-0.025	-3.92	-0.044	-1.06	0.057	5.12
Retail Trade	-0.175	-10.48	-0.188	-38.73	-0.230	-6.56	-0.175	-19.63
Finance, Insurance, and Real Estate	0.022	1.09	0.119	18.63	0.043	1.23	0.122	13.18
Services Business & Other, excluding Health	-0.078	-5.09	-0.106	-24.11	-0.087	-2.54	-0.056	-6.47
Health Services	-0.080	-4.03	-0.006	-0.76	-0.070	-2.02	0.035	3.87
Contractor Employment Share in MSA (in percent)*	0.005	6.43	0.013	55.80	0.005	6.67	0.014	59.49
Adj. R-Square	0.2476		0.3258		0.2917		0.3508	
Dependent Mean (Log Hourly Wage)	2.600		2.839		2.519		2.567	
Sample Size	23,725		207,507		28,717		174,452	

*The partial regression coefficient for this variable is the change in the log wage for a 1 percentage point change in the share.
SOURCE: Federal contractor employment data are from the *Equal Employment Advisory Council Handbook* (2002). All other data are based on the 2000 Census of population microdata files.

PART IV

Measuring Labor Market Discrimination Today

8

Labor Market Discrimination and Wage Gaps in the 2000s

Although earnings differentials between African Americans and whites and between men and women have narrowed over the years, they have by no means disappeared. But how much of the current minority–white wage gap and the current gender wage gap is due to labor market discrimination? Or can those wage gaps be explained by other factors such as differentials in work-related skills? These are crucial questions for the direction of civil rights policy and we address them in this chapter. Our discussion will include not only wage gaps between African Americans and whites and men and women but additionally wage gaps experienced by ethnic and racial minorities, and we will focus our discussion on conditions since the year 2000.

Unfortunately there is no barometer for directly detecting and measuring labor market discrimination. As noted in chapter 4, the number of charges of discrimination brought by individuals to the EEOC each year is only a minuscule fraction of the number of protected workers in the labor force—less than a fraction of 1 percent in each category of discrimination. Moreover, the EEOC regularly finds that a majority of charges filed by individuals show "No Reasonable Cause" to believe that discrimination had occurred. Although suggestive of a near-absence of discrimination by employers, the low rate of claims could understate the extent of discrimination in the labor market if fear of retaliation by employers is a deterrent to filing by those who are experiencing discrimination. Yet, retaliation has been added as an additional discriminatory offense, and a legal industry has arisen that seeks out and supports employees who believe they have experienced discrimination. The low number of EEOC filings could also be explained by workers pursuing other means to address discrimination, such as using their company's internal procedures for handling discrimination complaints or by simply finding another job.

Because of the inherent difficulty of directly measuring the prevalence of discriminatory behavior by employers, analysts have turned to empirical studies that seek to measure the extent to which racial and gender wage differences can be attributed to differences in employee productivity. The component of racial and gender wage differences that cannot be attributed to the measured productivity factors provides a rough indication of the effect of labor market discrimination on the earnings of minorities and women. This is a very rough measure, because our ability to explain how much of earnings differences are due to discrimination is dependent on our ability to measure productivity accurately. Measures of human capital such as years of school completed are readily obtained from standard sources such as census data. But differences in years of schooling, although usually correlated with earnings differences, are an extremely imperfect measure even of cognitive skills, in part because schools vary considerably in quality and in part because even within a quality-of-school category, student achievement varies because of differences in parental endowments and personal traits.

Measures of cognitive development, such as those revealed in test score data, are not widely available. When available, they are useful but imperfect measures of individual productivity. Other aspects of individual productivity, such as leadership ability and reliability, are generally unavailable. The typical survey has no way to measure those characteristics objectively, although they likely influence success in the labor market. Among groups with a significant proportion of immigrants, ability to speak English is an important aspect of productivity and can now be roughly measured with census data. Other aspects of acculturation are more difficult to assess.

Gender differences in productivity present the greatest challenge to measurement. Labor market outcomes differ between women and men in large part because of differences in lifetime career paths, a consequence of differences in gender roles within the family.[156] Consequently, an analysis of the gender gap requires detailed data on lifetime work experience. In addition, women's continuing family responsibilities influence their preferences for work situations that allow for more flexibility and less intensity. Men and women may therefore make different trade-offs between pay and job amenities.

We utilize several data sources for our estimates. One is the American Community Survey (ACS), a recently developed survey product of the U.S. Census Bureau. The ACS provides large samples of the population with enough observations to estimate earnings differentials between whites and minorities, separately by sex, even those from small population groups. We are therefore able to include non-Hispanic blacks and American Indians as well as Hispanics and Asians by country of origin—all of whom are groups that are protected minorities under Title VII. We provide results for 2005 and 2009 using the ACS.

One drawback of the ACS, a drawback shared by the decennial census and the Current Population Survey, is that it provides only limited measures of productivity-related factors. For example, it does not have information on lifetime work experience, an important omission for understanding the gender gap in earnings. A strong point of the National Longitudinal Survey of Youth, 1979 cohort (NLSY79), our second major data source, is that it provides information on key productivity-related characteristics such as lifetime work experience and test scores that allow for measurement of cognitive achievement. The NLSY79, however, does not provide large enough samples for analysis of small minority groups, though it has oversampled Hispanics and African Americans.

In the two major sections of this chapter we use statistical analysis to determine how much of the currently observed wage gaps between minority and white workers and between female and male workers might be attributed to productivity factors.

Wage Differences between Minorities and Whites

In this section we start with our findings based on the 2005 and 2009 ACS. The large sample size enables us to analyze the wage gaps between white non-Hispanics and sixteen racial and ethnic groups. Separate racial and ethnic analyses are provided for men and women. We then turn to the NLSY79 data to analyze the sources of wage differences between African Americans and whites, as well as between Hispanics and whites, in 2000 when the cohort was 35–43 years of age and in 2008 when the cohort had reached the ages of 43–51. We again analyze men and women separately.

FIGURE 8-1

AVERAGE HOURLY EARNINGS OF ASIAN, BLACK, AND HISPANIC MEN
AS PERCENT OF HOURLY EARNINGS OF NON-HISPANIC WHITE MEN,
FULL-TIME WORKERS AGES 25–54, 1979–2010

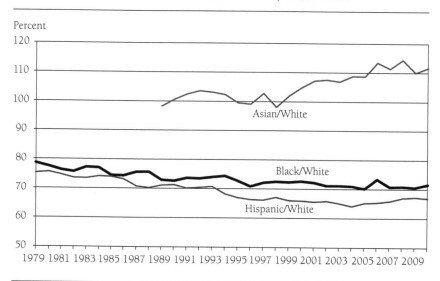

NOTE: Average hourly earnings were calculated from CPS ORG microdata. Earnings tabulations are restricted to those who worked full-time (35 hours or more per week).

Racial and Ethnic Wage Differentials: Results from the ACS. The various ethnic and racial minorities differ considerably both in their earnings and with respect to their skills. Since men and women have different career paths on average, we will consider these differentials separately, first for men and then for women.

Racial and ethnic differentials among men. Figure 8-1 shows the trend in the average hourly wage of three broad groups of minority men (Asian, African American, and Hispanic) as a percent of the wage of white men of the same ages (25–54). Note that throughout this chapter the racial designation of white always refers to white non-Hispanics. As a group, Asian men's average hourly wage rates were about the same or slightly above the hourly wages of white men between 1989 and 1999 and have risen well above the white male rate since 1999, reaching a 12 percent advantage in 2010. The Hispanic–white wage ratio declined fairly steadily from 75 percent in 1975 to about 65 percent in 2000 where it has remained. The black–white hourly wage ratio declined from 79 percent in 1979 to 73 percent in 1989 and has stayed at about that level up through 2010.

To what extent are these earnings differences explained by differences in skills that can be measured in U.S. Census Bureau surveys? The explanatory analysis is enriched by using a more detailed breakdown of the non-white groups. The Census Bureau divides Asians into subgroups of Chinese, Japanese, Asian Indian, Korean, Vietnamese, Filipino, and Other Asian. It also divides Hispanics into subgroups of Mexican, Puerto Rican, Cuban, Dominican, Other Central American, South American, and other Hispanic.

Using the 2005 and 2009 ACS we employ multiple regression analysis (ordinary least square [OLS] log wage regressions) to control statistically for the effects on wages of education and other factors that influence earnings. The results are shown in table 8-1, which displays wage differentials (expressed as ratios of hourly earnings) between each group and the reference group of white men.[157] We show results for two models, each of which takes into account an increasing number of explanatory variables. The variables included in each model are indicated at the bottom portion of the table, which displays an "X" for the particular variable included. Model I shows the effect of adjusting for age, geographic region, metropolitan/central city location, schooling, part-time work, and type of employer (government, non-profit, private); model II additionally adjusts for the number of years in the United States and proficiency in English.

Table 8-1 presents the hourly wage in each racial or ethnic group as a percent of the hourly wage of white men. Results using the 2005 ACS are shown in the first column and results using the 2009 ACS are shown alongside in the second column. The initial wage ratios, unadjusted for any skill factors, stayed the same or increased a bit between 2005 and 2009. We report the ratios for 2009, noting any significant change.

The wage ratios vary considerably among the groups. Most of the Asian groups of men earn more than white men. The wages of Asian Indian and Japanese men are the highest of any group: 41 percent and 24 percent respectively higher than the wages of white, non-Hispanic men in 2009. Chinese and Korean men earned 14 percent to 8 percent higher wages than white men. However, the group "Other Asian" (including Thai, Hmong, Pakistani, and Cambodian groups) earn only about 89 percent as much as white men.

TABLE 8-1

MINORITY/WHITE WAGE RATIOS FOR DETAILED RACIAL
AND ETHNIC GROUPS OF MEN (AGES 25–54) BEFORE AND
AFTER CONTROLLING FOR SKILL-RELATED CHARACTERISTICS

	Unadjusted (No control)		Model I		Model II	
	2005	2009	2005	2009	2005	2009
Race/Ethnicity Indicators						
American Indian	77	78	87	86	87	87
Black non-Hispanic	74	74	83	81	83	82
Chinese	113	114	89	90	98	99[NS]
Japanese	120	124	95	97[NS]	101[NS]	104[NS]
Asian Indian	128	141	99[NS]	106	105	113
Korean	108	108	86	86	96	94
Vietnamese	88	88	88	88	98[NS]	97[NS]
Filipino	93	96	84	86	89	90
Other Asian	82	89	80	86	86	91
Mexican	62	65	82	84	92	92
Puerto Rican	81	82	91	91	95	94
Cuban	89	85	91	88	100[NS]	96[NS]
Dominican	69	67	79	78	89	86
Other Central American	60	61	79	81	91	92
South American	79	83	79	84	90	93
Other Hispanic	79	86	89	90	94	93
Control Variables						
Age			X		X	
Region, MSA, Central City			X		X	
Schooling			X		X	
Work part-time			X		X	
Type of employer			X		X	
Yrs. since migration to U.S.					X	
English-speaking ability					X	

NOTE: The ratios shown were estimated from OLS regressions of an individual's log hourly wage rate on a set of explanatory variables including an indicator variable (or variables) specifying race/ethnicity, with white non-Hispanic as the omitted reference category. The anti-log of the partial regression coefficients of these indicator variables yields the wage ratios. The other variables controlled are indicated above for each model. The sample is retricted to wage and salary workers who worked 20 hours or more a week and 26 weeks or more a year. Hourly wages are obtained by dividing annual earnings by the product of weeks and hours worked during the year.
SOURCE: Public Use Microdata, American Community Survey (ACS), 2005 and 2009.
"NS" indicates not significant at 1% level.

We find that all of the Hispanic groups earn less than white non-Hispanic men and Asian men. Mexicans, Dominicans, and other Central Americans have the lowest earnings of any group shown: about one-third below those of white men. Cubans, Puerto Ricans, and those from South America have the highest earnings among Hispanics, but still earn about 15–18 percent less than white men. African American and American Indian men earn 22–26 percent less than white men.

Model I shows the effect of adjusting for age, geographic division, metropolitan/central city location, schooling, part-time work, and type of employer (government, nonprofit, private). Asians tend to live in high-wage areas and have much more education than most other groups. More than half of Asian men hold bachelor's or advanced degrees. Once differences in geographic location and education are taken into account, the earnings advantage of Asian men over white men is largely eliminated.

Hispanic groups, on the other hand, have relatively low levels of schooling: almost half of Hispanic men have not completed high school, and only 9 percent are college graduates. Consequently their earnings converge significantly with those of white (non-Hispanic) men when education variables are added to the model. The differential between Mexican and white men is cut in half, although the change for other Hispanic groups with stronger education backgrounds is less dramatic. The wages of African American and American Indian men relative to those of white men also rise when account is taken of differences in years of schooling.

A relatively large proportion of Asians and Hispanics are immigrants. In model II we add variables indicating the number of years since migrating to the United States and self-reported English language proficiency. This adjustment raises the wage ratios for Hispanics and Asians. At this final step, the wages of the Asian groups are mostly either slightly above or below those of white men. The wages of Asian Indians, still the highest earning group, are 13 percent above those of whites. The wage gap for Hispanic men is sharply reduced. In 2009 the wages of all Hispanic groups except for Dominicans are more than 90 percent as high as those of white men. Cuban men essentially reach parity with white men.

Groups with a significant proportion of immigrants present particular difficulties for analysis because of cultural differences among them that may influence the speed of assimilation. Such differences are only partly captured by measures of years of schooling and self-reported measures of English-speaking ability. Different cohorts of migrants from the same country can differ because of selection factors. Second-generation and higher-order-generation immigrants are likely to be more assimilated. We present additional analysis of Hispanic and black men later in this chapter using the superior measures of skills available in the NLSY79 data.

Racial and ethnic differentials among women. The hourly wage ratios of ethnic/racial groups to whites are relatively higher for women than is the case among men. As shown in figure 8-2, Asian women have earned more than white women in every year between 1989 and 2010 and their wage advantage rose sharply after 2002. To understand better the effect of differences in skill on these wage ratios we replicate for women the analysis conducted for men, again looking at a wider array of groups within the broad categories. The results are given in table 8-2.

Although the patterns of wage differentials among the different groups of women are similar to those of men, the size of the gaps between white women and black and Hispanic women is, for the most part, strikingly smaller than the parallel gap among men, a pattern suggested in figure 8-2. In the ACS for 2009, the unadjusted black–white ratio among men is 74 percent, and among women it is 86 percent (table 8-2). The differential with white non-Hispanic women is also much smaller than the male gap for all subgroups of Hispanic women. The adjustments in model I (which include schooling and geographic location) raise the ratios for groups with less education than white women (e.g., African American and Mexican women) and lower the ratios for groups with superior education (e.g., Japanese and Asian Indian women). After adjusting for all the variables in model II, which adds to model I immigration and English-speaking skills, the gaps among non-Asian women are further reduced and the wage ratios are mostly on the order of 95 percent for all groups except American Indians (88 percent), Dominicans and African Americans (93 percent), and Cuban women (who are at parity with white women).

The Asian–white differentials are quite similar for women and men. Asian women, like Asian men, typically earn more than their white counterparts because of their higher education levels. After adjusting for schooling and the migration and language variables in model II, Asian women still appear to earn more than white women (up to 10 percent more both for Chinese and for Asian Indian women).

FIGURE 8-2

AVERAGE HOURLY EARNINGS OF ASIAN, BLACK, AND HISPANIC WOMEN
AS PERCENT OF HOURLY EARNINGS OF NON-HISPANIC WHITE WOMEN,
FULL-TIME WORKERS AGES 25–54, 1979–2010

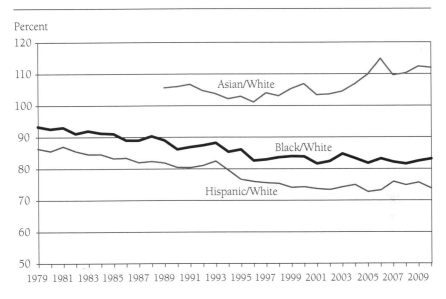

NOTE: Average hourly earnings are derived from CPS ORG microdata. Earnings tabulations are restricted to those who worked full-time (35 hours or more per week).

In general, given the limited availability of detailed productivity measures in the ACS, it remains difficult to say with certainty how much, if any, of the current earnings differentials could be due to labor market discrimination. In fact, including all variables, among men, most Asian groups earn about as much as or more than white men, and among women the Asian groups mostly earn more than white women.

Once we adjust for all the variables considered, most Hispanic men earn 90 percent as much as white (non-Hispanic) men (Cubans are at parity, and the gap for Mexicans and Puerto Ricans is extremely small). Among women, the adjusted Mexican–white wage ratio rises to 96 percent and the Cuban and Puerto Rican ratios reach parity. The adjusted black–white wage ratio is 93 percent.

TABLE 8-2

MINORITY/WHITE WAGE RATIOS FOR DETAILED RACIAL AND ETHNIC GROUPS
OF WOMEN (AGES 25–54) BEFORE AND AFTER CONTROLLING
FOR SKILL-RELATED CHARACTERISTICS

	Unadjusted (No control)		Model I		Model II	
	2005	2009	2005	2009	2005	2009
Race/Ethnicity Indicators						
American Indian	82	81	89	88	89	88
Black non-Hispanic	86	86	93	92	93	93
Chinese	121	124	97	100[NS]	107	110
Japanese	121	123	96	96	100[NS]	99[NS]
Asian Indian	122	131	98[NS]	103	105	110
Korean	107	109	92	94	102[NS]	103[NS]
Vietnamese	89	88	94	95	105	107
Filipino	115	117	97	99[NS]	102	104
Other Asian	88	89	90	90	96	96
Mexican	72	73	89	90	96	96
Puerto Rican	92	91	97	96	100[NS]	98[NS]
Cuban	98	94	97	94	104	101[NS]
Dominican	71	74	79	83	89	93
Other Central American	68	69	84	87	94	96
South American	85	87	83	86	94	95
Other Hispanic	84	90	94	94	97	96
Control Variables						
Age			X		X	
Region, MSA, Central City			X		X	
Schooling			X		X	
Work part-time			X		X	
Type of employer			X		X	
Yrs. since migration to U.S.					X	
English-speaking ability					X	

NOTE: The ratios shown were estimated from OLS regressions of an individual's log hourly wage rate on a set of explanatory variables including an indicator variable (or variables) specifying race/ethnicity, with white non-Hispanic as the omitted reference category. The anti-log of the partial regression coefficients of these indicator variables yields the wage ratios. The other variables controlled are indicated above for each model. The sample is restricted to wage and salary workers who worked 20 hours or more a week and 26 weeks or more a year. Hourly wages are obtained by dividing annual earnings by the product of weeks and hours worked during the year.
SOURCE: Public Use Microdata, American Community Survey (ACS), 2005 and 2009.
"NS" indicates not significant at 1% level.

In this broad overview we find that after we control for readily measured variables such as age, region, residence in a city, part-time work, years of schooling, class of employer (government, nonprofit, and private), migration history, and self-reported English-speaking ability, the remaining differentials between whites and minorities are small or eliminated. The largest between-group wage differential that remains after adjusting for these characteristics is that between African American and white men: a ratio of 83 percent. Among women the African American–white differential is smaller: 93 percent. The wage gap between white women and minority women is generally smaller than the parallel wage gaps for men. In fact, white women earn less than Asian women as well as less than Cuban women, once we account for differences in migration and English-speaking ability.

Black–White and Hispanic–White Wage Gaps: Results from the NLSY79. We now turn to the much richer data provided in the NLSY79 data for a more nuanced analysis of the black–white and Hispanic–white wage gaps among male and among female workers and of the gap in wages between women and men. We start with black–white and Hispanic–white differences.

The NLSY79 cohort was first interviewed in 1979 (at ages 14–22) and was initially re-interviewed each year (more recently every other year). Detailed information was obtained on lifetime work experience, education, and many other individual characteristics and behaviors of relevance to labor market outcomes. One unique variable of considerable value is the individual's score on the Armed Forces Qualification Test (AFQT), which was administered to survey participants in 1980. The test reflects differences in cognitive skills that are influenced by the quality as well as the quantity of schooling and by human capital acquired in the home.

We report on results from both the 2000 survey taken when the cohort was 35–43 years of age and the 2008 survey when the cohort had reached ages 43–51. Our sample of wage and salary workers was 5,399 in 2000 and 4,673 in 2008. Attrition as well as some movement in and out of the labor force led to the change in sample size between 2000 and 2008. African Americans and Hispanics were oversampled by the survey, allowing for adequate samples for analysis of these groups. Because the initial cohort was fixed, recent immigrants are not present in the dataset.

Wage gaps among men. To estimate the effect of differences in character-istics on the wage differential between black and white men and Hispanic and white men, we use a methodology similar to that employed in the preceding analysis of data from the ACS. White men are again restricted to white non-Hispanic men, although for convenience we continue to refer to them simply as whites. We again use multiple regression analysis to examine the effect of different explanatory variables on the individual's hourly wage rate.[158] The variables that we include are the characteristics of individuals that are likely to affect productivity and therefore wages.

The key characteristics and their mean values for white, African Ameri-can, and Hispanic men are displayed in table 8-3 for 2000 and 2008. Due to attrition, the sample for men declined by 15 percent for white men, 18 percent for black men, and 24 percent for Hispanic men. There was, however, little change for most characteristics, the main exceptions being years of work experience (which is expected to increase over an eight-year period) and the wage rate, which also increased after adjusting for infla-tion.[159] In our analysis we use detailed breakdowns of schooling completed. Hispanic men have the lowest levels of schooling: In 2008, almost 7 percent completed fewer than 10 years of schooling; another 18 percent completed 10 or 11 years and may have attended the twelfth grade but never gradu-ated high school; another 36 percent completed high school with a diploma or a GED but never attended college. About 27 percent of Hispanic men attended college but only 12 percent of those who attended college ever graduated with a BA level or higher degree.

African American men have completed more schooling then Hispanic men, particularly at the high school level. About 21 percent never com-pleted high school, but another 40 percent ended their schooling with a high school diploma or a GED. About the same percentage of African American men as Hispanic men attended college, but a somewhat larger percentage attained a bachelor's or advanced degree.

White men have considerably more education than either African Americans or Hispanics. Only 11 percent were high school dropouts. More than half of the white men attended college and close to 60 percent of those who attended obtained a bachelor's or advanced degree.

The education obtained by the three groups is likely to differ in qual-ity because of differences in family income and other aspects of family

TABLE 8-3
SELECTED CHARACTERISTICS OF MEN BY RACE (NLSY79)

	2000 (Ages 35–43)			2008 (Ages 43–51)		
	White	Black	Hispanic	White	Black	Hispanic
Hourly rate of pay [1]	22.1	15.8	18.1	24.1	16.9	19.5
Region (%)						
Northeast	17.3	14.0	15.2	26.8	20.0	15.9
North Central	34.9	17.1	7.1	30.5	16.3	6.8
South	31.4	61.5	31.0	26.9	56.6	31.6
West	16.4	7.4	46.6	15.8	7.0	45.7
Education (Highest Level Attained, %)						
<10 yrs.	4.3	4.1	9.3	2.9	2.6	6.8
10–12 yrs (no diploma or GED)	8.3	14.9	19.8	7.8	18.4	17.9
HS grad (diploma)	32.8	35.8	27.4	31.8	34.9	28.3
HS grad (GED)	4.1	7.9	6.2	4.1	5.4	7.8
Some college	21.6	23.9	26.4	22.8	25.4	26.8
BA or equiv. degree	20.7	10.9	7.9	21.5	10.1	9.6
MA or equiv. degree	5.9	2.1	1.9	7.0	3.2	2.3
Ph.D or prof. degree	2.3	0.4	1.2	2.2	0.3	0.5
AFQT percentile score	55.4	24.1	33.6	57.1	24.2	33.3
Work Experience						
Avg. years worked in civilian jobs since age 18 [2]	17.83	15.87	17.28	24.92	22.66	24.35
Avg. years worked in the military since 1978 [2]	0.48	0.83	0.44	0.73	1.11	0.65
Sample size	1416	759	519	1199	625	396

[1] Hourly rate of pay in 2008 dollars (geometric mean).
[2] Years are full-year equivalents based on total weeks worked divided by 52.
NOTE: Characteristics above are for wage and salary workers included in the regression analysis.
SOURCE: National Longitudinal Survey of Youth (NLSY79).

background. Years of schooling can be a poor proxy for cognitive skills when the quality of schools attended and family background differ among groups. One variable unique to the NLSY79 and of considerable value to the measurement of skill is the individual's score on the AFQT administered to nearly all survey participants in 1980 when they were 15–23 years of age. The AFQT is a component of a larger test of vocational aptitude developed by the military many decades ago to determine eligibility for service and for job placement within the service. The test is a measure of verbal and mathematical skills and has been validated over the years as an effective and unbiased predictor of job performance.[160] Of course, in common with any test of skill or achievement, the aptitude it measures is influenced by the quantity and quality of schooling, by the home environment from early childhood, as well as by intrinsic abilities.[161] Mean test scores on the AFQT are shown in table 8-3 and they differ considerably by race. On average, in 2008, the white men in the sample were reported to have scored at the 57th percentile, African Americans at the 24th percentile, and Hispanics at the 33th percentile.

We also take account of differences in work experience and include measures of total weeks worked in civilian employment since age 18 (divided by 52 to convert to full-year equivalents) and total weeks served in the military since 1978 (also divided by 52). Close to 17 percent of African American men served in the military, compared to 8.5 percent for Hispanic men and 9.6 percent for white men. Partly for this reason, black men accumulated fewer years of civilian employment than white or Hispanic men. However, the average combined total lifetime employment of African American men is lower than that of the other two groups. Thus the average years of work by black men was 16.7 in 2000, 1.6 years lower than the average years worked by white men. Hispanic men worked only 0.6 year less than white non-Hispanic men. All three groups added a little more than seven years to their work experience by 2008, and the differentials among the groups remained about the same.

The male black–white wage ratio in the NLSY79 sample was 71 percent and the male Hispanic–white ratio was 82 percent in 2000. In 2008 both ratios were about a percentage point lower. In table 8-4 we show how these ratios change when we control for different groups of characteristics. We group the variables into three stages, each of which builds on the prior level,

TABLE 8-4

EXPLAINING THE BLACK–WHITE AND HISPANIC–WHITE
WAGE GAPS AMONG MEN

	Black-White Wage Ratio		Hispanic-White Wage Ratio	
	2000 (Ages 35–43)	2008 (Ages 43–51)	2000 (Ages 35–43)	2008 (Ages 43–51)
Unadjusted hourly wage ratio (in %)	71.2**	70.1**	82.0**	80.9**
Hourly wage ratio controlling for:				
1). Schooling	83.0**	82.0**	91.5**	91.4**
2). Variables in 1) plus AFQT	94.0**	95.8	97.9	100.6
3). Variables in 2) plus work experience	102.1	99.9	97.4	100.0

NOTE: The log wage ratios are exponentiated log wage differentials, which are the partial regression coefficients of dummy (0, 1) variables for black (Hispanic) from a series of OLS regressions containing the explanatory variables noted. The reference group is white non-Hispanic. All regressions starting with stage 1 also control for age, MSA, central city, and region. The analysis is restricted to wage and salary workers. The statistical significance of the black and Hispanic coefficients is indicated as follows (two-tailed test):
     **significant at the 5% level or less. All other ratios are not statistically significant.
SOURCE: National Longitudinal Survey of Youth (NLSY79).

to observe the effects on the wage ratio of adding particular factors. Stage 1 controls for differences in age, geographic location, and schooling; stage 2 additionally controls for AFQT score; and stage 3 additionally controls for civilian and military work experience.

We found that, for 2008, the unadjusted hourly wage rate of black men is about 70 percent of the unadjusted white male wage rate, leaving a differential or gap of 30 percent (table 8-4). When we control for differences in age, geographic location, and schooling, the black–white ratio rises to 82 percent both because of differences in schooling and because a larger proportion of African American than of white men live in the South, where wages are lower (stage 1).

After adding a variable measuring AFQT score (stage 2) the black–white wage ratio jumps to 96 percent, leaving a gap of only 4 percent (100 minus the ratio) and is no longer statistically significant. The effect of AFQT scores on the wage ratio is so large because the differential in scores is large: African American men scored at the 24th percentile and white men at the 57th, and the effect of a percentile point increase in AFQT score on wages is large for both African Americans and whites. Our findings with respect to the explanatory power of the AFQT variable are similar to those of Neal and Johnson (1996) and O'Neill (1990), who analyzed the same NLSY79 cohort when the survey participants were still in their twenties.[162] The black–white hourly wage ratio rises above 100 percent and the gap is eliminated when we control for differences in civilian and military work experience (model 3).

Table 8-5 shows the effect on the black–white wage ratio of the same series of regression adjustments for two subsets of men: those who completed no more than high school and those who are college graduates or more. The initial, unadjusted wage ratios are somewhat higher within education group but the effects of moving from stage 1 to stage 3 are similar to what we observed for the total group. The effect of AFQT is similarly large. For college graduates the wage gap is eliminated in 2008 with the addition of AFQT in stage 2 (in 2000 the wage ratio rises to 95, not 100 percent, but is not statistically significant). With all of the variables added in stage 3, the black–white wage gap is no longer of statistical or practical significance for either of the education groups in both 2000 and 2008.

The differential between Hispanic and white men (table 8-4) is smaller than the black–white gap before adding any explanatory variables (less than 20 percent overall and less than 10 percent for the subgroups of those who had at most a high school diploma and those who had completed college or had higher degrees (table 8-5). The addition of detailed schooling plus age and the geographic variables (stage 1) reduces the overall differential by half and marginally reduces the gaps for the high school and college groups since the grouping by education has already accounted for much of the education difference. The gap for Hispanic men is no longer statistically or practically significant for the total group as well as for the two education subgroups once AFQT scores are added (stage 2). The addition of the work experience variable has no significant effect on the outcome.

Our analysis of the NLSY79 data indicates that differences in schooling, scores on the AFQT, and lifetime work experience explain virtually all of the difference in hourly pay between African American men and white

TABLE 8-5

EXPLAINING THE MALE BLACK–WHITE AND HISPANIC–WHITE WAGE GAPS AT DIFFERENT EDUCATION LEVELS

	High School Graduate or Less				College Graduate or More			
	Black–White Wage Ratio		Hispanic–White Wage Ratio		Black–White Wage Ratio		Hispanic–White Wage Ratio	
	2000 (Ages 35–43)	2008 (Ages 43–51)	2000 (Ages 35–43)	2008 (Ages 43–51)	2000 (Ages 35–43)	2008 (Ages 43–51)	2000 (Ages 35–43)	2008 (Ages 43–51)
Unadjusted hourly wage ratio (in %)	78.3**	77.9**	91.8**	91.6**	77.0**	80.5**	94.3	94.1
Hourly wage ratio controlling for:								
1). Schooling	82.7**	82.7**	93.4**	92.9**	82.4**	84.8**	96.1	95.9
2). Variables in 1) plus AFQT	92.8**	94.7	100.3	101.5	95.1	100.9	101.9	104.3
3). Variables in 2) plus work experience	97.3	99.0	99.1	100.2	96.6	102.7	103.8	105.0

NOTE: The log wage ratios are exponentiated log wage differentials, which are the partial regression coefficients of dummy (0, 1) variables for black (Hispanic) from a series of OLS regressions containing the explanatory variables noted. The reference group is white non-Hispanic. All regressions starting with stage 1 also control for age, MSA, central city, and region. The analysis is restricted to wage and salary workers. The statistical significance of the black and Hispanic coefficients is indicated as follows (two-tailed test):

**significant at the 5% level or less. All other ratios are not statistically significant.

SOURCE: National Longitudinal Survey of Youth (NLSY79).

men. The difference in schooling and AFQT alone accounts for the pay difference between Hispanic men and white men. In our analysis of data from the ACS, we found significant residual wage gaps mainly because those data sources provide no standardized measure of actual attainment of cognitive skills or of accumulated work experience. Years of school completed are a weak proxy for actual educational attainment when standards for promotion and the attainment of diplomas and degrees vary widely. The AFQT provides a standardized measure of attainment, which reflects cognitive skills acquired in school and in the home.

Without including the AFQT or work experience variables, the ACS and the NLSY79 both indicate about the same adjusted black–white wage gap. In fact, comparing the results of models that include only age, geographic location, and schooling, we find that the black–white wage ratio using the ACS 2009 is 81 percent (model 1 of table 8-1), about the same as the ratio observed in the NLSY79 data (stage 1 of table 8-4).[163] It is the addition of the AFQT variable (and also the work experience variables) that set the NLSY79 results apart from the standard results using data like the ACS.

In sum, we find that differences in years of schooling and, more importantly, AFQT scores alone explain most of the black–white wage gap among men and all of the Hispanic–white wage gap. When years of work experience are included in the regression, the black–white gap is eliminated. The question remains, however, whether these results are reliable or instead reflect bias in the explanatory variables or other problems that typically confound statistical analysis of wage differentials.

First, do the explanatory variables themselves reflect employer discrimination? Differences in years of schooling and the AFQT are not likely to have been influenced by current employer discrimination, although societal discrimination had a crucial influence in the past on the educational attainment of African Americans, as we have shown in chapters 1 and 5. Because AFQT scores are likely influenced by early schooling and parental background, they too could have been affected by the lingering effects of early segregationist policies. However, those effects should not be confused with current employer discrimination.

Another question is whether it is appropriate to include work experience in an analysis of the wage gap that aims to determine the role of employer discrimination. It would be inappropriate if employer discrimination were an important reason for the lower employment of African American men. However, factors other than employer discrimination appear to be more important determinants of black–white employment differences. The relative decline in the employment of young African American men (particularly high school dropouts) that started in the 1970s and continued in the 1980s has been related to the broader decline in demand for low-skilled workers as well as to increased crime and incarcerations (Bound and Freeman 1992).

Using data from the NLSY79, we also find that African American men are much more likely than white men to have been incarcerated. In the 2000 survey, close to 13 percent of African American men had been interviewed in jail in at least one of the survey years (compared to 6 percent of Hispanics and 3 percent of whites). Incarceration directly reduces years of work experience and, if it lasts long enough, may lead to depreciation of work-related skills. It also makes it more difficult to obtain future employment. In an analysis of the determinants of lifetime work experience we found that jail experience had a strong and significant negative effect on work experience.

The argument is sometimes also made that employer discrimination takes the form of rewarding minorities less than whites for higher levels of work-related skills, which would appear as lower coefficients in our regression analysis. Lower returns to additional years of work experience and education (and, less plausibly, to higher scores on the AFQT) for minorities than for whites could be evidence of employer discrimination that might discourage investment in work-related skills.

To address these issues we have estimated separate regressions for African Americans, whites, and Hispanics and we report here on our findings of results for the major explanatory variables in 2000 (appendix table 8A-1). With respect to AFQT scores, we find that the wage gain associated with a 10 percentile point increase in the AFQT score is larger for African American and Hispanic men than it is for white men, suggesting that employers recognize and reward skill among minority men at least to the same extent as they do among white men (i.e., holding constant the variables indicated in Model 1, a 10 percentile point increase in the AFQT score increases the wage rates of African American and Hispanic men by about 6 percent and white men by about 5 percent). When work experience is added to the model, the return to AFQT is slightly smaller for all groups, presumably because AFQT scores are correlated with work experience. However, the same pattern by race is maintained and the coefficients remain robust and significant. The even stronger relation between the AFQT score and wage rates among African Americans and Hispanics than for whites is good evidence that the AFQT provides an unbiased measure of skills.[164] The question of bias in the AFQT, however, has been analyzed more directly by the U.S. Department of Defense, which uses it extensively as a tool for assigning military personnel to occupational training and tasks. Such tests have concluded that the AFQT predicts African American performance as well as it does white performance.[165]

Most men have at least a high school diploma or a GED (87 percent among whites, 81 percent among African Americans, but dropping to 71 percent among Hispanics). The differences in attainment are more pronounced at the post-secondary level, where white men are much more likely to graduate from college than African American or Hispanic men. Holding AFQT constant, increases in schooling through high school do not have a significant effect on earnings for any group. However, the increases in wages associated with college graduation and with attainment of higher degrees are large and roughly similar for all groups. White and Hispanic men have a higher return to college graduation than black men, while black men have higher returns at the master's, doctoral, and professional degree levels.

With regard to the return to work experience, holding constant education and AFQT, the wage gain associated with an additional year of civilian experience is somewhat lower for African Americans than for the other groups: about 4 percent for black men, 4.7 percent for white men, and 4.9 percent for Hispanic men. The return to a year of military service is lower than the return to a year of civilian work experience for all three groups.[166] The small black–white difference in work experience coefficients may be due to discontinuities in African American male employment that we have not accounted for in this analysis.[167]

When we take into account minority–white differences in characteristics and the difference in the wage premiums associated with these differences, we find that the single largest factor contributing to the wage gaps is the differential in the AFQT. The AFQT differential alone explains 45 percent of the black–white wage gap and half of the Hispanic–white gap. AFQT and education together account for two-thirds of the black–white gap and 89 percent of the Hispanic–white gap. Differences in geographic location and work experience fully explain the remaining gaps.[168]

We conclude from this analysis that labor market discrimination is not a likely cause of either the black–white or Hispanic–white wage gap among men. Nonetheless, these wage gaps are troubling, particularly the persistent black–white gap. Our analysis suggests that the source of the problem lies in the fact that black men on average accumulate less in the way of cognitive skills before they enter the labor market and less continuous work experience after entry. The public policy issue that we face is what should be done to help eliminate the productivity gaps. Some observers advocate eliminating the *effects* of the skill gap rather than acknowledging its existence and devoting the energy and other resources needed to closing it. That is essentially the approach of affirmative action. Other analysts and commentators, concerned about the problems of young African American men, have focused on the causes of the skill gap. Jencks and Phillips (1998a) comment that "if racial equality is America's goal, reducing the black–white skill gap would probably do more to promote this goal than any other strategy that could command broad political support." Researchers have increasingly turned their attention to the sources of the skill gap and to the study of ways to change the provision of schooling, as well as the environmental conditions and parental attitudes that have negative impacts on the development of skills from early childhood. For example, see Jencks and Phillips (1998b), Fryer and Levitt (2004), Heckman (2008).

Wage gaps among women. The initial unadjusted minority–white wage gaps are considerably smaller among women than those we observed for men. In 2008 the black–white wage ratio for men in the NLSY79 is 70 percent, while the ratio for women is 87 percent. The Hispanic–white wage ratio for men is 81 percent and for women 92 percent. We have analyzed the sources of the black–white and Hispanic–white wage differences among women using the same methodology that we applied to our analysis of wage gaps among men. We conduct wage regressions for all women (and separately for women with high school education and women who are college graduates) and use the coefficients of variables indicating African American race and Hispanic origin to estimate wage differentials between the two minority groups and the reference group of white women.

The salient characteristics of black, white, and Hispanic women are displayed in table 8-6. In addition to the variables used in our analysis of racial and ethnic differences among men we include two variables that are particularly relevant to women. One indicates whether the person ever had a spell out of the labor force due to family responsibilities, and the other is a measure of the proportion of total weeks worked part-time since age 22.

In 2008, black women were almost as likely as white women to have completed at least high school (87 percent for black women versus 91 percent for white women; only 80 percent of Hispanic women completed high school.) Similar to the comparison among men, education differences are more pronounced at the college level. About 32 percent of white women completed college or more, compared to 18 percent of black women and 16 percent of Hispanic women. All three groups of women slightly increased their educational attainment between 2000 and 2008. AFQT scores differ considerably by race and Hispanic origin among women, much as they did among men. The average percentile score on the AFQT was 54 percent for white women compared to 26 percent for black women and 31 percent for Hispanic women.

In terms of work experience, white women accumulated more years of work experience in civilian jobs since age 18 than African American or Hispanic women, but white women were much more likely to have worked part-time. (About 17 percent of the total time worked by white women was part-time, compared to 10 percent for black women and 12 percent for Hispanic women.) Black women accumulated more years in the military than white or Hispanic women.

The results of our regression analysis are shown in table 8-7. The results for women, as for men, are given sequentially in three stages, each of which adds new groups of independent variables. The initial unadjusted black–white earnings ratio was 87 percent in 2008, somewhat higher than in 2000. The earnings ratio rises to 94 percent after controlling for schooling and the geographic and age variables. The addition of the AFQT variable eliminates any disparity. In fact it raises the black–white ratio for women to 106.6 percent. Lifetime work experience has no additional effect. (It lowers the ratio slightly to 105.7 percent.)

In 2008, the unadjusted Hispanic–white hourly wage ratio among women was 92 percent (a gap of 8 percent). When we control for differences

TABLE 8-6
SELECTED CHARACTERISTICS OF WOMEN BY RACE (NLSY79)

	2000 (Ages 35–43)			2008 (Ages 43–51)		
	White	Black	Hispanic	White	Black	Hispanic
Hourly rate of pay [1]	16.5	13.7	15.1	17.3	15.0	15.9
Region (%)						
Northeast	17.2	13.5	13.8	25.8	16.5	13.4
North Central	32.6	18.8	8.1	30.7	18.6	7.5
South	33.3	61.2	33.9	29.5	58.9	36.5
West	16.9	6.6	44.1	14.1	6.0	42.6
Education (Highest Level Attained, %)						
<10 yrs.	1.8	2.8	7.5	0.9	2.1	7.3
10–12 yrs (no diploma or GED)	8.2	11.1	14.6	8.0	10.9	12.5
HS grad (diploma)	32.6	29.2	24.0	29.7	24.6	23.0
HS grad (GED)	3.6	5.3	5.7	3.3	4.2	5.0
Some college	26.0	36.6	34.2	26.5	40.2	36.2
BA or equiv. degree	19.7	12.2	8.5	20.7	13.4	9.1
MA or equiv. degree	7.4	2.5	4.7	10.1	4.1	5.9
Ph.D or prof. Degree	0.8	0.4	0.8	0.9	0.5	0.9
AFQT percentile score	53.0	24.5	30.1	54.1	25.8	30.6
Work Experience Variables						
Avg. years worked in civilian jobs since age 18 [2]	16.45	14.48	15.00	22.94	21.31	21.26
Avg. years worked in the military since 1978 [2]	0.04	0.10	0.05	0.06	0.12	0.03
Proportion of total weeks worked PT since age 22 (%)	16.87	9.65	12.04	16.73	9.75	11.58
% ever out of labor force due to family responsibilities	49.6	57.8	64.4	55.5	58.9	66.7
Sample size	1358	855	492	1236	778	439

[1] Hourly rate of pay in 2008 dollars (geometric mean).
[2] Years are full-year equivalents based on total weeks worked divided by 52.
NOTE: Characteristics above are for wage and salary workers included in the regression analysis.
SOURCE: National Longitudinal Survey of Youth (NLSY79).

TABLE 8-7

EXPLAINING THE BLACK–WHITE AND HISPANIC–WHITE
WAGE GAPS AMONG WOMEN

	Black–White Wage Ratio		Hispanic–White Wage Ratio	
	2000 (Ages 35–43)	2008 (Ages 43–51)	2000 (Ages 35–43)	2008 (Ages 43–51)
Unadjusted hourly wage ratio (in %)	82.8**	87.1**	91.2**	91.9**
Hourly wage ratio controlling for:				
1). Schooling	90.8**	94.3**	97.0	98.3
2). Variables in 1) plus AFQT	104.1*	106.6**	107.3**	107.5**
3). Variables in 2) plus work experience	105.4**	105.7**	106.5**	105.8**

NOTE: The log wage ratios are exponentiated log wage differentials, which are the partial regression coefficients of dummy (0, 1) variables for black (Hispanic) from a series of OLS regressions containing the explanatory variables noted. The reference group is white non-Hispanic. All regressions starting with stage 1 also control for age, MSA, central city, and region. The analysis is restricted to wage and salary workers. The statistical significance of the black and Hispanic coefficients is indicated as follows (two-tailed test):
   **significant at the 5% level or less
   *significant at the 10% level
SOURCE: National Longitudinal Survey of Youth (NLSY79).

in schooling and geographic location, the Hispanic–white ratio rises to 98 percent, leaving a gap of 2 percent (not statistically significant). With the additional control for differences in AFQT scores, the Hispanic–white wage ratio rises above 100 percent (to 107.5 percent without the work experience variables and slightly lower when the work experience variables are added).

In table 8-8 we show the results of the same set of black–white and Hispanic–white regressions conducted for women who attended or graduated from high school and women who attained a college degree or more. At the college level Hispanic women earned 16 percent more than white non-Hispanic women in 2008 before adjusting for any explanatory factors, and that result is not significantly altered by the addition of other factors. Black women earn almost as much as white women before adjusting for other factors, and that ratio rises above 100 once we add AFQT. Among the high school subgroup, the wage ratios for both black and Hispanic women exceed 100 once we adjust for AFQT.

TABLE 8-8
EXPLAINING THE FEMALE BLACK–WHITE AND HISPANIC–WHITE WAGE GAPS AT DIFFERENT EDUCATION LEVELS

	High School Graduate or Less				College Graduate or More			
	Black–White Wage Ratio		Hispanic–White Wage Ratio		Black–White Wage Ratio		Hispanic–White Wage Ratio	
	2000 (Ages 35–43)	2008 (Ages 43–51)	2000 (Ages 35–43)	2008 (Ages 43–51)	2000 (Ages 35–43)	2008 (Ages 43–51)	2000 (Ages 35–43)	2008 (Ages 43–51)
Unadjusted hourly wage ratio (in %)	85.6**	87.2**	94.4*	92.6**	85.3**	96.7	105.9	116.1**
Hourly wage ratio controlling for:								
1). Schooling	91.7**	93.7*	96.0	97.6	89.0**	97.7	101.3	107.8
2). Variables in 1) plus AFQT	105.7*	105.0	106.5*	105.7	96.6	105.9	107.3	114.5*
3). Variables in 2) plus work experience	108.7**	105.1	104.9	103.0	95.0	103.0	110.0	117.8**

NOTE: The log wage ratios are exponentiated log wage differentials, which are the partial regression coefficients of dummy (0, 1) variables for black (Hispanic) from a series of OLS regressions containing the explanatory variables noted. The reference group is white non-Hispanic. All regressions starting with stage 1 also control for age, MSA, central city, and region. The analysis is restricted to wage and salary workers. The statistical significance of the black and Hispanic coefficients is indicated as follows (two-tailed test):
**significant at the 5% level or less
*significant at the 10% level
SOURCE: National Longitudinal Survey of Youth (NLSY79).

Looking at the results of separate regressions for black, white, and Hispanic women allows us to examine regression coefficients to determine how the monetary returns to key variables vary by race and Hispanic ethnicity.[169] We find, as we did in the same comparison among men, that the increase in the wage rate associated with an increase in AFQT is not only large and significant for all groups but is much larger for black and Hispanic women than for white women. A 10 percentile point increase in the AFQT score raises the wage rate by about 8 percent for African American women, 7 percent for Hispanic women and 4 percent for white women when schooling, age, and geographic location are held constant (see appendix table 8A-3). The return to additional years of work experience is about the same for all three groups (marginally higher for black and Hispanic women). Black women have worked more years in the military than the other groups, and their return to military service is also higher. Part-time work has a negative effect on hourly pay. Black women are less likely to have worked part-time than the other groups, and their wage penalty for part-time work is larger than it is for the other groups. White women were much more likely to have worked part-time, but their penalty for doing so is not as large as it is for black women.

When we take into account minority–white differences in characteristics and the difference in the wage premiums associated with these differences, we find, as we did for men, that the single largest factor contributing to the wage gaps is the differential in the AFQT score. In fact, the AFQT differential alone explains 94 percent of the female black–white wage gap and more than explains the female Hispanic-white gap.[170]

In sum, our analysis of female wage differentials by race and Hispanic ethnicity provides no support for the view that the differences observed— which are smaller than those observed among men—are due to employment discrimination.

Do Audit Studies Reveal Discrimination Undetected by Traditional Research? Some analysts have tried to develop direct measures of individual employer discrimination by the use of "matched-pair" studies, also called "audit studies."[171] In our view these studies are limited in their ability to shed light on the question of the overall level of current labor market discrimination. However, the Equal Employment Opportunity Commission has plans for extending their use and so we briefly discuss the methodology and findings of audit studies.

In an audit study, researchers select pairs of applicants to apply for entry-level jobs where the pairs consist of two individuals—one black, one white—but otherwise supposedly matched on relevant credentials such as age and education. Assuming that the auditor pairs are well matched, the researchers take any difference in treatment by employers as a measure of discrimination.

The auditor pairs are actually actors—college students on vacation who pretend to be applicants. No actual employment can result from these searches. Moreover, they only audit job openings advertised in newspapers, which is not the main way that youths find jobs (Heckman and Siegelman 1993). The findings of audits generally indicate that fewer minorities than whites obtain job offers. A clever lawyer on a discrimination case may be able to turn these results into a convincing "gotcha." But what do these results really mean?

James Heckman (1998), in a wide-ranging critique of the relevance of audit studies, points out that the results, taken on face value, are less impressive than advertised. Reviewing the results of major audits in three cities involving black–white comparisons, Heckman shows that the predominant result was equal treatment: situations where the African American and white auditors were treated symmetrically (both got a job; neither got a job). In Chicago and Denver 86 percent of the audits were in the equal treatment category. Among those that were not equal, in Chicago whites got a job but African Americans did not in 10 percent of the audits; and African Americans got the job and whites did not in 5 percent of the audits. On net, only 5 percent of the audits indicated preferential treatment of whites. In Denver, just the opposite, whites were twice as likely to be rejected as African Americans, resulting in a finding of preferential treatment of African Americans in 4 percent of the audits. In Washington, the results were less favorable to African Americans. But the net percent of audits indicating white preference was still rather small, merely 13 percent.

But how credible are these results? Heckman finds two major flaws. One is methodological and relates to the extreme difficulty of measuring the productivity characteristics relevant to a firm and the likelihood that pairs will never be perfectly matched on all of these characteristics. As we have seen, more easily measured traits—education and age—are inadequate for determining productivity. We also wonder the extent to which the bias of the auditing researchers influences the behavior of the actors.

But the second limitation is perhaps more critical. Even if it were safe to assume that prejudiced individual employers could be isolated by this method, there still would be no obvious way to know if the relative number of these prejudiced employers is large enough and their prejudice significantly great enough to result in labor market discrimination—i.e., a black–white wage gap for equally productive workers.

One of the important insights from Gary Becker's seminal theory of discrimination is that the existence of some prejudiced employers need not result in effective labor market discrimination at the market level (Becker 1957/1971). According to Becker's model the extent to which minority wages are ultimately reduced by labor market discrimination depends on the intensity and distribution of tastes for discrimination among employers and the interaction of those factors with market structure and production conditions. In situations where a large majority of employers are not prejudiced, the minority worker population may be able to avoid discrimination altogether, as they can find jobs in firms in which employers do not have a "taste" for discrimination. Moreover, if nondiscriminating firms were subject to production conditions that allow constant or increasing returns to scale, then in the long run nonbigoted firms would employ all the minority workers even if there had been an initial situation in which some minority workers had to work for employers with a taste for discrimination. Thus wage rates of minorities initially might be below their true productivity but in the long run, as they were absorbed by employers with no taste for discrimination, their wages would rise to a level equal to white workers of the same productivity. However, if nonprejudiced firms were a minor presence in the market relative to the size of the minority population, then their impact on reducing the effects of labor market discrimination would be minimal. That was the likely situation that prevailed in much of the South prior to passage of the 1964 Civil Rights Act.

Given the trends described in chapters 5 and 6 and the analysis in this chapter, it is likely that the relative number of bigoted firms in today's economy is not large enough to outweigh the effects of the much larger group of nonprejudiced employers who are willing to pay the same wage to equally productive African American and white employees.

The Gender Gap in Wages

Although the gender gap in pay has narrowed considerably since the late 1970s, women's hourly pay was only 79 percent of men's in 2000 among the NLSY79 cohort, who had reached ages 35–43 by that year.[172] Yet the women and men in the NLSY79 have approximately the same amount of schooling and scores on the AFQT test. Gender differences in productivity, however, arise for reasons other than differences in cognitive skills. The most important source of the gender wage gap is the difference in human capital acquired through labor market experience and in job choice, both of which reflect the relative importance of home and market activities in the lives of women and men.

The division of labor in the family is less delineated than it once was. A majority of married women with children now work. Nonetheless, women still assume greater responsibility for child rearing than men, and that responsibility influences the extent and continuity of market work as well as choice of occupation and preferences for working conditions that facilitate the combination of work in the market and housework.[173] These gender differences in preferences translate into wage differences, partly because they lead to differences in human capital acquired on the job and partly because flexible schedules at work, a less stressful work environment, and other working conditions compatible with meeting the demands of home responsibilities are likely to come at the price of lower wages.

The Trade-off between Work in the Market and Housework. The labor force participation of women has greatly increased over the years.[174] Yet even today labor force data show the strong effect of the presence of children, particularly young children, on women's work participation. Among parents of children under the age of six, 58 percent of women were employed in 2009 compared to 88 percent of men. Among parents of children whose youngest child was ages 6–17, 72 percent of women were employed compared to 86 percent of men. Thus many women are out of the labor force during a time of life when labor market skills would otherwise be acquired.[175]

Even if they are in the labor force, women with children differ from working men with respect to hours spent at work. As shown in figure 8-3,

FIGURE 8-3

EMPLOYMENT STATUS OF WOMEN AND MEN
WITH CHILDREN BY AGE OF CHILDREN, 2009

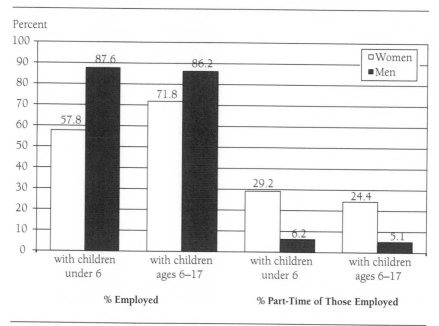

SOURCE: Data derived from Employment Characteristics of Families, Table 5, 2009. U.S. Department of Labor, Bureau of Labor Statistics.

in 2009, 29 percent of women with children under the age of six worked part-time compared to 6 percent of men with similarly aged children. The percentage of women working part-time is reduced to 24 percent when their children reach ages 6–17, while the percent part-time among men falls a little to 5 percent. Gender differences in hours are also present among full-time workers, in that women are less likely than men to work long hours in a week: in 2010, 25 percent of male full-time workers but only 14 percent of female full-time workers worked 41 hours or more a week.[176]

Are women steered into part-time jobs by prejudiced employers harboring stereotyped views of women? Polls on job preferences indicate that free choice, not employer choice, is the reason for the gender difference in part-time work. Results of a recent poll conducted by the Pew Research

TABLE 8-9
WHAT WORKING SITUATION WOULD BE IDEAL FOR YOU?
RESULTS FROM A 2007 PEW RESEARCH CENTER SURVEY

	Ideal Situation Would Be			
	Not working %	Part-time work %	Full-time work %	N
Have children under 18				
Fathers	16	12	72	343
Mothers	29	50	20	414
Mothers with children under 18				
Employed full-time	21	49	29	187
Employed part-time	15	80	5	75
Not employed	48	33	16	153

SOURCE: From "Fewer Mothers Prefer Full-time Work" in *A Social and Demographic Trend Report*, Pew Research Center, p. 3, July 12, 2007.

Center (2007) show that in answer to the question "What would be the ideal situation for you—working full-time, working part-time, or not working at all outside the home?" Fifty percent of all mothers of children under age 18 responded that part-time would be ideal, 20 percent said full-time, and 29 percent said not working at all. In contrast, 72 percent of fathers preferred full-time work, 12 percent part-time work, and 16 percent no work (table 8-9). Even among mothers who were employed full-time, 49 percent said that their ideal would be part-time work, while 80 percent of mothers working part-time said that part-time was their ideal and only 5 percent indicated a preference for full-time work. These results are not an anomaly. Over the years periodic polls on job preference have found similar results.[177]

Data collected by the Department of Labor's American Time Use Survey (ATUS) provide further insight into the trade-offs that women and men make in apportioning their time among market work, housework, and other activities. The ATUS collects information from individuals who keep detailed diaries, recording how they spend their time during a twenty-four-hour period. Table 8-10 displays our tabulations from the combined

TABLE 8-10

AVERAGE HOURS SPENT PER DAY IN CHILD CARE, WORK, AND OTHER
ACTIVITIES BY AGE OF YOUNGEST CHILD, FOR EMPLOYED WOMEN AND MEN
AGES 20–44 REPORTING TIME USE ON A WEEKDAY, 2003–2004
ANNUAL AVERAGES, ATUS DATA

Age of youngest child:	Currently employed and work on the diary day				
	<1	1–5	6–12	13–17	No Child
Women					
Household work	2.4	1.6	1.9	1.8	1.4
Primary child care	3.1	2.3	1.5	0.5	0.1
Market work	7.2	7.6	7.7	8.4	8.2
Socializing, sports, eating, and other	3.8	4.7	5.4	5.8	6.3
Sleeping	7.5	7.9	7.5	7.4	8.1
Total hours with children in respondent's care*	8.7	6.9	6.2	NC	NA
Men					
Household work	1.0	0.9	1.0	0.9	1.0
Primary child care	1.1	1.1	0.8	0.3	0.0
Market work	9.9	9.5	9.5	9.8	8.9
Socializing, sports, eating, and other	4.4	5.0	5.2	5.3	6.4
Sleeping	7.5	7.5	7.6	7.7	7.6
Total hours with children in respondent's care*	3.7	4.1	3.7	NC	NA

NOTE: Means are weighted. NC: Data not collected for children over 12 years of age. NA: Not applicable.
*Total waking hours in a day spent with children in a primary or a secondary capacity.
SOURCE: Pooled 2003 and 2004 data from the American Time Use Survey (ATUS).

2003–4 ATUS for employed men and women ages 20–44 who reported their time use on a weekday.[178]

The table shows the allocation of hours among five categories of primary activity: sleeping, housework, childcare, market work, and socializing, sports, and all other activities. The time allocations are given separately according to the age of the youngest child (<1, 1–5, 6–12, and 13–17) as well as for those who have no children under age 18 present in the household. Primary activities are mutually exclusive, so with allowance for rounding error, the time spent in the four activities plus sleeping adds up to 24 hours.

We report data for those who are currently employed, kept a diary on a weekday, and were employed on the diary day. Time spent on childcare is measured in two ways—hours during the day spent on primary childcare when it is the main activity and total hours spent with children present in either a primary capacity or a secondary capacity while engaged in other activities. (Total hours were not collected for children after they reached age 13.)

Several distinct patterns of time use stand out. No matter how measured, working mothers devote significantly more time to childcare than fathers. Hours spent on childcare by both mothers and fathers decline as children age. Working mothers of infants spent 3.1 hours on primary childcare and those hours declined to 2.3 when the youngest child was ages 1–5 and to 1.5 once the child reached school age (6–12), falling to only 0.5 hour when the youngest child was a teenager. Over the same span, fathers of infants devoted 1.1 hours to primary childcare, falling to 0.8 hours by the time the youngest child reached ages 6–12.

Mothers also spent more time on household work than fathers on a workday: 2.4 hours when the child was an infant, declining to somewhat less than 2 hours when children were more than infants. Fathers spent about an hour on household work and that did not vary by age of child.[179]

Fathers more or less make up for the lower hours spent on childcare and household work by working in the market longer hours during the day. Comparing mothers and fathers who worked on the diary day, we find that men spent 9.5 to 10 hours on market work, and those hours did not vary much with age of youngest child. Mothers, however, somewhat increased their work time from 7.2 hours when the youngest child was an infant to 8.4 hours when the youngest child reached ages 13–17.

Primary childcare understates the total burden of childcare because responsibility for children does not end when a parent does housework or other activities. It is striking that total time spent with children in the mother's care is considerable even on a day when the mother worked: 8.2 hours for mothers with an infant, declining to 6.2 hours when the child reached ages 6–12. Fathers spend about 4 hours of total time with children in their care on an average workday, and that time does not vary with age of child.

The ATUS data demonstrate that women continue to be responsible for a disproportionately large share of household work and childcare after they enter the market. The burden of household responsibilities affects more than desired hours on the job. In an important extension of his work on the economics of the family, Gary Becker (1985) has developed a model of the allocation of energy.[180] Becker's analysis shows how the energy demands of childcare and housework reduce the energy available for market work. Women who are heavily engaged in childcare and other household work could be expected to choose less-demanding and consequently lower-paying jobs.

Analyzing the Gender Pay Gap with NLSY79 Data. It is a challenge to estimate the determinants of the gender gap because differences in standard variables such as schooling are not likely to be important sources of the gender gap. The NLSY79 is superior to most other data sources because it provides detailed information on lifetime patterns of work participation. Although differences in lifetime work patterns have received considerable attention as a source of the gender gap, another significant source of wage differentials is what Adam Smith, in his *Wealth of Nations,* termed "Inequalities arising from the Nature of the Employments themselves." Smith observed that the "agreeableness and disagreeableness of the employments themselves" are one of the principal circumstances that make up for "small pecuniary gain in some employments and counterbalance a great one in other" (Smith 1776).[181] Those nonpecuniary characteristics of employments surely may be evaluated differently by women and men. For example, occupations and individual firms differ in the extent to which they provide part-time work or otherwise accommodate flexible work schedules, characteristics that are likely to be more highly valued by women than by men. To the extent these amenities are costly for employers to provide, jobs with amenities will be paid for with lower wages.

Jobs with disamenities, such as exposure to hazards or an unpleasant environment, are likely to require a pay premium. A large and growing literature in psychology, sociology, and economics has studied the risk-taking tendencies of men and women in many domains, including physical danger and financial risk.[182] It is fair to say that the general finding is that women are more risk-averse than men. In addition, men and women may differ in their attitudes toward work involving dirty or otherwise unpleasant physical conditions. Physical differences are likely to affect aptitude for certain work, for example, jobs requiring extremely heavy lifting, although the proportion of jobs requiring hard physical labor has declined sharply over time.

Another source of differences in financial rewards among occupations is the extent to which skills depreciate during periods of withdrawal from work. The rate of depreciation will vary depending on the rate of technological change and obsolescence of the skills acquired. Since women are more likely than men to expect to take career breaks for childrearing, they are more likely to avoid training for occupations with a larger financial penalty for withdrawal.[183]

Although women and men are more likely than they once were to work in the same occupation, large differences still prevail in their occupational distributions. In 2010 women were 45 percent of all full-time workers.[184] Women were 55 percent of all professional workers, but within the professions women continue to be concentrated in different fields. Women were 72 percent of education and library workers, 64 percent of psychologists, 48 percent of biologists but only 25 percent of workers in computer and mathematical occupations and 12 percent of architects and engineers. These percentages are close to women's representation in the same fields of college and graduate degrees (see chapter 6). In nonprofessional occupations, women make up 73 percent of office and administrative support occupations and 71 percent of cashiers but make up a tiny proportion of workers in many blue-collar occupations: 2 percent of construction and extraction workers, 3.7 percent of installation, maintenance, and repair workers, fewer than 1 percent of crane and tower operators.

We estimate that over the period 1994–2001, among all narrowly defined (three-digit) occupations as defined by the Bureau of the Census, 53 percent of women or men would have to change their occupation to produce gender equality in occupational distributions.[185] To assess the effect on wages of gender differences in occupational choice, we have incorporated in our wage analysis measures of the characteristics of each person's occupation based on additional information on the characteristics of each three-digit level occupation. Our analysis of the gender gap follows the same procedures used in our analysis of racial and ethnic differences. The key variables and their mean values for all men and women are given in table

8-11; table 8-12 shows the effect on the gender gap of controlling for different sets of explanatory variables from a series of log wage regressions.[186] Results are shown for the full sample of male and female workers as well as for subsets of the sample disaggregated by education. Results are also given for married men and women as well as for those who never had a child and never married and can be assumed to be free of family responsibilities (an assumption corroborated by our time use data in table 8-10).

We display the results as female–male hourly wage ratios.[187] The unadjusted hourly wage ratio for the full sample of men and women is 79.0 percent in 2000 and 77.4 percent in 2008 when the cohort is older. Using the 2000 data we find that the ratio is essentially unchanged after including education, AFQT score, and geographic location (stage 1). The addition of three work experience variables, however, reduces the gender gap by almost half and the wage ratio rises to 89 percent (stage 2). The work experience variables include weeks worked in civilian jobs since age 18 (converted to years by dividing by 52), weeks worked in the military divided by 52, and the proportion part-time of total weeks worked. On average, women have worked about two years less than men in military and civilian jobs combined. Moreover, close to 14 percent of the weeks worked by women were part-time compared to 5 percent for men.

As a proxy for commitment to home responsibilities we add in stage 3 a variable indicating whether the worker had ever withdrawn from the labor force citing child-care or family responsibilities as the reason. Such labor force withdrawal is associated with an 8 percent reduction in the wage rate for men as well as women. However, 55 percent of women and only 13 percent of men have ever withdrawn because of family responsibilities. We also add variables indicating whether the person's job is in government employment, the nonprofit sector, or the private sector. Nonprofit jobs offer more part-time work and are more likely to allow for flexible schedules and possibly a more relaxed ambience than work in the for-profit sector. But such amenities come at a cost to employers and are therefore associated with lower pay. As shown in table 8-11, women are more likely than men to work in the nonprofit and government sectors. The addition of the class of worker variables combined with the labor force withdrawal variable raises the hourly wage ratio by 2.3 percentage points to 91 percent. The final set of variables measure particular characteristics of each person's

TABLE 8-11
SELECTED CHARACTERISTICS OF MEN AND WOMEN (NLSY79)

	2000 (Ages 35–43)		2008 (Ages 43–51)	
	Female	Male	Female	Male
Hourly rate of pay[1]	15.3	19.4	16.3	21.0
% Hispanic	18.2	19.3	17.9	17.8
% Black	31.6	28.2	31.7	28.2
Education (Highest Level Attained, %)				
< High school	13.5	17.6	12.2	16.1
HS grad (diploma)	30.0	32.6	26.9	32.0
HS grad (GED)	4.5	5.6	3.9	5.1
Some college	30.8	23.2	32.6	24.2
BA or equiv. degree	15.3	15.5	16.3	16.2
MA or equiv. degree	5.3	4.1	7.5	5.1
Ph.D or prof. degree	0.7	1.5	0.8	1.4
AFQT percentile score	39.8	42.4	40.9	43.6
Work Experience Variables				
Avg. years worked in civilian job since age 18[2]	15.57	17.17	22.12	24.18
Avg. years worked in military since 1978[2]	0.06	0.57	0.07	0.83
Proportion of total weeks worked PT since age 22 (%)	13.71	4.95	13.60	4.11
% ever out of labor force due to family responsibilities	54.9	13.0	58.6	14.3
% in gov't job	21.6	14.4	26.7	17.5
% in nonprofit job	10.0	4.9	14.1	5.2
OCC. Characteristics of Person's 3-digit OCC.				
Specific Vocation Preparation (SVP) required in occup. (months)	27.0	28.8	26.0	28.7
% in OCC. involving:				
Hazards (0,1)	1.3	8.4	1.1	10.0
Fumes (0,1)	0.4	4.3	0.6	10.2
Noise (0,1)	8.0	30.7	7.1	32.8

(continued)

TABLE 8-11 (*continued*)
SELECTED CHARACTERISTICS OF MEN AND WOMEN (NLSY79)

	2000 (Ages 35–43)		2008 (Ages 43–51)	
	Female	Male	Female	Male
% in OCC. involving:				
Strength (0,1)	9.2	21.5	8.7	17.8
Weather extreme (0,1)	3.3	18.8	2.7	22.1
% using computers	55.7	41.5	56.7	44.0
% using computer for analysis	14.3	13.9	14.9	15.2
% using computer for word proc.	34.5	23.6	41.9	30.4
Risk of unemployment	0.8	1.1	0.8	0.9
Rate of transition to out of labor force	1.0	0.8	1.0	0.8
% female in OCC.	63.5	27.0	64.2	26.9
Sample size	2,705	2,694	2,453	2,220

[1] Hourly rate of pay in 2008 dollars (geometric mean).
[2] Year equivalents are total weeks of work divided by 52.
NOTE: Characteristics above are for wage and salary workers included in the regression analysis. Model also controls for age, central city, MSA, region, and occupation missing.
SOURCE: National Longitudinal Survey of Youth (NLSY79) merged with measures of occupational characteristics (3-digit level) from the September 2001 CPS, the March CPS, the CPS ORG, and the *Dictionary of Occupational Titles* (1991).

three-digit occupation. The characteristics are expected to have an effect on wages because they are associated with on-the-job investment or with particular amenities or disamenities. The occupational characteristics included in our analysis are listed in table 8-11 along with the mean values for men and women separately. Measures of months of Specific Vocational Preparation (SVP) required for the job and other occupational characteristics were derived from the *Dictionary of Occupational Titles* (U.S. Employment Service 1991) and from special supplements pertaining to computer use on the job from the Current Population Survey (CPS). A variable measuring the level of transition out of the labor force and another measuring the risk of unemployment in the occupation were estimated using data from the March CPS.

There is a problem with the occupational data, most of which are derived from the *Dictionary of Occupational Titles* created in 1991. The individual characteristics of each occupation are related to the three-digit

TABLE 8-12
EXPLAINING THE GENDER WAGE GAP:
FEMALE-MALE HOURLY WAGE RATIOS (NLSY79)

	All		By Schooling Level (2000)	
	2000 (Ages 35–43)	2008 (Ages 43–51)	High School Graduate or Less	College Graduate or More
Unadjusted hourly wage ratio (in %)	79.0	77.4	79.5	75.0
Hourly wage ratio controlling for:				
1). Schooling, AFQT	79.4	77.0	79.4	78.3
2). Variables in 1) plus work experience	88.6	88.2	92.8	83.4
3). Variables in 2) plus labor force withdrawal due to family responsibilities and type of employer	90.9	90.7	94.2	88.7
4). Variables in 3) plus occupational characteristics	92.0	91.0	93.0	92.5
5). Variables in 4) plus percent female in occupation	92.4	93.4	94.7	92.5
Alternative step:				
4A) Variables in 3) plus percent female in occupation	96.7	96.5	94.7	92.5

NOTE: All female coefficients are significant at the 10% level or lower. The log wage ratios are exponentiated log wage differentials, which are the partial regression coefficients of dummy (0, 1) variables for female from a series of OLS regressions containing the explanatory variables noted. The reference group is male. All regressions starting with stage 1 also control for age, MSA, central city, and region.
SOURCE: National Longitudinal Survey of Youth (NLSY79) merged with measures of occupational characteristics (3-digit level) from the September 2001 CPS, the March CPS, and the *Dictionary of Occupational Titles* (1991).

occupations as classified at that time. The characteristics of occupations may well have changed. The coding scheme for occupations has changed significantly. Consequently the occupations of NLSY79 participants may be quite imperfectly linked to the occupational descriptions we use. As an alternative we use a variable measuring the percent female in a three digit occupation, contemporaneously matched with the individual's occupational code. In earlier research occupational characteristics similar to those shown in table 8-12 were found to explain most of the variation in the percent female across 327 three-digit occupations (Cavallo and O'Neill 2004; O'Neill 1983).

The hourly wage ratio rises only slightly to 92 percent when the occupational characteristics enumerated in table 8-12 are added in stage 4. In stage 5 we add a variable that measures the percent female in the respondent's three-digit occupation. That addition barely affects the ratio, which rises to 92.4 percent. However, when we drop occupational characteristics and simply add percent female in the occupation, the female–male wage ratio increases to 97 percent (alternative, step 4-A). Because of the measurement difficulties described, the occupational characteristics measure may not be able to capture occupational differences as well as the percent female variable.

Although measures of occupational dissimilarity between men and women have declined since the 1970s, the occupational distributions of women and men are still very different. As shown in table 8-11, the women in our 2008 NLSY79 sample, on average, worked in occupations in which the percent female was 64 percent; men worked in occupations in which the percent female was 27 percent. These occupational differences are sometimes viewed as evidence of discrimination.[188] However, the occupations that women choose are strongly predicted by characteristics that are compatible with women's dual roles as workers and homemakers.[189] The addition of the variable measuring the percent female in an occupation has only a limited additional effect on wages because it is highly correlated with the other occupational and personal characteristics that have already been accounted for in the analysis. In fact, in a log wage regression based only on the female sample, the percent female is not statistically significant and bears a positive sign (appendix table 8A-3). The variable is negative and significant only for men. The results for the year 2008, also shown in table 8-12, are similar to the results for 2000 when the cohort was eight years younger.

Table 8-12 also provides results for two subgroups of the NLSY79 sample, differing by education level. The results for the high school group (those attaining a high school diploma or GED or with less schooling) are similar to those described above for all women and men. The unadjusted female–male ratio for this group was 79.5 percent in 2000. However, gender differences in work experience are more important for the high school group than for all women and men and alone account for two-thirds of the gender wage gap for this group. At the third stage, which also includes spells of labor force withdrawal and type of employer (government, non-profit or private sector), the female-male ratio reaches 94 percent.

The results for college graduates differ somewhat from those of the other groups. The unadjusted wage gap is larger (a ratio of 75 percent in 2000) in part because gender differences in skills among college graduates are somewhat larger. Men are more likely to receive doctoral and professional degrees, and among college graduates men have higher AFQT scores than women (73rd versus 64th percentile). Although the gender difference in years worked is slight at the college graduate level, the difference in part-time work is as large as for the high school group. Moreover, women who are college graduates are less likely to work in the private sector than other women, or men at any education level. (Seventeen percent of female college graduates work in the nonprofit sector and 42 percent work in government compared to 8 percent of men in nonprofits and 22 percent in government.) A college education appears to give women access to jobs with working conditions that allow them either to work part-time or to work full-time but under conditions more complementary with care of family, such as the long vacations of teachers.

Controlling for education, AFQT and work experience raises the ratio for college graduates to 83 percent (stage 2). But once account is taken of gender differences in withdrawal for family reasons and type of employer, the ratio among college graduates rises to 89 percent. Adding occupational characteristics brings the ratio up to 92.5 percent. Occupational characteristics are important at the college level and often reflect choice of college major. Brown and Corcoran (1997) find that adding information on field of college major to an analysis of the gender gap in pay among college graduates that also controls for work history and other factors reduces the gap to 6 percent (a female-male wage ratio of 94 percent).

Tables 8-13 and 8-14 further highlight the relative importance of family responsibilities versus labor market discrimination by comparing the gender gap for two groups at polar extremes: currently married men and women, and men and women who were never married and never had a child. Married women's hourly wage was about 74 percent of the wage of married men in 2000 (72 percent in 2008). Married men have somewhat

TABLE 8-13
SELECTED CHARACTERISTICS OF MEN AND WOMEN BY MARITAL STATUS (NLSY79)

| | Currently married | | | | Never married and never had a child | |
| | 2000 (Ages 35–43) | | 2008 (Ages 43–51) | | 2000 (Ages 35–43) | |
	Female	Male	Female	Male	Female	Male
Hourly rate of pay [1]	16.1	21.8	23.7	17.1	17.8	16.4
% Hispanic	19.8	19.5	17.5	18.1	15.8	17.1
% Black	20.5	21.0	21.7	21.6	35.5	29.0
Education (Highest Level Attained, %)						
< High school	11.5	14.0	8.9	13.0	5.4	16.8
HS grad (diploma)	30.9	32.4	27.6	30.9	18.7	28.7
HS grad (GED)	3.2	4.6	2.6	4.1	3.0	3.0
Some college	29.6	23.4	32.2	25.0	35.0	25.2
BA or equiv. degree	17.6	18.4	19.1	19.0	28.1	20.1
MA or equiv. degree	6.7	5.3	8.9	6.5	7.4	4.5
Ph.D or prof. degree	0.6	2.0	0.8	1.6	2.5	1.8
AFQT percentile score	44.2	47.3	46.0	47.7	49.2	42.6
Work Experience Variables						
Avg. years worked in civilian job since age 18 [2]	16.20	17.88	22.64	24.80	17.47	16.01
Avg. years worked in military since 1978 [2]	0.06	0.59	0.06	0.90	0.07	0.27
Proportion of total weeks worked PT since age 22 (%)	15.78	3.90	15.74	3.30	10.51	9.51
% ever out of labor force due to family responsibilities	54.6	10.2	58.0	11.4	16.3	12.9

% in gov't job	22.2	16.9	28.5	18.9	24.1	9.0
% in nonprofit job	11.2	5.0	15.4	5.2	11.8	8.4
OCC. Characteristics of 3-digit OCC.						
Specific Vocation Preparation (SVP) required in occup. (months)	28.9	32.9	28.0	32.5	32.7	26.4
% in OCC. involving:						
Hazards (0,1)	1.4	7.7	0.7	9.0	0.0	6.6
Fumes (0,1)	0.3	3.8	0.4	9.2	0.5	3.3
Noise (0,1)	6.5	29.3	6.2	30.2	7.4	26.4
Strength (0,1)	8.4	18.9	6.8	15.4	4.9	21.9
Weather extreme (0,1)	2.8	17.4	2.2	20.4	3.9	18.6
% using computers	58.6	46.1	59.8	48.7	62.0	41.9
% using computer for analysis	15.0	16.1	15.9	17.6	17.8	13.3
% using computer for word proc.	37.3	27.2	44.8	34.4	39.0	24.3
Risk of unemployment	0.7	1.0	0.8	0.9	0.7	1.1
% female in OCC.	65.0	27.2	65.8	27.2	63.0	32.5
Rate of transition to out of labor force	1.0	0.7	1.0	0.8	1.0	0.9
% female in OCC.	65.0	27.2	65.8	27.2	63.0	32.5
Sample size	1532	1674	1357	1419	203	334

1) Hourly rate of pay in 2008 dollars (geometric mean).

2) Year equivalents are total weeks of work divided by 52.

NOTE: Characteristics above are for wage and salary workers included in the regression analysis. Model also controls for age, central city, MSA, region, and occupation missing.

SOURCE: National Longitudinal Survey of Youth (NLSY79) merged with measures of occupational characteristics (3-digit level) from the September 2001 CPS, the March CPS, the CPS ORG, and the *Dictionary of Occupational Titles* (1991).

TABLE 8-14

EXPLAINING THE GENDER WAGE GAP: FEMALE-MALE HOURLY
WAGE RATIOS BY MARITAL STATUS (NLSY79)

	Currently married (with or w/o children)		Never married and never had a child
	2000 (Ages 35–43)	2008 (Ages 43–51)	2000 (Ages 35–43)
Unadjusted hourly wage ratio (in %)	73.6	72.1	107.9[ns]
Hourly wage ratio controlling for:			
1). Schooling, AFQT	74.1	71.4	98.1[ns]
2). Variables in 1) plus work experience	82.7	82.9	93.7[ns]
3). Variables in 2) plus labor force withdrawal due to family responsibilities and type of employer	85.6	87.3	95.9[ns]
4). Variables in 3) plus occupational characteristics	87.7	88.3	98.7[ns]
5). Variables in 4) plus percent female in occupation	87.9	91.3	97.3[ns]
Alternative step:			
4A) Variables in 3) plus percent female in occupation	91.3	93.6	101.5[ns]

NOTE: All female coefficients are significant at the 10% level or lower unless indicated with "ns" (not statistically significant). The log wage ratios are exponentiated log wage differentials, which are the partial regression coefficients of dummy (0, 1) variables for female from a series of OLS regressions containing the explanatory variables noted. The reference group is male. All regressions starting with stage 1 also control for age, MSA, central city, and region.

SOURCE: National Longitudinal Survey of Youth (NLSY79) merged with measures of occupational characteristics (3-digit level) from the September 2001 CPS, the March CPS, and the *Dictionary of Occupational Titles* (1991).

higher AFQT scores and education than married women, have more years of work experience (civilian and military) and are much less likely to work part-time (table 8-13). They are more likely to be responsible for financial support of the family and, as shown in the ATUS data, men with children spend a much larger proportion of their time at work and have a much lower burden of home responsibilities than women with children. One might expect that married men make job and career choices that assign a higher value to monetary awards than would married women who must balance the rewards of time with children against financial rewards from market work. Although we control for many variables, we have no data on time spent on household tasks and childcare in the NLSY79 data base and no way to incorporate more subtle differences in preferences. In 2000 the wage ratio comparing married women to married men rises to 88 percent after adjusting for all of our measured variables (stage 5); in 2008 when the group was older the ratio rises to 91 percent with the stage 5 specifications. The variable, percent female in the occupation, has a more powerful effect when it is used alone, as in the alternative step 4A, which excludes the detailed characteristics of occupations. The ratio at model 4A was 91 percent in 2000 and 94 percent in 2008.

At the opposite pole we compare the earnings of never-married men and never-married women who never had a child. Never-married men do not the bear the responsibility for the financial support of a family as do most married men. And never-married women who never had a child do not have the responsibility for children that mothers bear, though they are more likely to be responsible for their own financial support. Never-married women without children have stronger credentials than never-married men without children with respect to education and somewhat higher AFQT scores and years of work experience. They are somewhat more likely to work part-time than never-married men. The typical occupational differences still prevail, however, as never-married women work in occupations that are 63 percent female (almost the same percent as married women) compared to 32.5 percent among never-married men. (But note that married men are much less likely to work in female-dominated occupations than never-married men.)

Not surprisingly, given the stronger education and work profile of never-married women, the unadjusted gender gap for this group is actually positive; the women earned about 8 percent more than their male counterparts in 2000. When we control for differences in characteristics, the gender gap in favor of women is eliminated. The wage ratio is 99 percent when we add occupational characteristics (stage 4) and rises back over 100 percent when we measure occupation as the percent female in the worker's occupation (alternative step 4). Neither ratio is significant. (These results are for 2000; the sample for 2008 was too small to yield reliable results.)

These results lend support to the view that the factors underlying the gender gap in pay primarily reflect choices made by men and women, given their different roles in the family, rather than labor market discrimination against women due to their sex. Of course, it is still possible that men who have never married have unobservable negative productivity factors that selected them into this group in the first place. The fact that they have never married could reflect personal characteristics that would also lower their productivity in the labor market. However, the same could be true of never-married women. We do not know the proportion of men or of women who are unmarried by choice, dedication to a career, or because of negative personality traits.

The comparison of male and female earnings and the interpretation of the gender gap in pay are further complicated by gender differences in the effects of certain variables on earnings. However, the variables involved are not those that have sometimes aroused suspicion of bias. As shown in separate wage regressions for women and men, the coefficients measuring the pecuniary returns to standard human capital variables such as schooling and years of work experience are similar for women and men (see appendix table 8A-3). However, coefficients differ considerably by sex when the variable is one that is likely to have a different meaning for women and men. For example, the variable measuring the proportion of weeks worked part-time is negatively associated with earnings for both men and women; but the size of the effect is much larger for men. Whether one works for a nonprofit employer is negatively associated with earnings for both men and women, and again the effect is much stronger for men. The variable measuring the percent female in the individual's occupation is negatively related to earnings for both women and men, but the effect for women is weak and never statistically significant, while the effect for men is usually larger in magnitude than it is for women and is also statistically significant.

How can these findings be explained? Women are likely to choose part-time work and nonprofit work because they offer more flexibility and perhaps, in the case of nonprofit work, less stress. However, women who work part-time are more likely to have chosen part-time work as a long-term adjustment to home responsibilities. Moreover, some occupations allow for transition from full-time work to part-time work and back again (e.g., nursing and real estate sales). A smaller proportion of men work part-time than women, and those who do are more likely to report that their part-time work is due to inability to find a full-time job. Under these circumstances men working part-time are more likely than women to accept a pay cut below their usual work. Such considerations would explain why wage data from the Bureau of Labor Statistics typically show that women working part-time earn considerably more than part-time men.[190]

When it comes to full-time work within the private for-profit sector, women may seek job situations that offer more flexibility in schedules, although we have no easy way to detect that with the available data. In that case the difference in work situations between full-time work in profit or nonprofit employment may be less stark for women than for men.

Because of gender differences in coefficients, such as those noted above, the adjusted wage ratio differs depending on whether male or female coefficients are used to evaluate the effect of adjusting for several of the variables. As shown in appendix table 8A-4, the unadjusted gap, expressed as the ratio of women's to men's hourly wage, was 79 percent in 2000. Using male regression coefficients the ratio rises almost to 100 percent when all variables are included; using female coefficients it rises to 92 percent.

Which are the more appropriate coefficients to use? The answer depends on the degree to which our data accurately measure differentials in personal and job characteristics and the effects of those differentials on wages. Without better data, all we can conclude is that labor market discrimination is unlikely to account for a differential of more than 5 percent but may not be present at all. The results of the analysis comparing men and women who never married nor had a child also suggest no differential.

A number of recent studies have analyzed gender differences in earnings focusing on those with higher degrees. Those studies rely on unusually detailed survey instruments and take account of gender differences in life cycle work experience. Their findings are generally consistent with the results of our analysis of the gender gap among college graduates. Bertrand, Goldin, and Katz (2009) focus on male and female MBA graduates from a top U.S. business school. Using regression analysis, they found that, when they included all graduates, the annual earnings ratio unadjusted for any explanatory variables except for cohort and year was 75 percent.[191] Adjusting for hours worked per week raises the ratio to 84 percent. The ratio jumps to 91 percent after adding the effect of MBA grade point average

(GPA) and concentration in finance courses (women have lower grades and are less likely to have taken finance courses). Once account is taken of work experience and career breaks, the wage ratio reaches 96 percent and is no longer statistically or substantively significant.

Black, Haviland, Sanders, and Taylor (2008) analyze gender wage differences comparing white non-Hispanic men with four groups of college-educated women (white non-Hispanic, Hispanic, Asian, and black). The observed unadjusted gaps are on the order of 74 percent expressed as wage ratios. Their statistical methodology differs from the standard regression analysis in that they match men and women for comparability on certain key characteristics. After matching for age, highest degree, and field of major the ratio rises to 83 percent or to 92 percent depending on the group. When the authors further restrict the match to women with "high labor force attachment," the gender wage gap is essentially eliminated for Hispanic and Asian women and is reduced to 9 percent for white women and 12 percent for black women (implying wage ratios of 91 percent and 88 percent, respectively). Black et al. do not appear to have accounted for detailed data on hours worked on current job or measures of differences in cognitive skills (at the college level women have lower SAT scores and GPAs than men; the sizes of these female–male gaps vary by race).

The results of statistical analysis of the gender gap are clearly dependent on access to information on lifetime work patterns, measures of cognitive skills other than years of school completed, and details of job characteristics and personal preferences that are not available in most data sets. Bertrand, Goldin, and Katz (2009) utilize an unusually complete dataset and find no substantive differences in pay between male and female MBAs once differences in characteristics are taken into account. We generally find little or no difference in pay among more heterogeneous samples of men and women.

Despite the evidence of economic research that discrimination is unlikely to play a significant role in explaining the gender pay gap, organizations such as the National Committee on Pay Equity continue to call for legislation that would directly impose measures to close the pay gap. The most recent example is the Paycheck Fairness Act, which though supported by President Obama failed to garner the votes to pass in the Senate (O'Neill, 2010). Paycheck Fairness is similar in spirit, and is generally supported by the same groups that have supported the implementation of "comparable worth" pay systems. Comparable worth is a mechanism for raising women's pay directly by requiring a firm to equalize pay between occupations dominated by women and occupations dominated by men when these occupations are determined by job evaluations to be of "comparable worth." Since there is no uniform way to rank occupations by worth, a comparable-worth policy would ultimately lead to politically administered wages that would depart from a market system of wage determination. Ironically, if implemented, it would likely impede women's progress. Women have been moving into nontraditional occupations such as medicine, law, and even engineering. Apart from the gross inefficiencies it would breed, these pay distortions would discourage women and men from investing in the skills to enter these higher paying fields.

Comparable worth has been rejected in the courts, notably by the Ninth Circuit Federal Court of Appeals in 1985 (*AFSCME v. Washington*).[192] Overturning the decision of the district court in the state of Washington, the court upheld the state's right to base pay on market wages rather than on a comparable worth job evaluation, writing: "Neither law nor logic deems the free market system a suspect enterprise." The judge who wrote the decision was Anthony Kennedy, now a member of the U.S. Supreme Court.[193]

Conclusions

Several lessons can be drawn from this survey of group differences in earnings. One is that it can be highly misleading to use earnings differentials alone to determine the extent of labor market discrimination. Groups vary in productivity, sometimes considerably, because of their particular advantages and disadvantages with respect to such factors as educational attainment and immigrant status. In the case of the gender gap, differences in preferences for working conditions are an additional source of pay differentials. Women are more likely to assume responsibility for child rearing than men, and as a result they acquire less work experience in the market and are more likely to place a high value on shorter hours and flexible work situations, which usually involve a wage trade-off. Those factors explain most and in some cases all of the variation in earnings among racial and ethnic minorities and between women and men.

Labor market discrimination is a minimal source of wage differentials. However, this does not mean that discrimination in society has been eliminated. Prejudiced individuals clearly exist, as we are sharply reminded when acts of violence occur against Asians, African Americans, and other minorities. Some individual employers and managers are prejudiced. However, as Gary Becker (1957/1971) has taught us, as long as the pool of nonprejudiced employers is large enough, those employers who would discriminate against women and minorities have little effect on their market opportunities and wages.

APPENDIX TABLE 8A-1

MEANS AND PARTIAL REGRESSION COEFFICIENTS OF EXPLANATORY VARIABLES FROM
SEPARATE LOG WAGE REGRESSIONS FOR BLACK, WHITE, AND HISPANIC MEN AGES 35–43 IN 2000 (NLSY79)

	Mean			White				Black				Hispanic			
				M1		M2		M1		M2		M1		M2	
	White	Black	Hisp.	Coef.	t-stat	Coef.	t-stat	Coef.	t-stat	Coef.	t-stat	Coef.	t-stat	Coef.	t-stat
Education: Highest Level Attained															
<10 yrs.	0.043	0.041	0.093	-0.051	-0.68	-0.036	-0.49	0.069	0.80	0.024	0.30	-0.064	-0.81	-0.082	-1.08
10–12 yrs (no diploma or GED)*	0.083	0.149	0.198	—	—	—	—	—	—	—	—	—	—	—	—
HS grad (diploma)	0.328	0.358	0.274	0.064	1.33	0.009	0.19	0.072	1.51	0.005	0.12	-0.007	-0.12	-0.063	-1.10
HS grad (GED)	0.041	0.079	0.062	-0.018	-0.24	0.031	0.43	0.042	0.62	0.078	1.22	-0.080	-0.87	-0.077	-0.89
Some college	0.216	0.239	0.264	0.236	4.42	0.215	4.13	0.205	3.76	0.151	2.89	0.085	1.32	0.068	1.11
BA or equiv. degree	0.207	0.109	0.079	0.419	7.31	0.427	7.66	0.335	4.88	0.294	4.51	0.355	3.77	0.369	4.13
MA or equiv. degree	0.059	0.021	0.019	0.524	7.14	0.561	7.84	0.634	5.29	0.624	5.48	0.465	2.94	0.484	3.23
Ph.D or prof. degree	0.023	0.004	0.012	0.645	6.50	0.780	8.00	1.302	5.07	1.359	5.58	0.593	2.95	0.774	4.02
AFQT percentile score (x.10)	5.538	2.411	3.360	0.046	7.63	0.039	6.49	0.058	6.68	0.048	5.80	0.059	6.04	0.046	4.91
Work Experience (Year Equivalents)															
Weeks worked in civilian job since age 18 ÷ 52	17.828	15.865	17.279			0.047	9.17			0.040	9.20			0.049	7.55
Weeks worked in military since 1978 ÷ 52	0.483	0.835	0.436			0.033	4.31			0.028	4.00			0.036	2.89
Adj. R-square				0.296		0.337		0.287		0.359		0.262		0.335	
Dependent mean (Log hourly wage)				2.898				2.559				2.700			
Sample size				1,416				759				519			

NOTE: Model also controls for age, central city, MSA, and region. The analysis is restricted to wage and salary workers employed within the past month.
*Reference group.
SOURCE: National Longitudinal Survey of Youth (NLSY79).

APPENDIX TABLE 8A-2

MEANS AND PARTIAL REGRESSION COEFFICIENTS OF EXPLANATORY VARIABLES FROM SEPARATE LOG WAGE REGRESSIONS FOR BLACK, WHITE, AND HISPANIC WOMEN AGES 35–43 IN 2000 (NLSY79)

	Mean			White				Black				Hispanic			
				M1		M2		M1		M2		M1		M2	
	White	Black	Hisp.	Coef.	t-stat	Coef.	t-stat	Coef.	t-stat	Coef.	t-stat	Coef.	t-stat	Coef.	t-stat
Education: Highest Level Attained															
<10 yrs.	0.018	0.028	0.075	-0.261	-2.51	-0.186	-1.89	-0.069	-0.75	0.010	0.12	-0.130	-1.55	-0.059	-0.76
10–12 yrs (no diploma or GED)*	0.082	0.112	0.146	—	—	—	—	—	—	—	—	—	—	—	—
HS grad (diploma)	0.326	0.292	0.240	0.042	0.85	-0.033	-0.70	0.148	3.10	0.035	0.77	0.102	1.60	-0.003	-0.06
HS grad (GED)	0.036	0.053	0.057	-0.087	-1.10	-0.075	-1.00	-0.025	-0.34	-0.018	-0.27	0.071	0.77	0.077	0.92
Some college	0.260	0.366	0.342	0.163	3.10	0.082	1.64	0.213	4.34	0.072	1.52	0.208	3.35	0.106	1.84
BA or equiv. degree	0.197	0.122	0.085	0.378	6.45	0.286	5.09	0.352	5.61	0.197	3.29	0.418	4.67	0.319	3.89
MA or equiv. degree	0.074	0.025	0.047	0.504	7.20	0.396	5.92	0.514	5.35	0.362	3.78	0.485	4.54	0.386	3.92
Ph.D or prof. degree	0.008	0.004	0.008	0.841	5.61	0.763	5.36	0.726	3.01	0.531	2.36	0.734	3.35	0.854	4.27
AFQT percentile score (x.10)	5.298	2.445	3.006	0.042	6.64	0.032	5.27	0.080	9.71	0.063	7.98	0.070	7.19	0.043	4.65
Work Experience Variables															
Weeks worked in civilian job since age 18 ÷ 52	16.453	14.482	14.999			0.030	8.43			0.030	8.96			0.033	7.39
Weeks worked in military since 1978 ÷ 52	0.045	0.096	0.051			0.029	1.27			0.058	3.07			0.049	1.80
Proportion of total weeks worked PT since age 22	0.169	0.097	0.120			-0.174	-2.72			-0.287	-2.86			-0.052	-0.45
Labor force withdrawal due to family responsibilities (0,1)	0.496	0.578	0.644			-0.098	-3.28			-0.037	-1.17			-0.120	-2.72
Adj. R-square				0.255		0.336		0.324		0.415		0.344		0.458	
Dependent mean (log hourly wage)				2.606				2.416				2.514			
Sample size				1358				855				492			

NOTE: Model also controls for age, central city, MSA, and region. The analysis is restricted to wage and salary workers employed within the past month.
*Reference group.
SOURCE: National Longitudinal Survey of Youth (NLSY79).

Appendix Table 8A-3

MEANS AND PARTIAL REGRESSION COEFFICIENTS OF EXPLANATORY VARIABLES FROM SEPARATE LOG WAGE REGRESSIONS FOR MEN AND WOMEN AGES 35–43 IN 2000 (NLSY79)

| | Means | | Female | | | | Male | | | |
| | Female | Male | M1 | | M2 | | M1 | | M2 | |
			Coef.	t-stat	Coef.	t-stat	Coef.	t-stat	Coef.	t-stat
Race										
Hispanic (0,1)	0.182	0.193	0.063	2.57	0.060	2.61	-0.025	-1.02	-0.018	-0.75
Black (0,1)	0.316	0.282	0.053	2.42	0.066	3.14	-0.022	-0.92	0.005	0.20
Education: Highest Level Attained										
<10 yrs.	0.031	0.052	-0.089	-1.76	-0.078	-1.64	-0.028	-0.65	-0.025	-0.60
10–12 yrs (no diploma or GED)*	0.103	0.124	—	—	—	—	—	—	—	—
HS grad (diploma)	0.300	0.326	-0.003	-0.10	-0.008	-0.27	-0.018	-0.65	-0.013	-0.50
HS grad (GED)	0.045	0.056	-0.015	-0.34	-0.046	-1.12	0.027	0.63	0.015	0.38
Some college	0.308	0.232	0.090	2.99	0.060	2.09	0.166	5.31	0.123	4.08
BA or equiv. degree	0.153	0.155	0.276	7.61	0.216	6.19	0.373	10.23	0.260	7.08
MA or equiv. degree	0.053	0.041	0.391	8.49	0.348	7.76	0.562	10.84	0.446	8.62
Ph.D or prof. degree	0.007	0.015	0.758	7.47	0.654	6.71	0.806	10.60	0.639	8.53
AFQT percentile score (x.10)	3.981	4.238	0.042	9.92	0.032	7.84	0.042	9.92	0.029	7.04
Work Experience Variables										
Weeks worked in civilian job since age 18 ÷ 52	15.565	17.169	0.030	13.85	0.023	11.13	0.038	12.54	0.034	11.39
Weeks worked in military since 1978 ÷ 52	0.062	0.573	0.046	3.53	0.040	3.22	0.025	5.15	0.020	4.46
Weeks PT ÷ total weeks workd since age 22	0.137	0.050	-0.203	-4.24	-0.084	-1.81	-0.779	-7.90	-0.540	-5.70
Labor force withdrawal due to family responsibilities (0,1)	0.549	0.130	-0.081	-4.16	-0.082	-4.46	-0.080	-3.14	-0.066	-2.74

(continued)

APPENDIX TABLE 8A-3 (*continued*)

MEANS AND PARTIAL REGRESSION COEFFICIENTS OF EXPLANATORY VARIABLES FROM SEPARATE LOG WAGE REGRESSIONS FOR MEN AND WOMEN AGES 35–43 IN 2000 (NLSY79)

	Means		Female				Male			
			M1		M2		M1		M2	
	Female	Male	Coef.	t-stat	Coef.	t-stat	Coef.	t-stat	Coef.	t-stat
Employment Type										
Gov't employer (0,1)	0.215	0.144			-0.030	-1.50			-0.027	-1.13
Nonprofit employer (0,1)	0.100	0.049			-0.056	-2.13			-0.121	-3.20
OCC. Characteristics of Person's 3-digit OCC.										
SVP required in occup. (months) (DOT)	26.961	28.773			0.001	2.44			0.003	5.43
Hazards (0,1) (DOT)	0.013	0.084			0.327	4.66			0.131	3.97
Fumes (0,1) (DOT)	0.004	0.043			-0.293	-2.27			-0.075	-1.72
Noise (0,1) (DOT)	0.080	0.307			0.005	0.18			0.019	0.83
Strength (0,1) (DOT)	0.092	0.215			0.011	0.37			-0.049	-1.99
Weather extreme (0,1) (DOT)	0.033	0.188			0.120	2.56			0.000	-0.01
Prop. using computers (CPS)	0.557	0.415			0.157	2.19			0.045	0.49
Prop. using computer for analysis (CPS)	0.143	0.139			0.497	4.62			0.258	2.22
Prop. using computer for word proc. (CPS)	0.345	0.236			-0.255	-3.19			-0.007	-0.06
Relative rate of transition to unemployment	0.772	1.092			-0.022	-1.11			-0.023	-1.91
Relative rate of transition to OLF	1.046	0.789			-0.144	-7.30			-0.073	-3.57
% female in OCC. X 0.1. (CPS ORG)	6.348	2.695			0.005	1.08			-0.019	-3.55
Adj. R-square			0.392		0.464		0.403		0.467	
Dependent mean (log hourly wage)			2.529				2.764			
Sample size			2704				2694			

NOTE: Model also controls for age, central city, MSA, region, and whether occupation was missing. The analysis is restricted to wage and salary workers employed within the past month.

*Reference group.

SOURCE: National Longitudinal Survey of Youth (NLSY79) merged with measures of occupational characteristics (3-digit level) from the September 2001 CPS, the March CPS, the CPS ORG, and the *Dictionary of Occupational Titles* (1991).

APPENDIX TABLE 8A-4

EXPLAINING THE SOURCE OF THE GENDER WAGE GAPS (NLSY79 IN 2000)

	Using male coefficients		Using female coefficients	
	M1	M2	M1	M2
Unadjusted female/male hourly wage ratio (%)	79.0	79.0	79.0	79.0
Percent explained by:				
Age, race, region, central city, MSA	1.0	0.8	0.8	0.5
Education level	−1.1	−0.9	−0.6	−0.4
AFQT	0.9	0.7	0.9	0.7
Work experience	12.4	9.9	7.6	5.6
Labor force withdrawal due to family responsibilities	2.9	2.5	2.9	2.9
Nonprofit, government		0.7		0.4
Occupational characteristics:				
Investment related				
SVP (Specific Vocational Preparation)		0.5		0.2
Computer usage		−0.4		−0.2
Compensating differences				
Disamenities (physical)		0.4		2.3
Unemployment risk; labor force turnover		0.2		2.2
TYP: % female in occupation		6.4		−1.2
Adjusted female/male hourly wage ratio (%)	95.1	99.9	90.7	92.1

NOTE: The results are derived from Appendix Table 8A-3, which shows separate regressions for men ages 35–43 by race and by model using NLSY79 data. The results are given under two assumptions. One uses the male coefficients and the other uses female coefficients to evaluate the effects of the explanatory variables on wages. The hourly wage ratios are the anti-log of the log hour wage.

SOURCE: National Longitudinal Survey of Youth (NLSY79) merged with measures of occupational characteristics (3-digit level) from the September 2001 CPS, the March CPS, the CPS ORG, and the *Dictionary of Occupational Titles* (1991).

Notes

1. The Paycheck Fairness Act fell short of the votes necessary for passage in the Senate in November 2010. Its supporters hope it will be passed in an upcoming session. See O'Neill (2010).

2. U.S. Census Bureau (1918). In 1860 about 97 percent of African American slaves lived in the South. Among the small minority who were freemen, about half lived in the South and half in the North. In the North about one-third of African Americans were slaves. In the South, 94 percent were slaves.

3. The discussion in this paragraph is from Welch (1973), who draws some of his information from Bond (1966).

4. See Thernstrom and Thernstrom (1997) and Bullock (1967).

5. Harlan dissent, *Plessy v. Ferguson*, 163 U.S. 537 (1896).

6. *Brown v. Board of Education of Topeka*, 347 U.S. 483 (1954).

7. For additional detail see Virgil A. Clift (1966).

8. U.S. Commission on Civil Rights (1986).

9. Margo (1986) finds that factors such as black–white differences in parental literacy, occupational status, and wealth, account for half the black–white gap in school attendance.

10. Measured as the percent enrolled of youth ages 5–19, the African American rate increased from 45 percent in 1910 to 75 percent in 1950; the white rate from 61 percent in 1910 to 79 percent in 1950. U.S. Commission on Civil Rights (1986).

11. See U.S. Commission on Civil Rights (1986), table 4.7.

12. Ibid.

13. In 1953, African American students in the South attended school 96 percent as many days as white students and were in classes with the same number of students per teacher as whites. The largest racial gap in measured resources was in the salary of teachers. Teacher salaries (per student day) for the teachers of African American children were only 90 percent as much as those who were teachers of white students. U.S. Commission on Civil Rights (1986).

14. Note too that the schooling measures shown in table 1-2 refer to workers ages 25–54 and therefore include the records of older African American men who lived in the South in the Jim Crow era, when access to schooling was extremely limited. The schooling measures in table 1-1 indicate higher levels of schooling in 1940 and

larger gains for both African Americans and whites between 1940 and 1960 because the data are restricted to younger persons, those ages 25–29, who had higher levels of schooling than older workers.

15. See Maloney (1995) for an interesting comparison of the advance of African American workers in northern meat-packing and steel industries before World War II. African Americans were more readily hired and eventually promoted to higher levels according to Maloney because of the less rigid internal structure that allowed for greater turnover and therefore for lower costs of experimentation with new employees.

16. We use hourly earnings to measure the black–white wage ratio for women because women frequently work part-time, a factor that would cause variability in weekly wages unadjusted for hours worked per week. Because the percentage of men who work part-time is low, we are able to use average weekly earnings as our wage measure for men.

17. For example, fewer than 1 percent of African American women worked as textile operatives in the South in 1960 compared to 11 percent of southern white women. Outside the South, 6 percent of African American women worked as textile operatives compared to 4 percent of white women.

18. The March on Washington was proposed by A. Philip Randolph, the African American activist, labor leader, organizer of the Brotherhood of Sleeping Car Porters in 1925, and later the founder of the Leadership Conference on Civil Rights. See the account by John Hope Franklin (1966), 78.

19. In 1945, the Ives-Quinn law in New York established the State Commission Against Discrimination (later the State Commission for Human Rights). The model for the New York commission was the National Labor Relations Board, an individual, single-mission agency that could hold hearings, investigate, and ultimately issue orders enforceable in court. See Graham (1990), 20–21.

20. Landes (1968) found a positive statistical effect of state FEPC laws on the earnings of African Americans but also an increase in African American unemployment.

21. See Graham (1990), 16–7, for a discussion of Eisenhower's Contract Committee, which replaced President Truman's Contract Compliance Committee.

22. "Affirmative action" was used as far back as the Wagner Act of 1935 where it was used in the context of defining the authority of the National Labor Relations Board to redress an unfair labor practice. See Graham (1990), chapter 1.

23. The addition of sex was a late change proposed by Congressman Howard Smith, not a fan of the legislation, who moved to add "sex" to the list of groups protected by Title VII saying, "This bill is so imperfect, what harm will this little amendment do?" By some accounts, however, he was a proponent of women's rights and joined forces with Congresswoman Martha Griffiths to get the amendment passed. See Graham (1990), 136.

24. *Heart of Atlanta Motel v. U.S.,* 379 U.S.241 (1964).

25. *Wards Cove Packing Co. Inc. v. Atonio* (490 U.S. 642, 1989).

26. *Griggs v. Duke Power Co.*, Supreme Court 401, U.S. 424, argued Dec 14, 1970.

27. During the debates over Title VII, Senator Clifford P. Case (R-NJ) and Senator Joseph Clark (D-Pa.), who were shepherding the legislation on the Senate floor, strongly responded to the concerns of wavering senators by saying that "no court could read title VII as requiring an employer to lower or change the occupational qualifications he sets for employees simply because proportionately fewer Negroes than whites are able to meet them." In addressing the issue of the Motorola case, Senator Case called it a "red herring"; Senator Humphrey noted that Motorola was only the decision of a hearing examiner and was never affirmed by a full board or the court. See Richard Epstein, who also notes: "No supporter of title VII defended the hearing examiner's decision in Motorola as a desirable outcome. Everyone sought to explain why it could not happen under Title VII." (Epstein 1992, 187–90).

28. The labor department serviced the other departments and was responsible for janitorial services in the plant. It was the lowest paid department.(*Griggs v. Duke Power Co.*, 420F.2d 1228, 4th Cir.1970)

29. Ibid, 1229.

30. Ibid, 1225.

31. Quoted from the opinion of the court in *Griggs v. Duke Power*. Note too that the EEOC had written an amicus brief in support of the plaintiffs, which likely influenced the decision.

32. Graham notes that the letter was drafted on January 27, 1979 but was not sent. However, it was Pemberton who drafted the amicus brief for the EEOC. He believed that *Griggs* was a weak case and believed that a stronger case for finding tests unlawful could be found. But he was nonetheless a soldier for disparate impact and despite doubts about the case was willing to risk a try.

33. As noted above, the Kennedy order was the first to state that contractors should take "affirmative action" to guard against discrimination. But nothing was said about special preferences for minority workers.

34. Executive Order No. 11246, September 28, 1965, 30 F.R. 12319.

35. Before setting its sights on Philadelphia, the OFCC tried to apply its pre-award enforcement strategy to construction in St. Louis, San Francisco, and Cleveland. Problems arose in each case (such as a large union walkout in St. Louis followed by a lengthy Department of Justice suit).

36. As vice president in the Eisenhower administration, Richard Nixon chaired the committee coordinating Eisenhower's executive order and developed a plan resembling the Philadelphia Plan. It was never implemented, but Nixon's earlier interest may have come to fruition when he adopted his own Philadelphia Plan during his presidency. He was obviously conflicted on the issue of quotas, which he often denounced in political appearances.

37. From remarks by Assistant Secretary of Labor Arthur Fletcher at signing of Philadelphia Plan, Philadelphia, Pennsylvania, June 27, 1969. Quoted in Graham (1990), 326–7.

38. *Bollinger v. Sharpe* (347 U.S. 497 [1954]) was a parallel case to *Brown v. Board of Education* and used the Fifth Amendment rather than the Fourteenth because the Fifth applied in the District of Columbia while the Fourteenth did not.

39. In *Contractors Association of Eastern Pennsylvania v. Secretary of Labor*, a contractors' association brought a case raising the objection that the Philadelphia Plan violated the Civil Rights Act by requiring racial quotas and was unauthorized by Congress. A federal district judge granted the Department of Justice's motion to dismiss the suit, ruling that the plan was a necessary move to eliminate segregated employment that violated federal policy. See Graham (1990), 141.

40. See www.dol.gov/esa/regs/compliance/ofccp/aa.htm, Section C, Affirmative Action Requirements, subsection 1, July 9, 2003.

41. Robertson's comment is quoted in Epstein (1992), 186. The quote was taken from 110 Cong. Rec. 7419 (1964).

42. All private firms (nonfederal contractors of one hundred employees or more and federal contractors of fifty employees or more) must submit annual EEO-1 reports. All the reports go to the EEOC, which can use them both in carrying out investigations of charges of discrimination brought by individuals and for "commissioner charges" (see chapter 4). The order for collection of these annual reports was promulgated by EEOC soon after the passage of Title VII in 1964. Since the original intent of Congress was to prohibit the enforcement of quotas on firms, Title VII would appear to prohibit the EEOC from requiring firms to submit racial composition statistics. But bureaucrats sympathetic to affirmative action at EEOC managed to circumvent the language of Section VII, and the EEO-1 reporting system was created. See the discussion in Graham (1990), 193–7 and Thernstrom and Thernstrom (1997).

43. See www.dol.gov/esa Federal Contractor Selection System (FCSS)—Questions and Answers.

44. See Equal Employment Advisory Council (2002). The EEAC's handbook describes the targeting method and provides data on the number of workers in federal contractor firms within MSA and industry categories classified by sex and minority status thereby enabling firms to compare themselves with others in their MSA. The OFCCP tends to keep from public scrutiny various important aspects of their enforcement procedures, and that tendency is repeated when it comes to revealing the details of how the hundreds of CRs that it completes each year are settled (see our discussion of table 3-1).

45. The most recent public statement by the OFCCP about its targeting procedure was posted on its website on April 8, 2007. Aside from general statements that its targeting procedure uses data from a number of sources, it still does not reveal the procedures it uses to combine the data to target individual firms. Most significantly there is no mention of its use of the *relative* position of contractors EEO-1 distribution rather than comparing it with actual labor market availability. It also asserts that it has added a "mathematical model" to its procedure but does not say how this addition

alters the procedures we have just described. There is no way to tell what the research firm, Westat, actually did from the statement that "Westat thoroughly analyzed data from five years of OFCCP compliance evaluations to formally identify and characterize relationships between reported EEO-1 workforce profiles and findings of discrimination." But what were the "relationships between reported EEO-1 profiles" and findings of discrimination? These profiles were already designed to do that. How were they altered? Again OFCCP is essentially silent.

46. Leonard (1985), passim.

47. Again, as with information on how they carry out their targeting procedures, the OFCCP no longer reveals the outcomes of their annual Compliance Reviews on their publicly accessible blog. We called the OFCCP and were told by its staff (Mr. Thomas Wells) that we would have to file a request for the data under the Freedom of Information Act. Since the possible time lag would be very large and there is no guarantee that we would even be granted permission—although the reason why information like this should require such elaborate protection from public scrutiny is not obvious—we decided to proceed with the data shown in table 3-1.

48. *Federal Contract Compliance Manual*, vol. 1, Chapter II, Desk Audit, 92–3, U.S. Department of Labor, Employment Standards Administration, Office of Federal Contract Compliance (volume was last updated in Nov. 1998).

49. Ibid., 101.

50. Ibid., Chapter III, Onsite Review Procedures, 262.

51. See *Federal Register*, part VI, June 16, 2006; Part VI, OFCCP; Interpreting Nondiscrimination Requirements of Executive Order 11246 (With Respect to Systemic Compensation Discrimination; Notice)

52. Ibid, 35140.

53. *Federal Register*, volume 76, number 237 (Friday, December 9. 2011)

54. U.S. Department of Labor, Press Release, December 8, 2011, available at: http://www.dol.gov/opa/media/press/ofccp/OFCCP20111614.htm.

55. See Thomas DeLeire (2000) and Acemoglu and Angrist (2001). For an analysis of the issues raised by the ADA, see Walter Y. Oi (1991) and Sherwin Rosen (1991).

56. See U.S. EEOC 2006b.

57. On April 4, 2006, the EEOC put out a press release entitled, "EEOC Makes Fight Against Systemic Discrimination a Priority" (U.S. EEOC 2006c). The EEOC had adopted recommendations from an internal task force report on "strengthening the approach to investigating and litigating systemic cases." The task force was led by Commissioner Leslie Silverman and was endorsed by then-Chair of the EEOC Cari Dominguez. The full task force report is available on the EEOC website at http://www.eeoc.gov/abouteeoctaskforce reports/systemic.htm. More recently the EEOC has stated its plan to incorporate its E-RACE objective with the systemic initiative.

58. See EEOC 2006a Section 15: Race and Color Discrimination (example 7), issued 4/19/06.

59. Examples of such cases are *Keeley v. Cisco Systems et al.*, U.S. District Court, N.D., Dallas Division, Civ A. 301cv1504d, Aug 8, 2003; *Steve R. Spain v. Mecklenburg County School Board*, U.S. Court of Appeals of the Fourth Circuit no 01-2282, Dec. 23, 2002; *Hickerson v. Coxcom Inc.*, U.S. District Court, E.D. Louisiana, No. Civ A., 02-0762, Nov 20, 2002; and *Caswell v. Federal Express Corporation*, U.S. District Court, N.D., Texas, Dallas Division, No. Civ. A., 30-1757, Dec. 31, 2002.

60. The EEOC manual now opines: "While the Commission considers it a violation of the Title VII for an employer to allow females but not males to wear long hair, successful conciliation of these cases will be virtually impossible in view of the conflict between Commission's and the various courts' interpretations of the statute. Therefore the Commission has decided that it *will not* continue the processing of charges in which males allege that policy which prohibits men from wearing long hair discriminates against them because of their sex" (emphasis added).

61. Securities Industry and Financial Markets Association (2003).

62. The characteristics of these jobs are a deterrent. For example, they demand long hours, employment continuity and frequently involve risk. See chapter 8 for further discussion of gender differences in job choice.

63. The suit claims that Walmart discriminates against women in pay and promotion. After losing its argument before the Ninth Circuit to stop the class action from going forward, Walmart is appealing the case to the Supreme Court. The plaintiffs have argued essentially that one Walmart store is like another in terms of its discriminatory behavior to women. Their discrimination case is based on findings of sociologists who believe that firms like Walmart treat women according to stereotyped views of their abilities. The EEOC filed an amicus brief in support of the plaintiffs when the case was before the Ninth Circuit.

64. See http//www.walmartclass.com/public_home.html.

65. See *Wal-Mart Stores Inc. v. Dukes et al.*, June 2011. Specifically, the court in a 5-4 decision held that the commonality requirement for forming a class is not met by generalized questions that do not meaningfully advance the litigation and is not met where named plaintiffs and putative class members have not suffered the same injury. In addition, and in a unanimous decision, the court found that individual monetary claims, including those for back pay, could not be certified under Rule 23.

66. Civil Rights Act of 1964 (703[e]). See also Epstein (1992), who points out the origin of BFOQ (1992, chapter 14).

67. Ibid., Section 625.

68. *Diaz v. Pan American World Airways Inc.*, 442 F. 2d 385, 3 EPD para 81665/Fifth Circuit, 1971.

69. Quoted from the court record in Franze (1998).

70. Cited in Thomas (1998).

71. *EEOC v. Turtle Creek Mansion*, 1995 WL478833 N.D.Tex. (1995). See Franze, 1998.

72. Franze (1998) notes that the EEOC expert was the same in both cases. But the Texas court in *Mansion* found the EEOC expert's analysis to be "fatally flawed" because the broad occupational categories available in the census did not reflect the qualifications needed for the job. Perhaps *Mansion* simply used a more skilled lawyer than did *Joe's*.

73. *Forts v. Ward*, 621 F .2d 1210, 1216-1217, 23 EPD para 30,935/2nd Circuit 1980.

74. See Case No. CV-04-4731 SI.

75. The law was amended after a divided Supreme Court in the case of *Dewey v. Reynolds Metals Company* upheld a U.S. Court of Appeals decision questioning the validity of EEOC regulations requiring employers to act affirmatively to accommodate religious practice. The decision seemed to imply that if an employee's religious practice came into conflict with a neutral workplace rule, the employee would have to choose between the practice of his or her faith and his or her job.

76. U.S. EEOC (2006a), section 15, V-B. Although Section 15 is directed at "Race and Color Discrimination," the section on disparate impact applies to all groups.

77. See 42 U.S.C, 2000e-2(k) (disparate treatment provision of Title VII); 29 C.F.R. Part 1607 (Uniform Guidelines on Employee Selection Procedures); see also *Griggs v. Duke Power Co.*, 401 U.S. 424 (1971).

78. *Griggs*, 401 U.S, at 431.

79. Ibid., 432.

80. The disparate impact exemption for bona fide seniority systems and certain other bona fide systems is in section 703(h) of Title VII. (The manual also notes the Title VII exemption from disparate impact challenge rules regarding the employment of substance abusers.)

81. See *Watson v. Fort Worth Bank and Trust*, 487 U.S. 977, 990–91 (1988).

82. See 42 U.S.C. 2000e-2(k)(1)(B)(i).

83. See 42 U.S.C. § 2000e-2(k)(1)(A)(i). If a policy or practice used at a certain point of the selection process has a discriminatory impact, the employer must justify the discriminatory policy or practice even if later stages of the selection process eliminate the disparate impact when looking at the selection process as a whole. See *Teal*, 457 U.S. at 453–5.

84. See 42 U.S.C. §§ 2000e-2(k)(1)(A)(ii) & (k)(1)(C).

85. Uniform Guidelines on Employee Selection Procedures, 29 C.F.R. §1607.

86. See the extensive discussion on disparate impact and test validation in Epstein (1992).

87. In a statement presented at a meeting of the EEOC on employment testing and screening (May 16, 2007), Jeffrey Stern, an EEOC attorney, mentioned that only 2 of the 51 African American applicants (4 percent) passed the apprenticeship selection test, compared to 108 out 292 white applicants (37 percent). The period of time for these results was not given.

88. 382 F.3d 680 (7th Cir. 2004).

89. 29 C.F.R. (1607.4).

90. Lawrence Ashe, Statement in *Recent Developments in Scored Test Case Law,* EEOC, Meeting of May 16, 2007.

91. *Green,* 523 F.2d at 1298-99

92. The leading case on arrest records is *Gregory v. Litton Systems,* 316 F.Supp.401, 2EPD 10,264 (C.D. Cal. 1970, modified on other grounds, 472 F. 2d 631, 5 EPD 8089 (9th Cir. 1972).

93. Two recent cases filed are *EEOC v. Peoplemark, Inc.,* 2008 and *EEOC v. Freeman,* 2009.

94. No analysis is given of the reason for the decline in the percentage of women passing the test which led to the decline in women among new hires. It is possible that women who ordinarily would not have applied for these meat-packing jobs chose to do so after hearing about the EEOC activity and the possibility of joining the class. The women who failed the test and were rejected for jobs each received more than $50,000 in compensation.

95. Rosenblum (2005).

96. U.S. EEOC 2006a, section 13-V Language Issues, example 17.

97. Ibid.

98. http://archive.eeoc.gov/litigation/02annrpt.html.

99. Ibid., section 13-V, English-only rules.

100. Ibid., example 20.

101. Epstein (1992). See also Paul (1990).

102. The EEOC adds that "the principles involved here continue to apply to race, color, religion or national origin."

103. 561 F.2d 983, 984 (D.C. Cir.1977).

104. On the same day the Court also ruled on *Faragher v. City of Boca Raton,* 524 U.S. 775 (1998), a case that raised similar issues to those in *Ellerth.* In *Faragher,* as in *Ellerth,* the court determined that even in the absence of any quid pro quo the employer could be held guilty of vicarious liability if supervisors created a hostile work environment through the use of lewd language and offensive touching and even if the employee never reported the incidents to the employer.

105. No. 97-569. Argued April 22, 1998, decided June 26, 1998.

106. The three incidents alluded to in the Court's summary are: after telling Ellerth she should "loosen up," Slowik made a crude reference to Ellerth's breasts and then said, "Kim, I could make your life very hard or very easy at Burlington"; during a promotion interview, Slovik commented that Ellerth was not "loose enough" and rubbed her knee; and, during a phone conversation, Ellerth asked Slowik's permission to fill a customer's request, whereupon he said that he did not have time to deal with her request unless she told him what she was wearing. Ellerth interpreted these comments as veiled threats. But no direct propositioning for any type of sex act is ever reported by Ellerth, and the major touching was the knee rub mentioned above. The harassment was mainly the constant verbal comments about her legs and clothing, combined with sexual jokes and comments.

107. See the discussion in Ranney (1997).

108. These are the details found in U.S. EEOC (2004a) (http://archive.eeoc.gov/litigation/04annrpt/index.html). No additional information is given.

109. See the discussion of the *Sears* case in Epstein (1992). The explanation for the statistical discrepancy was hotly debated by the two opposing academic experts. Professor Rosenberg (for Sears) took the position that differences in the characteristics of commissioned and noncommissioned jobs and women's preferences for the work-related conditions in noncommissioned jobs explained the difference, not discrimination. Professor Kessler-Harris (for EEOC) then had to justify the position that women and men did not differ in their preferences for types of jobs—a much more difficult proposition to defend. See Part IV, where we discuss the role of gender differences in preferences and its effects on labor market outcomes.

110. Wise (2005) reports that Burger King had terminated forty-two employees in response to complaints of harassment between 1990 and 2000.

111. Data tabulated by the authors from the Current Population Survey show that women are only about 16 percent of those working forty-one hours a week or more in securities sales (largely stockbrokers) in the securities industry. That statistic was 16 percent in 1997–9 and remained at that level through 2008–9 with the exception of the years 2000–1. Those were the years of the case against Smith Barney (with the notorious "boom-boom room"). The affirmative action campaign seems to have produced a temporary increase in women. But the fundamental reasons women do not flock to these jobs are the tough time and energy demands, not discrimination.

112. They cite a 2005 Gallup poll conducted with input from the EEOC. Gallup found that 15 percent reported they had been discriminated against in their workplace for some reason in the past twelve months. Discrimination was self-defined, however and a significant portion reported that the reason for the discrimination included nepotism/favoritism, sexual orientation, language, education, pay, and jealousy, none of which is prohibited by federal law. When these reasons are omitted, the proportion drops to 9 percent. The response rate to the survey was only 23 percent. In a survey such as this, those who are likely most eager to respond are those with a grievance.

113. Note that starting in 1987, when the relevant data became available, we show the earnings of African Americans both as a percentage of all whites and as a percentage of white non-Hispanics.

114. Data for 1939 were estimated from microdata files of the 1940 Census and refer to the median annual wage and salary earnings of full-time year-round workers. Data for 1955–2010 are U.S. Census Bureau estimates from the March Current Population Surveys and refer to median income of full-time year-round workers from 1948–66 for men (1955–66 for women) and to full-time year-round earnings for 1967–2010. (We estimated full-time year-round income for men for the period 1948–54 based on annual income data for all workers, a procedure that was not feasible for women.) The measure for 1939 excludes the self-employed, but the self-employed are included in all other years.

115. These statistics refer to the total population. The proportion of the working population living in the South in 1940 by race is somewhat smaller.

116. See U.S. Commission on Civil Rights (1986), table 5.3. These wage rates do not adjust for differences in the quality of education or other factors that could affect pay.

117. See chapter 1 for additional detail.

118. With respect to the comparison with whites, it should be noted that the trend for whites after 1980 depends on how white is defined. After 1980 the immigration of Hispanics began to increase and the rate of increase grew rapidly over the next two decades. Because a majority of Hispanics are classified as white and Hispanic immigrants have much less schooling than most other groups, the inclusion of Hispanics as white pulls down the school completion rate for all whites and increasingly so as the share of Hispanics in the population increased. Starting in 1995 the census began to provide education data for white non-Hispanics. The education data in table 5-1 refer to all whites including white Hispanics through 1990 and is restricted to white non-Hispanics starting in 1995.

119. Initially African American men did not increase their rates of college going as much as did white men. The World War II GI bill had increased the college attainment of white men and African American men born outside the South much more it had helped southern African American men (Turner and Bound, 2003). Segregation in southern colleges and universities and limited space in the African American colleges are believed to have been significant factors restricting college attendance of African American men in that period.

120. See chapter 1 for a brief discussion of these differences. Also see Welch (1973) and the U.S. Commission on Civil Rights (1986). The school resources considered include differences in the length of the school term, class size, and teacher salaries.

121. See Commission on Civil Rights (1986), table 4.9, for a summary of black–white differences in standardized test scores on different tests administered at different grade levels between 1960 and 1982. The average difference was about one standard deviation. A recent report of the College Entrance Examination Board (2002) found that among college-bound seniors who took the SAT, African American students scored about 100 points behind whites in 2002 on both the verbal and math tests (a slight widening in the differential since 1992).

122. The AFQT is sometimes referred to as an IQ test. But it is not an IQ test, as it is strongly affected by quality of schooling and environmental background. The genetically inherited component is unknown. Within education and race categories the AFQT varies by such things as region of the country. Scores on the army Alpha test (a precursor to the AFQT), used to test recruits for the World War I draft, also varied dramatically between southern and northern recruits of the same age, race, and education. For example, among fourth-grade graduates the median score of southern African Americans on the army Alpha was 36 percent of the score of the native white draft, while the median score of northern African Americans (presumably educated in

superior northern schools) was 85 percent of the white score. See National Academy of Sciences (1921), Memoir XV.

123. Although six states passed Fair Employment Practices Acts in the late 1940s, joined by seven more in the 1950s, most of the country was without legislation barring labor market discrimination in the years before 1960, the period that we discuss here.

124. The decennial census provides earnings data for the prior calendar year, although the demographic characteristics of the individuals are reported as of the time of the interview in the census year. In most tables we refer to the earnings data by the census year (that is, 1940, 1950, etc.). The wage ratios reported were calculated from the Census Public Use Microdata Set (PUMS) 1940–2000. The wage measures exclude self-employed workers, active military, and students and include only those who worked more than twenty-six weeks during the year and worked thirty-five hours or more in a week. We report hourly wage for women rather than weekly wage because a larger proportion of women work part-time and the percent part-time is variable among women.

125. The 1950s were years of rapid growth in real hourly earnings, a consequence of rapid gains in labor productivity. The annual average rate of increase in the real earnings of white men was 3.8 percent, the highest of any decade between 1940 and 1980. The rate of increase for African American men was not quite as rapid—3.4 percent a year, which is why the relative earnings ratio declined. The African American annual rate of growth in earnings was higher both absolutely and relative to whites in the 1940s and 1960s (U.S. Commission on Civil Rights, 1986, table 1.1).

126. The index of dissimilarity is calculated as the sum of the difference in the African American and white proportions in each occupation (like the proportions shown in table 6.2) divided by two. If the occupational distributions of African Americans and whites were completely different the index would be 100; if exactly the same it would be zero.

127. Cunningham and Zalokar (1992) provide more detailed occupational distributions and show that white women professionals were largely teachers and nurses; clerical workers dominated clerical and sales.

128. The dissimilarity index measures the proportion of African American or white workers who would have to change jobs for the occupational distributions of both groups to be identical. An index of 100 percent implies the most extreme occupational difference. An index of zero implies that the occupational distributions of both groups are identical.

129. In 1940 only 26.5 percent of white women ages 25–54 were in the labor force compared to 44 percent of black women. (See chapter 1, table 1-2.) The white women who worked were the most highly educated of any group. White women greatly increased their labor force participation between 1940 and 1960 as more married women and women with less work experience entered the labor force. This helps explain the decline in the proportion of white women employed

in professional occupations between 1940 and 1960. African American women also increased their labor force participation but by a smaller amount, and their relative education standing increased.

130. The commission analysis also included industrial sector (agriculture, private non-agriculture and government), potential work experience (based on age), and marital status.

131. In the *American Negro Reference Book* (1966), Davis reports that 84 percent of the African Americans and 33 percent of the whites entering the army between March 1941 and December 1942 scored in the two lowest categories of the AGCT, while only 4.5 percent of the African Americans and 35 percent of the whites scored in the highest two categories.

132. Quoted in Davis (1966).

133. Executive Order 9981 was issued from the White House by President Truman on July 26, 1948 (Davis, 1966).

134. See Davis (1966); Thernstrom and Thernstrom (1997).

135. Thernstrom and Thernstrom (1997, table 2, 141) report on the results of several surveys of whites in the South and North. Among the findings for the South: in 1942 2 percent thought that African American and white students should attend the same schools—by 1956 the percentage had risen to 15 percent, in 1964 to 31 percent; on eliminating separate sections on buses and streetcars, 4 percent said yes in 1942, 27 percent in 1956 and 52 percent in 1963; on being indifferent if an African American family of the same education and income as their own moved into their block, 12 percent said "make no difference" in 1942, 38 percent in 1956, 51 percent in 1963. Responses by whites in the North started at a much higher level. In 1942, about 40 percent said they favored school and residential integration, 57 percent were against segregated buses and streetcars; those sentiments were strengthened in 1956 and 1963, by which time a large majority supported integration.

136. Ibid.

137. The FEPCs were found to have a small positive effect on the black–white wage gap. See below for further discussion.

138. Smith and Welch separately and jointly have written extensively on black–white wage differences and the role of education. Smith and Welch (1989) is a summary of their work.

139. The black unemployment rate has been consistently higher than the white rate, and that differential has widened over time. However, the unemployment gap was considerably smaller in the South than in the non-South throughout the period 1940–1960 and that differential continued at least to 1980 (U.S. Commission on Civil Rights 1984, chapter 2). One explanation for the seeming puzzle is that there was more wage flexibility in the South because of less unionization and a smaller proportion of firms covered by minimum wages. With less wage flexibility, discrimination can take the form of reducing employment rather than paying equal wages. Thus the

FEPAS, in seeking equal pay, may have caused racial differences in unemployment. For further discussion see Gilman (1965).

140. Also see the important research by Jacob Mincer on the determinants of married women's labor force participation. As Mincer (1962) shows, women's labor market participation is influenced by their opportunity costs as well as by the income effect of husband's income. As women have gained more education their opportunity cost of staying home has increased and women have responded by increasing their market work participation. Increases in the incomes of married men, however, have a negative effect on women's market work making the net outcome difficult to predict.

141. Butler and Heckman attribute the relatively rapid decline in black male labor force participation to the expansion of transfer programs—disability and welfare—which reduced the incentive to work and coincided with the civil rights activities of the 1960s and 1970s.

142. The particular assumptions used to adjust for selectivity make a difference to the results, as Chandra (2000) shows. Chandra estimates black–white wage ratios for each decade between 1940 and 1990 using data from the decennial censuses and compares the observed change in the ratio from 1950–90 with that of ratios adjusted for employment dropouts. He uses three methods for the adjustment. Replicating Brown's method (which assumes that non-workers would have had wages below the median) produces the largest correction—a rise in the ratio from 1950–90 of only 3 percentage points compared to the observed unadjusted rise of 13 percentage points over the same period. The smallest correction (assuming the dropouts are similar to the average) is minimal and a third is in-between.

143. As reported in U.S. Commission on Civil Rights (1986), a change in estimating procedure leads Jonathan Leonard to find much larger effects in Leonard (1985) than in Leonard (1984) though both studies cover the same time period.

144. See the summaries of the studies in U.S. Commission of Civil Rights (1986), Butler and Heckman (1977), Donohue and Heckman (1991), and the discussion by Smith and Welch (1984) of their own work.

145. See O'Neill and Hill (1992) for evidence on intercohort changes in lifetime work experience and how they have differed between white and African American women.

146. The average hourly wage depicted in figure 6-1 is based on data from the Current Population Survey's Outgoing Rotation Groups (ORG). The data are collected monthly from all wage and salary workers and are based on a question concerning wages on the individual's current job, reported as the usual hourly wage for those paid by the hour and for others derived from questions on usual weekly earnings and usual hours worked (and other time frames and respective hours for other pay periods). An hourly wage can be derived from the decennial census by dividing annual wage and salary income during the prior calendar year by the product of usual hours and weeks worked during the year. Recall is not likely to be as accurate for this derived measure. The ORG data are available starting in 1979.

147. Gary Becker's (1981) seminal analysis of the family demonstrates how strong economic incentives underlie the observed division of labor in the family.

148. Labor force participation of married women in 1900 is from Goldin (1984). Hours worked in the home in 1900 are from Lebergott (1976).

149. In the mid-1950s the total fertility rate of women ages 14–49 reached 3.6. By 1975 it had declined to 1.8.

150. As shown in figure 6-2, the male labor force participation rate declined slightly over time for those ages 25–54. The decline began in the late 1960s and was more pronounced for men with relatively low education.

151. Using a broader measure of schooling, O'Neill (1985) finds that in 1952 women in the labor force had completed 1.6 more years of schooling than men, measured as median years of school completed by men and women in the labor force ages 18 and over. This difference declined to 0.7 year by 1959 and was almost erased by 1969, remaining at 0 through 1983.

152. Also see Blau and Kahn (1997) and Wellington (1993).

153. Equal Employment Advisory Council (2002). The Equal Employment Advisory Council is an organization that aids contractor firms in meeting goals and timetables by providing them with comparative data.

154. Smith and Welch (1976) estimated the effect of the OFCCP on the relative wages of minorities using time series data for the period 1967–74 and found that the rate of increase in African American relative wages was greater in the nonfederal contractor sector.

155. The results based on MSAs as the unit of analysis are sensitive to the universe of MSAs included in the analysis. As noted, because the geographic boundaries of MSAs changed between 1990 and 2000, it was necessary to realign the data. When we omitted MSAs with a low percentage of blacks, the C/T variable had an effect closer to that of the industry/region analysis.

156. The pervasiveness of gender differences in lifetime career paths is underscored in Goldin and Katz (2008). The authors find that even female graduates of Harvard, 60 percent of whom had attained at least one professional degree or doctorate, took career breaks after the birth of a child, and had more total months of non-employment and were less likely to work full-time, full-year when compared with male Harvard graduates (60 percent versus 90 percent).

157. The hourly wage ratios were derived from OLS regressions of an individual's log hourly wage rate on a set of explanatory variables including a "dummy" variable (0,1) indicating the individual's race/ethnicity with white non-Hispanic as the omitted reference category. The anti-log of the partial regression coefficients of the variable indicating race/ethnicity yields the wage ratios.

158. The earnings of all persons in the sample were converted into an hourly wage unless they were paid on an hourly basis. For example, a weekly salary is converted into an hourly wage by dividing by the hours worked each week. The regressions are OLS in which the logarithm of the hourly wage is regressed on a set of explanatory variables.

159. Attrition occurs because of deaths as well as because participants cannot be located or, when located, choose not to participate. The composition of the sample can also change because some participants who had dropped out rejoin the panel.

160. We use the NLSY79 version reported in 1989, which includes scores on reading comprehension, word knowledge, arithmetic reasoning, and mathematical knowledge. For a discussion of recent validation tests conducted by the National Academy of Sciences in conjunction with the Department of Defense, see Neal and Johnson (1996).

161. Herrnstein and Murray (1994) assign a causal role to genetic factors in explaining differences in the AFQT and refer to the test as an IQ test. Many analysts, however, have found that AFQT scores are significantly affected by environmental factors. See, for example, Korenman and Winship (1995), Fryer and Levitt (2004), Heckman (2008).

162. The AFQT was administered to the NLSY79 sample just once: in 1980, when the cohort was 15–23 years of age. Test score results are affected by age and schooling at the time of the test, although the precise effect is difficult to assess because we do not have readings on the AFQT for the same individual at different stages in their lives. We hold constant age and completed education in 2000 in our analyses—an implicit adjustment. Neal and Johnson (1996) adjust scores for age, but not for education at time of test. O'Neill (1990) holds constant both years of schooling completed at time of test and since the test.

163. The large influx of immigrants between 1979, the year in which the NLSY79 cohort was selected, and 2000, the census year, makes it difficult to compare census and NLSY79 results for Hispanics. As noted, the NLSY79 cohort is fixed as of 1979.

164. Similar findings on the return to AFQT by race were reported by O'Neill (1990) and Neal and Johnson (1996) when the cohort was younger.

165. Neal and Johnson (1996) discuss a large study of the relation between AFQT scores and performance in the military conducted by the National Academy of Sciences in conjunction with the Department of Defense. The study concluded that the AFQT predicted performance in the military as well for African Americans as for whites.

166. The lower return to military service could reflect less relevance of military skills to civilian jobs, since we exclude the active military from our wage sample. However, the subject bears further investigation into the timing of exit from the military and other circumstances of military service. For example, those who recently separated may be experiencing transitional problems.

167. In other analyses we have found that the work experience coefficients converge when we add a variable indicating jail time.

168. The statistics discussed in this paragraph are results from an analysis in which we use the difference in characteristics and evaluate them using the partial regression coefficients derived from separate log wage regressions for white, black, and Hispanic men. The separate regressions are shown in appendix table 8A-2. We refer here to

the results using the minority coefficients because they presumably do not reflect an upwards bias due to discrimination. Note that the analysis shown in tables 8-5 and 8-6 are based on pooled regressions in which the coefficients are implicitly based on the average coefficients of the three groups.

169. See appendix table 8A-1a for regression results.

170. The statistics discussed in this paragraph are results from an analysis in which we use the difference in characteristics and evaluate them using the partial regression coefficients derived from separate log wage regressions for African American and Hispanic women. The separate regression results for women are shown in appendix table 8A-2. We refer here to results using the minority coefficients because they presumably do not reflect an upward bias. Note that the analyses shown in tables 8-7 and 8-8 are based on pooled regressions in which the coefficients are based on an average of the coefficients for whites, blacks, and Hispanics.

171. Holzer and Neumark (2000) review the audit study literature in their broad review of the entire literature that might bear on the efficacy and efficiency of affirmative action.

172. See chapter 6 for a detailed discussion of the narrowing of the gender gap over the years.

173. A growing literature has investigated how women's greater attachment to child rearing influences human capital acquisition as well as energy for work. See Mincer and Polachek (1974), Mincer and Ofek (1982), and Becker (1985). For recent work on the "motherhood wage penalty" see, for example, Anderson, Binder, and Krause (2003) and Waldfogel (1995).

174. See chapter 6 for discussion of the changes in women's participation and participation profiles over the past century.

175. These are the most recent data, but they are influenced by the recession. Data for 2006 show a similar pattern but somewhat higher employment rates for both sexes.

176. See U.S. Department of Labor, BLS (2011), *Highlights of Women's Earnings in 2010*, Report 1031, July, table 5.

177. Similar polls conducted by the Pew Center show similar results. A Gallup survey published in *Newsweek* (1986) also indicates similar preferences.

178. Respondents were assigned either a weekday or a weekend day for their diary day. In this table we show results for those assigned a weekday. We focus on weekday reports because work is much more likely to occur on weekdays than weekends.

179. In line with popular impressions, ATUS data show that the type of household work differs by gender. Women specialize more in traditional housework and food preparation, men in lawn and garden care.

180. Becker (1985).

181. Part 1 of book 1, chapter 10 of *The Wealth of Nations* by Adam Smith, 1776 is entitled "Inequalities arising from the Nature of the Employments themselves." In the text, Smith lists five principal circumstances that give rise to wage differentials, the first of which is quoted here—"the agreeableness or disagreeableness of the employments

themselves." In one of the oft-cited examples from this part, he notes that "the most detestable of all employments, that of public executioner, is, in proportion to the quantity of work done, better paid than any common trade whatever."

182. For a broad survey of results from studies on gender differences in risk taking, see Byrnes, Miller, and Schafer (1999). For a study of the effect of physical risk on earnings see DeLeire and Levy (2004), who examine the tradeoff between wages and hazards and find that married women are much more risk-averse than men, requiring a larger compensating differential.

183. Mincer and Ofek (1982) demonstrated that women's wages deteriorate during periods of labor force withdrawal and found that the rate of depreciation is greater for more educated women who are more likely to have acquired significant market skills before withdrawal. McDowell (1982) estimated the costs of interrupted careers in several doctoral fields and found that women are less likely to be represented in fields such as physics where knowledge depreciates rapidly.

184. This statistic and those that follow are from U.S. Department of Labor, Bureau of Labor Statistics, *Highlights of Women's Earnings in 2010*, Report 1031, July 2011. Note that the occupational data refer to full-time workers.

185. This measure is usually referred to as the Duncan index of occupational segregation.

186. As before, the wage gap is estimated as the partial regression coefficient on a "dummy" variable indicating the sex of the worker. The gender coefficient is expressed as a wage ratio by taking the anti-log.

187. The log wage differential is converted to an hourly wage ratio by taking the anti-log of the coefficient.

188. One school of thought maintains that occupational segregation is the main mechanism through which discrimination is imposed. See the well-known work on the crowding hypothesis by Bergmann (1974).

189. Cavallo and O'Neill (2004) conduct an analysis of the determinants of the percent female in an occupation across three-digit occupations and find that variables compatible with women's constraints (such as the incidence of part-time work and of a long workweek and the extent of specific training required) explain most of the variation. Also see O'Neill (1983) for similar findings for an earlier period.

190. The median usual weekly earnings of women working part-time were 8 percent higher than those of men working part-time in 2008. In fact, when the earnings of women and men who worked the same number of hours per week are compared, wage ratios are higher and therefore the gender gap smaller than for the overall average, unadjusted for hours. Thus in 2008, among those working 35–39 hours per week the wages of women were 8 percent higher than men's; at 40 hours the female–male ratio was 87 percent and for those working 41 hours or more a week the ratio was 86 percent. And these statistics are not adjusted for any other characteristics. Similar results are reported for other years. (U.S. Department of Labor, Bureau of Labor Statistics, and U.S. BLS, *Highlights of Women's Earnings in 2008*, Report 1017, July 2009.

191. We have expressed the log earnings differential (Bertrand, Goldin, and Katz 2009, table 6) as a ratio by taking the anti-log.

192. *AFSCME v. Washington*, 770 F.2d 1401 (9th Cir. 1985).

193. For additional information about comparable worth, see O'Neill (1984) and O'Neill (1993).

References

Acemoglu, Daron, and Joshua D. Angrist. 2001. Consequences of Employment Protection? The Case of the Americans with Disabilities Act. *Journal of Political Economy*, 109: 915-957.

Ackman, Dan. 2001. EEOC Takes Up Morgan Stanley Case. *Forbes Magazine*, September 11.

Aigner, Dennis J., and Glen G. Cain. 1977. Statistical Theories of Discrimination in Labor Markets. *Industrial and Labor Relations Review* 30 (2): 175–87.

Anderson, Deborah J., Melissa Binder, and Kate Krause. 2003. The motherhood wage penalty revisited: experience, heterogeneity, work effort, and work-schedule flexibility. *Industrial and Labor Relations Review* 56 (2): 273–94.

Anderson, James D. 1988. *The Education of Blacks in the South*. Chapel Hill: University of North Carolina Press.

Antilla, Susan. 2002. *Tales from the Boom-Boom Room: Women vs. Wall Street*. New York: Bloomberg Press.

Ashe, Lawrence. 2007. Recent Developments in Scored Test Case Law. Paper presented to the U.S. Equal Employment Opportunity Commission, May 16.

Ashenfelter, Orley, and James Heckman. 1976. Measuring the Effect of an Antidiscrimination Program. In *Evaluating the Labor Market Effects of Social Programs*, ed. Orley Ashenfelter and James Blum, 46–84. Princeton NJ: Industrial Relations Section, Princeton University Press.

Autor, David H., Lawrence F. Katz, and Melissa S. Kearney. 2008. Trends in U.S. Wage Inequality: Revising the Revisionists. *Review of Economics and Statistics* 90 (2): 300–23.

Becker, Gary S. 1957/1971. *The Economics of Discrimination*. Chicago: University of Chicago Press.

———. 1981. *A Treatise on the Family*. Cambridge MA: Harvard University Press.

———. 1985. Human Capital, Effort, and the Sexual Division of Labor. *Journal of Labor Economics* 3: 33–58.

Belz, Herman. 1991. *Equality Transformed: A Quarter-Century of Affirmative Action*. New Brunswick NJ: Transaction Publishers.

Bergmann, Barbara. 1974. Occupational Segregation, Wages and Profits When Employers Discriminate by Race or Sex. *Journal of Human Resources* 17 (3): 371–92.

Bertrand, Marianne, Claudia Goldin, and Lawrence F. Katz. 2009. *Dynamics of the Gender Gap for Young Professionals in the Financial and Corporate Sectors.* Working Paper No. 14681. Cambridge MA: National Bureau of Economic Research.

Black, Dan, Amelia Haviland, Seth Sanders, and Lowell Taylor. 2008. Gender Wage Disparities Among the Highly Educated. *Journal of Human Resources* 42 (3) 630–59.

Blau, Francine D., and Lawrence M. Kahn. 1997. Swimming Upstream: Trends in the Gender Wage Differential in the 1980s. *Journal of Labor Economics* 15 (1): 1–42

Bond, Horace Mann. 1934. *The Education of the Negro in the American Social Order.* Reprint. New York: Octagon Books, 1966.

Bound, John, and Richard B. Freeman. 1992. What Went Wrong? The Erosion of Relative Earnings and Employment among Young Black Men in the 1980s. *Quarterly Journal of Economics* 107 (1): 201–32.

Bound, John, and George Johnson. 1992. Change in the Structure of Wages in the 1980's: An Evaluation of Alternative Explanations. *American Economic Review* 82 (3): 371–92.

Brown, Charles. 1984. Black–White Earnings Ratios Since the Civil Rights Act of 1964: The Importance of Labor Market Dropouts. *Quarterly Journal of Economics* 99 (1): 31–44.

Brown, Charles, and Mary Corcoran. 1997. Sex Based Differences in School Content and the Male-Female Wage Gap. *Journal of Labor Economics* 15 (3): 431–64.

Bullock, Henry Allen. 1967. *A History of Negro Education in the South from 1619 to the Present.* Cambridge MA: Harvard University Press.

Butler, Richard, and James J. Heckman. 1977. The Government's Impact on the Labor Market Status of Black Americans: A Critical Review. In *Equal Rights and Industrial Relations,* ed. Leonard J. Hausman and Farrell E. Bloch, 235–81. Madison WI: Industrial Relations Research Association.

Byrnes, James, David C. Miller, and William D. Schafer. 1999. Gender Differences in Risk Taking: A Meta-Analysis. *Psychological Bulletin* 125 (3): 367–83.

Cain, Glen G. 1986. The Economic Analysis of Labor Market Discrimination: A Survey. In *Handbook of Labor Economics,* vol. 1, ed. Orley Ashenfelter and Richard Layard, 693–785. Amsterdam: North-Holland.

Card, David, and Alan B. Krueger. 1992. School Quality and Black–White Relative Earnings: A Direct Assessment. *Quarterly Journal of Economics,* 107 (1): 151–200.

Catalyst. 2011. *Women CEOs of the Fortune 1000.* October. http://www.catalyst.org/publication/271/women-ceos-of-the-fortune-1000.

Cavallo, Alex, and June O'Neill. 2004. *Determinants of Gender Differences in Occupational Choice.* Paper presented at the annual meeting of the Society of Labor Economists, San Antonio, May 1.

CBS News, *60 Minutes.* 2009. The Look of Abercrombie & Fitch. February 11.

Chandra, Amitabh. 2000. Labor-Market Dropouts and the Racial Wage Gap: 1940–1990. *American Economic Review* 90 (2): 333–38.

Chay, Kenneth Y. 1998. The Impact of Federal Civil Rights Policy on Black Economic Progress: Evidence from the Equal Employment Opportunity Act of 1972. *Industrial and Labor Relations Review* 51: 608–32.

Clift, Virgil A. 1966. Educating the American Negro. In *The American Negro References Book*, ed. John P. Davis, 360–95. Englewood Cliffs NJ: Prentice-Hall.

College Entrance Examination Board. 2002. *College Board Annual Report*. New York: College Entrance Examination Board.

Cunha, Flavio, James J. Heckman, Lance Lochner and Dimitry Masterov. 2006. Interpreting the Evidence on Life Cycle Skill Formation. In *Handbook of the Economics of Education*, ed. E. A. Hanushek and F. Welch, 697–812. Amsterdam: North-Holland.

Cunningham, James S., and Nadja Zalokar. 1992. The Economic Progress of Black Women, 1940–1980: Occupational Distribution and Relative Wages. *Industrial & Labor Relations Review* 45 (3): 540–55.

Davis, John P., ed. 1966. *The American Negro Reference Book*. Englewood Cliffs, NJ: Prentice-Hall.

DeLeire, Thomas. 2000. The Wage and Employment Effects of the Americans with Disabilities Act. *Journal of Human Resources*, 35: 693-715.

DeLeire, Thomas, and Helen Levy. 2004. Worker Sorting and the Risk of Death on the Job. *Journal of Labor Economics* 22 (4): 925–94.

Donohue, John J., III, and James Heckman. 1991. Continuous versus Episodic Change: The Impact of Civil Rights Policy on the Economic Status of Blacks. *Journal of Economic Literature* 29 (4): 1603–43.

Doran, James. 2004. Morgan Stanley Settles Sex Lawsuit for $54m. *The Times Online*. July, 13.

Economist. 2004. Morgan Stanley Settles Sex Discrimination Lawsuit. July 15.

Elder, Larry. 2003. Is "All-American" Un-American? *Jewish World Review*, June 26.

Epstein, Richard. 1992. *Forbidden Grounds: The Case Against Employment Discrimination Laws*. Cambridge MA: Harvard University Press.

Equal Employment Advisory Council. 2002. *EEAC Handbook on the OFCCP Equal Employment Data System*. Washington, D.C.: Equal Employment Advisory Council.

Franklin, John Hope. 1966. A Brief History of the Negro in the United States. In *The American Negro References Book*, ed. John P. Davis, 1-95, Englewood Cliffs NJ: Prentice-Hall.

Franze, Laura M. 1998. Hiring by the Numbers. *Texas Lawyer,* June 22.

Freeman, Richard B. 1973. Decline of Labor Market Discrimination and Economic Analysis. *American Economic Review* 63 (2): 280–6.

Fryer, Roland G., Jr., and Steven D. Levitt. 2004. Understanding the Black–White Test Score Gap in the First Two Years of School. *Review of Economics and Statistics* 86 (2): 447–64.

Gilman, Harry J. 1965. Economic Discrimination and Unemployment. *American Economic Review*, 55: 1077-97.

Goldin, Claudia. 1984. The Historical Evolution of Female Earnings Functions and Occupations. *Explorations in Economic History* 21 (1): 1–27.

———. 1989. Life Cycle Labor Force Participation of Married Women: Historical Evidence and Implications. *Journal of Labor Economics* 7 (1): 20–47.

———. 1992. *Understanding the Gender Gap: An Economic History of American Women*. New York: Oxford University Press.

Goldin, Claudia, and Lawrence F. Katz. 2002. The Power of the Pill: Oral Contraceptives and Women's Career and Marriage Decisions. *Journal of Political Economy* 110 (4): 730–70.

———. 2008. Transitions: Career and Family Lifecycles of the Educational Elite. *American Economic Review* 98 (2): 363–9.

Goldin, Claudia, and Robert A. Margo. 1990. The Great Compression: The Wage Structure in the United States at Mid-century. *Quarterly Journal of Economics* 107 (1): 1–34.

Goldstein, Morris, and Robert Smith. 1976. The Estimated Impact of Anti-Discrimination Laws Aimed at Federal Contractors. *Industrial and Labor Relations Review* 29 (4): 523–43.

Graham, Hugh Davis. 1990. *The Civil Rights Era: Origins and Development of National Policy, 1960–1972*, Cambridge MA: Oxford University Press.

Harris, John F., and Kevin Merida. 1995. On Affirmative Action, New Perspectives Strain Old Alliances. *Washington Post*. April 5.

Heckman, James J. 1998. Detecting Discrimination. *Journal of Economic Perspectives* 12 (2): 101–16.

———. 2008. School, Skill, and Synapses. *Economic Inquiry* 46 (3): 289–324.

Heckman, James J., and Brook S. Payner. 1989. Determining the Impact of Federal Antidiscrimination Policy on the Economic Status of Blacks: A Study of South Carolina. *American Economic Review* 79 (1): 138–77.

Heckman, James, and Peter Siegelman. 1993. The Urban Institute Audit Studies: Their Methods and Findings. In *Clear and Convincing Evidence: Measurement of Discrimination in America*, ed. Michael Fix and Raymond J. Struyk, 187–258. Washington, D.C.: Urban Institute.

Heckman, James J., Jora Stixrud, and Sergio Urzua. 2006. The Effect of Cognitive and Noncognitive Abilities on Labor Market Outcomes and Social Behavior. *Journal of Labor Economics* 24 (3): 411–82.

Heckman, James J., and Kenneth I. Wolpin. 1976. Does the Contract Compliance Program Work? An Analysis of Chicago Data. *Industrial and Labor Relations Review* 29 (4): 544–64.

Herrnstein, Richard J., and Charles A. Murray, 1994. *The Bell Curve: Intelligence and Class Structure in American Life*. New York: Free Press.

Holzer, Harry, and David Neumark. 2000. Assessing Affirmative Action. *Journal of Economic Literature* 38 (3): 483–568.

Hymowitz, Carol, and Timothy Schellhardt. 1986. The Glass Ceiling: Why Women Can't Seem to Break the Invisible Barrier That Blocks Them from the Top Jobs. *Wall Street Journal.* March 24.

Jencks, Christopher, and Meredith Phillips. 1998a. America's Next Achievement Test: Closing the Black–White Test Score Gap. *American Prospect* 40 (September–October): 44–53.

———. 1998b. The BlackWhite Test Score Gap: An Introduction. In *The Black–White Test Score Gap*, ed. Christopher Jencks and Meredith Phillips, 1–51. Washington, D.C.: Brookings Institute.

Jones, Elizabeth, and Ivan G. Osorio. 2004. Tort Law "to Make Law." *CEI's Monthly Planet* 17 (6). Washington, D.C.: Competitive Enterprise Institute.

Juhn, Chinhui, Kevin M. Murphy, and Brooks Pierce. 1991. Accounting for the Slowdown in Black–White Wage Convergence. In *Workers and Their Wages: Changing Patterns in the United States*, ed. Marvin H. Kosters, 107–43. Washington, D.C.: AEI Press.

Kahn, Shulamit. 1991. *Does Employer Monopsony Power Increase Occupational Accidents? The Case of Kentucky Coal Mines.* Working Paper No. 3897. Cambridge MA: National Bureau of Economic Research.

Korenman, Sanders, and Christopher Winship. 1995. A Reanalysis of the Bell Curve. Working Paper No. 5230. National Bureau of Economic Research.

Landes, William M. 1968. The Economics of Fair Employment Laws. *Journal of Political Economy* 76 (4): 507–52.

Lebergott, Stanley. 1976. *The American Economy: Income, Wealth, and Want.* Princeton NJ: Princeton University Press.

Leonard, Jonathan. 1984. The Impact of Affirmative Action on Employment. *Journal of Labor Economics* 2 (4): 439–63.

———. 1985. Affirmative Action as Earnings Redistribution: The Targeting of Compliance Reviews. *Journal of Labor Economics* 3 (3): 363–84.

Lundberg, Shelly J., and Richard Startz. 1983. Private Discrimination and Social Intervention in Competitive Labor Markets. *American Economic Review* 73 (3): 340–7.

MacKinnon, Catharine A. 1979. *Sexual Harassment of Working Women: A Case of Sex Discrimination.* New Haven CT: Yale University Press.

Maloney, Thomas N. 1994. Wage Compression and Wage Inequality Between Black and White Males in the United States, 1940–1960. *Journal of Economic History* 54 (2): 358–81.

———. 1995. Degrees of Inequality: The Advance of Black Male Workers in the Northern Meat Packing and Steel Industries Before World War II. *Social Science History* 19 (1): 31–62.

Margo, Robert A. 1986. Educational Achievement in Segregated School Systems: The Effects of "Separate-but-Equal." *American Economic Review* 76 (4): 794–80.

————. 1995. Explaining black–white wage convergence, 1940–1950. *Industrial and Labor Relations Review* 48 (3): 470–81.

McDowell, John M. 1982. Obsolescence of Knowledge and Career Publication Profiles: Some Evidence of Differences among Fields in Costs of Interrupted Careers. *American Economic Review* 72 (4): 752–68.

Mehri, Cyrus. 2007. Testimony to the U.S. Equal Employment Opportunity Commission meeting on employment testing and screening, May 16. http://eeoc.gov/eeoc/meetings/archive/5-16-07/mehri.html

Mincer, Jacob. 1962. Labor Force Participation of Married Women. In *Aspects of Labor Economics*, ed. H. Gregg Lewis, 63–106. Cambridge MA: National Bureau of Economic Research.

————. 1974. *Schooling, Experience and Earnings*. New York: Columbia University Press for National Bureau of Economic Research.

Mincer, Jacob, and Haim Ofek. 1982. Interrupted Work Careers: Depreciation and Restoration of Human Capital. *Journal of Human Resources* 17 (1): 3–24.

Mincer, Jacob, and Solomon Polachek. 1974. Family Investment in Human Capital: Earnings of Women. *Journal of Political Economy* 82 (2): S76–S108, Part II.

Murphy, Kevin M., and Lawrence F. Katz. 1992. Changes in Relative Wages, 1963–1987: Supply and Demand Factors. *Quarterly Journal of Economics* 107: 35–78.

Murphy, Kevin M., and Finis Welch. 1992. The Structure of Wages. *Quarterly Journal of Economics* 107 (1): 285–326.

Myrdal, Gunnar. 1944. *The American Dilemma: The Negro Problem and Modern Democracy*. New York: Harper & Bros.

National Academy of Sciences. 1921. Memoir XV. *Psychological Examining in the United States Army*, ed. Robert M. Yerkes. Washington D.C.: Government Printing Office.

Neal, Derek, and William R. Johnson. 1996. The Role of Premarket Factors in Black–White Wage Differences. *Journal of Political Economy* 104 (5): 869–95.

Neumark, David, and Wendy A. Stock. 2001. *The Effects of Race and Sex Discrimination Laws*. Working Paper No. 8215. Cambridge MA: National Bureau of Economic Research.

Newsweek. 1986. How Women View Work, Motherhood, and Feminism. 107 (March 31), 51.

Oi, Walter Y. 1991. Disability and a Workable-Welfare Dilemma. In *Disability and Work: Incentives, Rights, and Opportunities*, ed. Carolyn L. Weaver, AEI Studies No. 516: 31-45. Washington, D.C.: AEI Press.

O'Neill, June. 1983. *The Determinants and Wage Effects of Occupational Segregation*. Washington D.C.: The Urban Institute Working Paper, March.

————. 1984. *An Argument Against Comparable Worth*, in U.S. Commission of Civil Rights. Comparable Worth: Issue for the 80's, vol. 1. June 1984.

————. 1985.The Trend in the Male–Female Wage Gap in the United States. *Journal of Labor Economics* 3 (1): S91–S116.

————. 1990. The Role of Human Capital in Earnings Differences Between Black and White Men. *Journal of Economic Perspectives* 4 (4): 25–45.

————. 1993. Comparable Worth. In *Fortune Encyclopedia of Economics*, ed. David R. Henderson. New York: Warner Books, Inc.

————. 2003. The Gender Gap in Wages, Circa 2000, *American Economic Review* 93 (2): 309–14.

————. 2010. Washington's Equal Pay Obsession. *Wall Street Journal*, November 18.

O'Neill, June, and Anne Hill. 1992. An Intercohort Analysis of Women's Work Patterns and Earnings. In *Research in Labor Economics*, vol. 13, ed. Ronald Ehrenberg, 215–86. Greenwich CT: JAI Press.

————. 1993. *Underclass Behaviors in the United States: Measurement and Analysis of Determinants*. Working paper, Center for the Study of Business and Government, Baruch College, City University of New York.

————. 2001. *Gaining Ground: Measuring the Impact of Welfare Reform on Welfare and Work*. Civic Report No.17, Manhattan Institute.

O'Neill, June, and Solomon Polachek. 1993. Why the Gender Gap in Wages Narrowed in the 1980s. *Journal of Labor Economics* 11 (1): 205–28.

Oppenheimer, Valerie. 1970. *The Female Labor Force in the United States: Demographic and Economic Factors Concerning Its Growth and Changing Composition*. Berkeley CA: Institute of International Studies, University of California.

Orlans, Harold, and June O'Neill, eds. 1992. Affirmative Action Revisited. *The Annals of the American Academy of Political and Social Science* 523.

Paul, Ellen. 1990. Sexual Harassment as Sex Discrimination: A Defective Paradigm. *Yale Law & Policy Review* 8 (2): 333–65.

Pew Research Center. 2007. From 1997 to 2007 Fewer Mothers Prefer Full-time Work. *A Social and Demographic Trend Report*. July 12.

Ranney, Frances J. 1997. What's a Reasonable Woman to Do? The Judicial Rhetoric of Sexual Harassment. *NWSA Journal* 9 (2): 1–22.

Rosen, Sherwin. 1991. Disability Accommodation and the Labor Market. In *Disability and Work: Incentives, Rights, and Opportunities*, ed. Carolyn L. Weaver, AEI Studies No. 516: 18-30. Washington, D.C.: AEI Press.

Rosenblum, Sarah, ed. 2005. *EEOC v. Dial Corporation*, What Went Wrong and Why? *Legal Fact Sheet* 4 (1).

Securities Industry and Financial Markets Association. 2003. *Annual Report on Diversity*. Washington D.C.: Securities Industry Association.

Silberman, Laurence. 1977. The Road to Racial Quotas. *Wall Street Journal*. August 11.

Smith, Adam. 1776/1977. *The Wealth of Nations*, ed. Edwin Cannan. Chicago: University of Chicago Press.

Smith, James P. 1984. Race and Human Capital. *American Economic Review* 74 (September): 685–98.

Smith, James, and Michael Ward. 1989. Women in the Labor Market and in the Family. *Journal of Economic Perspectives* 3 (1): 9–23.

Smith, James, and Finis Welch. 1977. Black/White Male Earnings and Employment: 1960–70. In *Distribution of Economic Well-Being*, ed. F. Thomas Juster, 233–302. Cambridge MA: National Bureau of Economic Research.

———. 1984. Affirmative Action and Labor Markets. *Journal of Labor Economics* 2 (2): 269–302.

———. 1986. *Closing the Gap.* Santa Monica CA: RAND Corporation.

———. 1989. Black Economic Progress after Myrdal. *Journal of Economic Literature* 27 (2): 519–64.

Taeuber, Alma F., and Karl E. Taeuber. 1966. The Negro Population in the United States. In *The American Negro References Book*, ed. John P. Davis, 96-160.

Taylor, Stuart. 1982. How Resolute is Reagan on Civil Rights? *New York Times*, October 10.

Thernstrom, Abigail, and Stephan Thernstrom. 1997. *America in Black and White: One Nation, Indivisible.* New York: Simon & Schuster.

Thomas, Cal. 1998. Big Government's Crab Grab. *The Jewish World Review.* August 18. www.jewishworldreview.com/cols/thomas081898.html.

Turner, Sarah, and John Bound. 2003. Closing the Gap or Widening the Divide: The Effects of the G.I. Bill and World War II on the Educational Outcomes of Black Americans. *The Journal of Economic History* 63 (1): 145–77.

U.S. Census Bureau, 1918. Census Report. *The Negro Population 1870–1915.*

U.S. Commission on Civil Rights. 1986. Clearinghouse Publication 91. *The Economic Progress of Black Men in America.*

U.S. Department of Labor. 1991. *A Report on the Glass Ceiling Initiative.*

U.S. Department of Labor, Bureau of Labor Statistics. 2009. *Highlights of Women's Earnings in 2008,* Report 1017, July.

———. 2011. *Highlights of Women's Earnings in 2010,* Report 1031, July.

U.S. Department of Labor, Employment Standards Administration, Office of Federal Contract Compliance Programs. 1998. *Federal Contract Compliance Manual*, vol. 1, chapter II–Desk Audit, 92–3.

———. 2006. *Interpreting Nondiscrimination Requirements of Executive Order 11246.* See *Federal Register*, Part VI, June 16, 2006 with Respect to Systemic Compensation Discrimination Notice.

———. Federal Contractor Selection System (FCSS)—Questions and Answers. http://www.dol.gov/ofccp/regs/compliance/faqs/fcssfaqs.htm.

U.S. Employment Service. 1991. *Dictionary of Occupational Titles.*

U.S. Equal Employment Opportunity Commission. 1990. *Policy Guidance on Current Issues of Sexual Harassment*, section C.3, 3/19/90.

———. 2000. *EEOC History, 35 Years of Ensuring the Promise of Opportunity.* http://www.eeoc.gov/eeoc/history/35th/history/index.html .

———. 2004a. *Annual Report of the Office of the General Counsel.*

———. 2004b. *EEOC Agrees to Landmark Resolution of Discrimination Case Against Abercrombie & Fitch.* News release, November 18. http://www.eeoc.gov/eeoc/newsroom/release/11-18-04.cfm.

———. 2005. *Litigation Settlements.*

———. 2006a. *Compliance Manual.*

———. 2006b. *Diversity in the Finance Industry.* News release, April 26. http://www.eeoc.gov/eeoc/newsroom/release/4-26-06.cfm

———. 2006c. *EEOC Makes Fight Against Systemic Discrimination a Priority.* News release, April 4. http://www.eeoc.gov/eeoc/newsroom/release/4-4-06.cfm.

———. 2007a. *Employment Testing and Screening.* http://eeoc.gov/eeoc/meetings/archive/5-16-07/index.html.

———. 2007b. *Phoenix Jury Awards $287,640 to Fired Muslim Woman in EEOC Religious Discrimination Lawsuit.* News release, June 4.

Waldfogel, Jane. 1995. The Price of Motherhood: Family Status and Women's Pay in a Young British Cohort. *Oxford Economic Papers* 47 (4): 584–610.

Welch, Finis. 1973. Education and Racial Discrimination. In *Discrimination in Labor Markets,* ed. Orley Ashenfelter and Albert Rees, 43-81. Princeton NJ: Princeton University Press.

———. 2003. Catching Up: Wages of Black Men. *American Economic Review* 93 (2): 320–5.

Wellington, Alison J. 1993. Change in the Male/Female Wage Gap, 1976-85. *Journal of Human Resources* 28 (Spring): 383–411.

Wise, Daniel. 2005. EEOC Charges Dismissed Against Burger King Owner. *New York Law Journal,* April 22.

Wolgemuth, Kathleen L. 1959. Woodrow Wilson and Federal Segregation. *Journal of Negro History* 44: 158–73.

Wright, Gavin. 1999. The Civil Rights Revolution as Economic History. *Journal of Economic History* 59 (2): 267–89.

Yerkes, Robert M., ed. 1921. *Memoirs of the National Academy of Sciences,* vol. 15, *Psychological Examining in the United States Army,* 27–90. Washington, D.C.: Government Printing Office.

Cases Cited

AFSCME v. Washington, 770 F.2d 1401 (9th Cir. 1985).

Barnes v. Costle, 561 F.2d 983, 984 (D.C. Cir. 1977).

Biondo v. Chicago, 382 F.3d 680 (7th Cir. 2004).

Blake v. City of Los Angeles, 595 F.2d 1367 (9th Cir. 1979).

Bollinger v. Sharpe, 347 U.S. 497 (1954).

Brown v. Board of Education of Topeka, 347 U.S. 483 (1954).

Brown v. F. L. Roberts, 419 F. Supp. 2d 7 (D. Mass. 2006).

Burlington Industries, Inc. v. Ellerth, 524 U.S. 742 (1998).

Caswell v. Federal Express Corporation, 210 P.3d 713 (2007).

Cloutier v. Costco Wholesale Corp., 390 F. 3d 126 (1st Cir. 2004).

Contractors Ass'n of Eastern Pa. v. Secretary of Labor, 442 F. 2d 159 (3rd Cir. 1971).

Dewey v. Reynolds Metals Company, 429 F. 2d 324 (6th Cir. 1970).

Diaz v. Pan Am. World Airways, Inc., 442 F. 2d 385 (5th Cir. 1971).

Dred Scott v. Sandford, 60 U.S. 393 (1857).

Dukes v. Wal-Mart, Inc., 509 F. 3d 1168 (9th Cir. 2007).

EEOC v. Alamo Rent-A-Car LLC, 432 F. Supp. 2d 1006 (Dist. Court, D. Arizona 2006).

EEOC v. Aldi, Inc. (Dist. Court, W.D. Pennsylvania 2009).

EEOC v. BlueGreen Corp. (N.D. Tex. June 14, 2004).

EEOC v. Caesar's Entertainment (Dist. Court, D. Nevada 2007).

EEOC v. Carrols Corporation (Dist. Court, N.D. New York 2005).

EEOC v. Craftex Wholesale and Distributors, Inc., & Ashcroft Leasing LLC (S.D. Tex. May 20, 2004).

EEOC v. Dial Corp., 156 F. Supp. 2d 926 (Dist. Court, N.D. Illinois 2001).

EEOC v. EQW Temps Inc.

EEOC v. Ford Motor Co. and United Automobile Workers of America (S.D. Ohio June 16, 2005).

EEOC v. Foster Wheeler Construction Inc., et al. (Dist. Court, N.D. Illinois 2002).

EEOC v. Freeman (D. Md. 2011).

EEOC v. Innovative Medical Research (D. Md. 2001).

EEOC v. Joe's Stone Crab, Inc., 969 F. Supp. 727 (Dist. Court, S.D. Florida 1997).

EEOC v. Kettering University (E.D. Mich. 2003).

EEOC v. Lawry's Restaurants, Inc. (C.D. Cal. 2009).

EEOC v. Milgard Manufacturing, Inc. (D. Col. 2004).

EEOC v. NEA, Alaska, 442 F.3d 840 (9th. Cir. 2005).

EEOC v. Peoplemark Inc. (W.D. Mich. 2011).

EEOC v. Premier Operator Services, Inc., 113 F. Supp. 2d 1066
   (Dist. Court, N.D. Texas 2000).

EEOC v. Red Robin Gourmet Burgers, Inc. (W.D. Wash. 2005).

EEOC v. Russell Enters., L.L.C., d/b/a McDonald's (E.D. Va. 2005).

EEOC v. Sears, Roebuck & Co., 628 F. Supp. 1264 (Dist. Court, N.D. Illinois 1986).

EEOC v. Taco Bell Corp., 575 F. Supp. 2d 884 (Dist. Court, W.D. Tennessee 2008).

EEOC v. Turtle Creek Mansion (N.D. Tex. 1995).

EEOC v. Watlow Batavia Inc. (N.D. Ill. 2000).

Faragher v. City of Boca Raton, 524 U.S. 775 (1998).

Forts v. Ward, 621 F. 2d 1210 (2nd Cir. 1980).

Gonzalez v. Abercrombie & Fitch Stores, Inc. (Dist. Court, N.D. California 2007).

Green v. Missouri Pacific Railroad Company, 523 F. 2d 1290 (8th Cir. 1975).

Gregory v. Litton Systems, Inc., 316 F. Supp. 401 (Dist. Court, C.D. California 1970).

Griggs v. Duke Power Co., 401 U.S. 424 (1971).

Hands v. DaimlerChrysler Corp., 282 F. Supp. 2d 645 (Dist. Court, N.D. Ohio 2003).

Harper v. Blockbuster Entertainment Corp., 139 F. 3d 1385 (11th Cir. 1998).

Harris v. Forklift Systems, Inc., 510 U.S. 17 (1993).

Heart of Atlanta Motel, Inc. v. United States, 379 U.S. 241 (1964).

Hickerson v. Coxcom Inc. (Dist. Court, ED Louisiana 2002).

Horace v. City of Pontiac, 624 F.2d 765 (6th Cir. 1980).

Keeley v. Cisco Systems et al. (Dist. Court, N.D. Texas 2003).

Kielczynski v. Village of LaGrange, Ill., 19 F. Supp. 2d 877 (Dist. Court, N.D.
   Illinois 1998).

Lanning v. Southeastern Pennsylvania Transp. Auth., 181 F. 3d 478 (3rd Cir. 1999).

McDonnell Douglas Corp. v. Green, 411 U.S. 792 (1973).

Meritor Savings Bank, FSB v. Vinson, 477 U.S. 57 (1986).

OFCCP v. Bank of America (ALJ case #97-ofc-16).

OFCCP v. Beverly Enterprises (ALJ case # 1999-ofc-11).

OFCCP v. Burlington Industries (ALJ case #90-ofc-103).

OFCCP v. Cambridge Wire Inc. (ALJ case #94-ofc-12).

OFCCP v. Greenwood Mills (ALJ case #84-ofc-39).

OFCCP v. Interstate Brands Corp. (ALJ case #1997-ofc-0006).

OFCCP v. Jacksonville Shipyards (ALJ case # 89-ofc-1).

OFCCP v. Jacor Inc. (ALJ case #95-ofc-17).

OFCCP v. Lawrence Aviation (ALJ case # 87-ofc-11).

OFCCP v. Loffland Brothers Co. (ALJ case #75-1).

OFCCP v. U.S. Airways (ALJ case #88-ofc-17).

Plessy v. Ferguson, 163 U.S. 537 (1896).

Rabidue v. Osceola Refining Co., 805 F. 2d 611 (6th Cir. 1986).

Ricci v. DeStefano, 557 U.S. 557 (2009).

Robinson v. Ford Motor Company (Dist. Court, S.D. Ohio 2005).

Sledge v. Goodyear Dunlop Tires North America, 275 F. 3d 1014 (11th Cir. 2001).

Steve R. Spain v. Mecklenburg County School Board (4th Cir. 2002).

Vanguard Justice Society, Inc. v. Hughes, 471 F. Supp. 670
   (Dist. Court, D. Maryland 1979).

Wal-Mart Stores, Inc. v. Dukes et al., 131 S. Ct. 2541 (2011).

Wards Cove Packing Co. v. Atonio, 490 U.S. 642 (1989).

Watson v. Fort Worth Bank and Trust, 487 U.S. 977 (1988).

Weiner v. Cuyahoga Community College District, 19 Ohio St. 2d 35 (1969).

West v. Abercrombie, et al.

Index

Abercrombie & Fitch case, 84–86
Ability tests, employment, *See* Testing (job), discriminatory
Acculturation of immigrants, 196, 201–2
Achievement tests as measure of skills, 130–31
Administrative law system of DOL, 57
Affirmative action
    Americans with Disabilities Act of 1990 (ADA), 60
    effect on economic status of target groups, overview, 178–82
    origin of term, 24
    See also EEOC (Equal Employment Opportunity Commission); OFCCP (Federal Contract Compliance Programs, Office of)
Affirmative Action Plan (AAP), 44–45
Affirmative action reports, requirements for, 37–38
African Americans, 3, 9–12
    See also Civil Rights Act of 1964; Desegregation efforts; Education; Wage gap, racial/ethnic
American Community Survey (ACS), 197
American Indians, 201
American Time Use Survey (ATUS), 225–26
Americans with Disablilties Act of 1990 (ADA), 60

Antidiscrimination law and policy
    Brown v. Board of Education of Topeka, 9, 12, 20
    changes after 1964
        affirmative action and quotas, 34–39
        Congressional actions, 29–30
        Court decisions, 31–34
    emancipation and reconstruction period, 10–12
    fair employment legislation (state level), 17, 22–23, 26–27, 143, 149–50
    See also Civil Rights Act of 1964; Discrimination categories
Aptitude testing, 32
Armed Forces Qualification Test (AFQT), 130–31, 160, 205, 208, 209–10, 213–15, 216–19, 235
Army General Classification Test (AGCT), 141
Arrest record and discrimination, 98–100
Asians, 5, 198–99
    See also Wage gap, racial/ethnic
Assistant Secretary of Labor for Wage and Labor Standards, 36
Athletes, black, 142
Attendance rates, school, 13–14
    See also Education
"Availability" of qualified minorities
    definitions, 38
    determining, 45, 52–53
    and OFCCP review targeting, 47, 58–59, 179

Baby boom, 170
Barnes v. Costle, 106
Beards and religious accommodation, 87
Becker, Gary, 222, 228
Bertrand, Marianne, 242
Biondi v. Chicago, 96–97
Birth control, 166
Black, Dan, 242
Body piercing and discrimination, 88, 89–90
Boll weevils, 12
Bona fide occupational qualifications (BFOQ), 79–86
"Boom-boom-room" case, 77
Brown, Charles, 154–55
Brown v. Board of Education of Topeka, 9, 12, 20
Brown v. F. L. Roberts, 90
Burger, Warren, 30–32, 33
Burger King, 116–17
Burlington Industries, Inc. v. Ellerth, 108–11
Business necessity, determining, 93–94
Butler, Richard, 154

Career commitment and gender wage gap, 76, 159, 175–76
Carter administration, 38
Chay, Kenneth Y., 158
Chicago Fire Department, 96–97
Child rearing and career choices, 76, 164–65, 223–28
Church of Bodily Modification (CBM), 89–90
Citizenship rights, 10
Civil Rights, U.S. Commission on, 23
Civil Rights Act of 1957, 23
Civil Rights Act of 1964
    effectivity of, overviews, 143–47, 149, 154–58, 176–77
    historical background, 9, 24–27
    passing of and Title VII, 24–29
Civil Rights Act of 1991, 76

Civil rights movement, overviews, 19, 24–25
Civil War, 10–12
Cloutier, Kimberly, 89–90
Cloutier v. Costco Wholesale Corp., 89–90
College completion rates, 14, 128–30, 171–75
    See also Degrees, advanced
Colorism, 118–19
Commerce Clause, 29
Commission Against Discrimination (New York), 23
Commission on Civil Rights, U.S., 23, 140
Commissioner's Charges, 115–16
Committee on Fair Employment Practice, 22
"Comparability," defining, 73
"Comparable worth" concept, 54–55, 243
Compensation discrimination, See Wage gap, gender; Wage gap, racial/ethnic
Compensatory damages, legislation for, 30
Compliance Officer (CO), 50
Compliance Review (CR) by OFCCP
    evaluation process, analysis of, 52–56
    evaluation process and outcomes, overview, 50–51
    process overview, 45
    targeting process, analysis of, 45–49, 58
Conciliation Agreement (CA), 50
Connor, Bull, 19
Consent decree (CD) v. court resolution, 70–71
Constitutionality issues, 29, 57
Construction labor market, desegregation of, 35–37
Conviction records and discrimination, 98–100
Cotton industry, 12

Credit history and discrimination, 100
Crime and African American labor
    force participation, 213
Criminal records and discrimination,
    98–100
Crock, Arthur, 26–27
Cultural/societal perspectives
    of immigrants, 201–2
    on women in labor force, 166–68
Cunningham, James S., 139
Customer preference and BFOQ, 80–81

Decennial census, use of, 53–54
Defense, Department of, 35
Degrees, advanced, 128–29, 173–75,
    241–42
Depreciation of skill, 229
Desegregation efforts
    construction labor market, desegre-
        gation of, 35–37
    early actions, 22, 23–24
    early actions/cases, 9, 12, 20
    fair employment legislation (state
        level), 17, 22–23, 26–27, 143,
        149–50
    Lockheed Aircraft, 25–26
Diaz v. Pan American World Airways Inc.,
    80–81
Directory of Occupational Characteris-
    tics, 232–34
Disabled workers, legislation for,
    29–30, 59–60
Discrimination, definitions, 43, 71–72,
    91–92
Discrimination, modern profile over-
    view, 195–97
Discrimination categories
    availability cases, 58–59
    EEOC impact overview, 117–19
    hiring practices, 30–33, 57–59, 93, 95
    overview, 71–72
    religious, 29, 65, 86–91, 118
    systemic, 55, 115–17

targeting procedures, OFCCP, 58
    See also Disparate impact discrimi-
        nation; Disparate treatment
        discrimination; Sexual
        harassment
Disparate impact discrimination
    and conviction records, 98–100, 118
    definitions, 91–92
    EEOC impact, 118, 119
    height and weight requirements,
        100–103
    and job testing, 30–34, 59, 94–98
    language requirements, 103–5
    measuring/determining, 92–94
    OFCCP determination of, 55–56
Disparate treatment discrimination
    and bona fide occupational qualifi-
        cations, case analysis, 79–86
    case analysis overview, 72–73
    definition under Title VII, 27
    EEOC impact, 118
    "glass ceiling," case analysis, 76–79
    in grooming policies, case analysis,
        75–76
    in hiring, case analysis, 74–75
Diversity in the Finance Industry, 117
Domestic servant employment, 139
Donohue, John, 148, 150
Dred Scott v. Sandford, 10
Dreiband, Eric, 84
Dress codes, discrimination in, 86–91
Due process, protection under, 10, 37

Earnings gap, See Wage gap, gender;
    Wage gap, racial/ethnic
Economic status of women and African
    Americans
    and effectivity of affirmative action,
        overview, 178–82
    occupational upgrading, analysis of,
        182–85
    racial differences overview, 15–19
    relative wages, analysis of, 185–91

The Economist, 78
Education
    attainment levels and gender wage
        gap, 171–75, 234–35
    attainment levels and race wage gap,
        13–15, 15–16, 127–30, 140,
        147–48, 206–8, 214, 216
    in Civil War Union, 11
    desegregation in, 9, 12, 20
    Fourteenth Amendment rights, 10
    limitations in South, 12–14
    school quality, effects of, 13–14,
        127, 130–31, 140–41, 148,
        208
    and wage premiums, 131–34,
        144–46t
Educational job requirements, 31–32,
    74
Educational wage premiums, 132–33
EEO-1 reports, 44, 179–91
EEOC (Equal Employment Opportu-
    nity Commission)
    analysis of, criteria for, 64
    charges by individuals, trends in,
        65–71
    effectivity of, overviews, 157–58
    enforcement approaches, 115–17
    formation of, 27
    impact of and future outlook, 117–19
    increase in authority of, 29
    and job testing, 33
    "reasonable accommodation" of reli-
        gious practices, 86–91
    role and jurisdiction overview,
        62–63
    See also Discrimination categories;
        Title VII of Civil Rights Act of
        1964
EEOC v. Alamo Rent-A-Car LLC, 87–88
EEOC v. Aldi, 91
EEOC v. BlueGreen Corp., 114
EEOC v. Caesars Entertainment Inc. et al.,
    106–7

EEOC v. Dial Corp., 101–2
*EEOC v. Fort Motor Co. and United and
    Automobile Workers of America,*
    94–96
EEOC v. Innovative Medical Research,
    103–4
EEOC v. Kettering University, 73–74
EEOC v. Lawry's Restaurants Inc., 81
EEOC v. Premier Operator Services Inc.,
    104–5
EEOC v. Red Robin Gourmet Burgers, Inc.,
    88–89
EEOC v. Sears, Roebuck & Co., 116
EEOC v. Taco Bell, 106
EEOC v. Watlow Batavia Inc., 104
"80 percent rule," 93
Eisenhower administration, 23
Ellerth, Kimberly, 108–11
Emancipation Proclamation, 9, 10–12
Employee productivity, measuring,
    196–97
Employment tests, *See* Testing (job),
    discriminatory
English language requirements, 103–5,
    196
Enrollment rates, school, 13–14
    See also Education
Epstein, Richard, 105
Equal Employment Advisory Council
    (EEAC) handbook, 46
Equal Opportunity Specialists (EOSs),
    55
Equal opportunity *v.* equal outcomes,
    5, 9, 21
Equal protection clause, 10
E-RACE (Eradicating Racism and Color-
    ism from Employment), 118–19
"Essential service," definition, 81
Evans, Medgar, 19

Fair employment legislation (state
    level), 17, 22–23, 26–27, 143,
    149–50

Fair Employment Practices Committee (FEPC), 21–22
Family roles and gender wage gap, 76, 164–66, 196, 223–28, 230, 235, 238–39
Farm employment, 139
Federal Contract Compliance, Office of (OFCC), 24, 34–39
Federal Contract Compliance Programs, Office of (OFCCP), See OFCCP (Federal Contract Compliance Programs, Office of)
Federal contracts, 22, 23–24, 25–26
    See also OFCCP (Federal Contract Compliance Programs, Office of)
Federal Rule of Civil Procedure, 23, 79
Federal service, segregation in, 20, 21
Field of study differential, 173–75, 176
    See also Degrees, advanced; Occupational differentials
Fifteenth Amendment, 10
Fitness tests and discrimination, 101–3
Fletcher, Arthur, 36, 39
Flight attendant cases, 80–81
Fourteenth Amendment, 10, 37
Fourth Amendment rights, 58
Freedmen's Bureau, 11
Freedom Riders, 19
Freeman, Richard, 154–55

Gender discrimination examples
    flight attendants, 80–81
    prison guards, 83
    waitstaff, 81–83, 85–86
    See also "Glass ceiling"; Wage gap, gender
"Glass ceiling," 76–79, 118
Glass Ceiling Commission, 76
"Goals and timetables" rules, 34, 38, 44–45
Goldin, Claudia, 242
Gonzalez, et al. v. Abercrombie, et al., 84–85

Graham, Hugh Davis, 34
Great Depression, 168
Green v. Missouri Pacific Railroad Company, 99–100
Greenbert, Jack, 34
Griggs v. Duke Power, 30–33, 93, 95
Grooming/appearance policies, discrimination in, 75–76, 86–91
Guards, prison and gender discrimination, 83

Hair length issues, 75–76, 90
Hands v. DaimlerChrysler Corp., 96
Harassment, racial, 114–15
Harassment, sexual, See Sexual harassment
Hardy, Charles, 113
Harlan, John Marshall, 11
Harper v. Blockbuster Entertainment Corp., 75
Harris, Teresa, 113
Harris v. Forklift Systems, Inc., 113
Harvey, Thomas, 114
Haviland, Amelia, 242
Heart of Atlanta Motel v. United States, 29
Heckman, James, 48, 148, 150, 154, 221–22
Height requirements and discrimination, 100–101
High school completion, 127–28, 129
Hijab, wearing of, 87–88
Hill, Herbert, 25
Hiring discrimination, 30–33, 57–59, 93, 95
    See also Disparate impact discrimination; Disparate treatment discrimination; Testing (job), discriminatory
Hispanics, 5, 73, 97, 158, 199
    See also Wage gap, racial/ethnic
Hooters, 83
"Hostile environment" sexual harassment, 107–8, 112–13

Hours worked, gender differences in, 162, 223–28
Human capital, 151, 196

Illiteracy, 14
Image discrimination, 84–86
"Immediate labor market area," defining, 52–53
Immigrants/non-white ethnicities
  acculturation of, 196, 201
  Asians, 5, 198–99
  Europeans, 12
  Hispanics, 5, 73, 97, 158, 199
  See also African Americans; Wage gap, racial/ethnic
International Association of Machinists (IAM), 25

Jim Crow South, 11–12, 126
Joe's Stone Crab case, 81, 82–83
Johnson, Lyndon, 24, 35
Juhn, Chinhui, 132
Julius Rosenwald Fund for education, 13
Justice, U.S. Department of, 23

Katz, Lawrence F., 242
Kemetic religion, 88
Kennedy, Anthony, 243
Kennedy administration, 24, 25
Kielczynski v. Village of LaGrange, 98
King, Martin Luther, 19
Ku Klux Klan, 11, 149

Labor, U.S. Department of (DOL), 35, 44
Labor force participation
  black v. white, 16–17, 151–52, 154–57
  and crime, 213
  and gender gap, 164–71
Language requirements, 103–5, 196
Lenning v. Southeastern Pennsylvania Transportation Authority, 102–3

Leonard, Jonathan, 48–49
Liability, employer (sexual harassment), 107–14
Lilly Ledbetter Fair Pay Act (2009), 30
Lincoln, Abraham, 10–12
Literacy rates, 14
Local demographics of labor market area, 43, 52–53
Lockheed Aircraft, desegregation of, 25–26
Lynchings, 11

MacKinnon, Catharine A., 105
Maloney, Thomas, 139, 140–41
Management positions and women, See "Glass ceiling"
Manion, Daniel, 109
"Manning tables," 35
Mansion on Turtle Creek case, 83
Margo, Robert, 140–41
Marital status and labor force participation, 166–68
Martens, Pamela, 77
Matched pair studies, 220–22
McDonald's, 87
McDonnell Douglas Corp. v. Green, 72
Mehri, Cyrus, 95
Meritor Savings Bank v. Vinson, 107–8, 111–12
Metropolitan Statistical Areas (MSAs), 46–48, 186–87
Migration, effects of, 12, 16, 126–27, 140, 147
Military, segregation in, 20, 21, 141–42
Minorities, See Immigrants/non-white ethnicities; Wage gap, racial/ethnic
Morgan Stanley case, 77–78
Motorola, testing practices of, 26–27, 31
Murphy, Kevin M., 132
Muslims and religious discrimination, 87–88

National Association for the Advancement of Colored People (NAACP), 25
National Committee on Pay Equity, 242
National Longitudinal Study of Youth, 197
National origin discrimination, 65, 103–5
New Jersey, 23
New York state, 22–23
New York Times, 26–27, 163
Niche markets and discrimination, 82, 84–86
Nixon, Richard, 23, 24, 36
Norton, Eleanor Holmes, 63
Notice of Proposed Rulemaking (NPRM) by OFCCP 2011, 59–60
Nur, Bilan, 87–88

Obama administration, 1, 242–43
Occupational categories of EEO-1 report, 44
Occupational differentials, 137–40, 173–75, 176, 182–85, 229–30, 232–34
O'Connor, Sandra Day, 113
OFCCP (Federal Contract Compliance Programs, Office of)
    creation of, 38–39
    disabled workers, legislation for, 29–30, 59–60
    effectivity of, overviews, 56–59, 155, 156–57, 178–82
    and occupational upgrading, 182–85
    procedures and review process overview, 44–45
    relative wages, effect on, 185–91
    role and overview, 44
    See also Compliance Review (CR) by OFCCP
OFCCP v. Jacor Inc., 59

OFCCP v. U.S. Airways, 59
Office of Federal Contract Compliance (OFCC), 24, 34–39
    See also Civil Rights Act of 1964
Older workers, legislation for, 29–30
O'Neill, June, 176
Outback Steakhouse case, 78

Park, Anna Y., 81
Part-time work and gender pay gap, 166, 224–25
"Pattern or practice" of discrimination, definition, 63
Paycheck Fairness Act, 1, 242–43
Pemberton, John, 34
Philadelphia Plan, 24, 35–37, 39
Physical strength requirements and discrimination, 100–103
Physically demanding jobs, 58, 82, 228–29
Pierce, Brooks, 132
Plessy v. Ferguson, 9, 12, 20
Polachek, Solomon, 176
Policy Guidelines on Current Issues of Sexual Harassment, 113
Posner, Richard, 109–10
Post 9/11 backlash, 87, 88
Pregnancy Discrimination Act, 65
Pregnant workers, legislation for, 29–30, 65
President's Committee on Equal Employment Opportunity (PCEEO), 24, 25
President's Committee on Government Contracts, 23–24
Pretextual discrimination, 72, 74, 79, 83, 92, 98, 102, 119
Prison guards, and gender discrimination, 83
Productivity (employee), measuring, 196–97
Productivity basis for hiring, 37–38
Promotion rates, school, 13–14

Qualification, determining, 53
Quid pro quo sexual harassment, 106–12
Quotas, employment, 26, 28, 34–39
    See also Affirmative action

Rabidue v. Osceola Refining Co., 112–13, 118
Racial wage gap, See Wage gap, racial/ethnic
Rastafarian religion, 87, 90
Reagan administration, 163
"Reasonable accomodation"
    of disabilities, 60
    of religious practices, 29, 86–91, 118
"Reasonable commute," defining, 52–53
Rehabilitation Act of 1973, 59–60
Religion, defining, 86
Religious discrimination, 29, 65, 86–91, 118
Reverse discrimination, 85–86, 96–97
Ricci v. DeStefano, 97, 119
"Right to sue" issuance, 65, 69
Risk taking behavior, 118, 228–29
Robertson, Absalom, 43
Robinson, Jackie, 142
Roosevelt (FDR) administration, 21, 22
Rosenwald Fund for education, 13
Rovner, Ilana, 109–10

Sanders, Seth, 242
SAT scores, black–white gap in, 131
Scalia, Antonin, 110–11
Scheduling and religious discrimination, 91
Schieffelin, Allison, 77–78
School, See Education
School quality, effects of, 13–14, 127, 130–31, 140–41, 148, 208
Schultz, George, 36, 37–38, 39
Screening, job, 33–34, 119
    See also Testing (job), discriminatory

Segregation
    in Jim Crow South, 11–12
    of military/federal service, 20, 21, 141–42
    in Southern industry, 19
    See also Desegregation efforts
Seniority concept, 92
Separate but equal provision, 11–12, 20
Service sector jobs, 166
Sexual harassment
    EEOC trends, 65
    "hostile environment" type, 107–8, 112–13
    interpretations of, 113–14
    overview and definitions, 105–6
    quid pro quo type, 106–12
Sexual Harassment of Working Women (MacKinnon), 105
Shiu, Patricia, 60
Silberman, Laurence, 37, 38
Silver, Roslyn, 87–88
Silverman, Leslie, 117
60 Minutes, 84
Skill depreciation, 229
Skill level
    and gender wage gap, 159, 164–75
    monetary return to, 131–34, 132–33, 148, 160
    and racial wage gap, 215
    See also Education; Work experience differential
Slavery, 10–12
Slowik, Ted, 108–9, 110
Smith, Adam, 228
Smith, James P., 147–48, 157, 179–80
Smith Barney case, 77
Southern v. Northern regional challenges
    1940 to 1960, 15–17, 19
    post–Civil Rights Act (1964), 149–51
    Reconstruction Period, 10–12
    See also Migration, effects of

Spanish language issues, 104–5
Specific Vocational Preparation (SVP), 232
Staats, Elmer, 36
State-level fair employment legislation, 17, 22–23, 26–27, 143, 149–50
Stereotyping, 74, 76, 114, 118
Strength requirements and discrimination, 100–103
Subjective criteria of OFCCP, 46, 58
Systemic discrimination, 55, 115–17
Systemic Task Force, 117

Tattoos and discrimination, 88–89
Taylor, Lowell, 242
Taylor, Sidney, 107–8
Technology, influence of, 166
Testing (job), discriminatory
    and disparate impact discrimination, 30–34, 93–94, 94–98, 119
    Motorola, 26–27
    strength requirements, 100–103
    and Title VII provisions, 27–28
Textile industry, 19, 150
Thirteenth Amendment, 10
Thomas, Clarence, 63
Thomas, Douglas, 110–12
Title VII of Civil Rights Act of 1964, 1–2, 27–29, 29–30
    See also Civil Rights Act of 1964; EEOC (Equal Employment Opportunity Commission)
Top tier occupational distributions, 182–85
    See also Occupational differentials
Tower, John, 27, 34, 37
Truman administration, 20

"Undue hardship," defining, 86
Unemployment, 26, 141, 149, 232
Unions, 22, 25, 35
Urbanization, 126–27

Vicarious liability, employer, 109
Vinson, Michelle, 107–8, 111–12
Violence, racial, 11–12

"Wage bubble," 157
Wage compression, 132, 141, 148–49
Wage discrimination, definitions, 54–55
Wage gap, gender
    post-1980 analysis, 175–76
    analysis of changes in, overview, 162–64
    educational attainment, 171–75
    modern analysis
        determinants assessment, 228–43
        overview, 223, 243–44
        women's choices, impact of, 223–28, 240–44
    work experience and labor force participation, 164–71
    See also Economic status of women and African Americans
Wage gap, racial/ethnic
    1940 to 1960, 17–19, 134–43
    1960 to 1980, 143–58
    post-1980, 158–61
    analysis of changes in, overview, 123–25
    educational attainment, effects of, 127–30, 144–46t, 147–48, 160
    migration, effects of, 12, 16, 126–27
    modern analysis
        audit study assessment, 220–22
        men, 198–202, 206–15
        overview, 197–98, 245–49t
        women, 202–5, 215–20
        school quality, effects of, 130–31
        wage structure and skill level, 131–34
    See also Economic status of women and African Americans

Wage premiums for education/skill
    level, 131–34, 132–33, 148, 160
Waitstaff cases, 81–83, 85–86
Wall Street and "glass ceiling" issues,
    76–77, 118
Wall Street Journal, 76
Walmart case, 78–79
Wartime demand for labor
    and African Americans, 12, 16–17,
        140, 141
    and women, 165–66
Washington Post, 39
Wealth of Nations (Smith), 228
Weight requirements and discrimina-
    tion, 100–102
Weight-lifting tests and discrimination,
    101–3
Welch, Finis, 147–48, 157, 179–80
West v. Abercrombie, et al., 84–85
Wilson, Woodrow, 20
Wirtz, Willard, 26, 35
Wolpin, Kenneth, 48

Women
    black–white wage gap
        1940 to 1960, 17–18, 18–19
        1940 to 2000, 144t, 146t
        educational attainment, 129
    "glass ceiling," 76–79, 118
    modern wage differential by race/
        ethnicity, 202–5
    and strenuous work, hiring for, 58,
        101–3
    See also Sexual harassment; Wage
        gap, gender
Wood, Diane, 109–10
Work experience differential
    and gender wage gap, 164–71, 235
    and racial wage gap, 208, 214
    and racial wage gap among women,
        19, 151–54, 159, 216
World War II, influence of, 12, 140,
    141–42, 165–66

Zalokar, Nadja, 139

About the Authors

June O'Neill is the Wollman Distinguished Professor of Economics at Baruch College, City University of New York (CUNY) and a professor at the CUNY Graduate Center. She is also an adjunct scholar at the American Enterprise Institute, a research associate of the National Bureau of Economic Research and a research fellow of the Institute of Labor Economics in Bonn, Germany. Between 1995 and 1999, she served as director of the Congressional Budget Office. Earlier, Dr. O'Neill held senior-level appointments at the U.S. Commission on Civil Rights, the Urban Institute, the President's Council of Economic Advisers, and the Brookings Institution. She was elected vice president of the American Economics Association in 1998. She received her Ph.D. in economics from Columbia University in 1970. Dr. O'Neill has published articles and books dealing with the determinants of income and wage differentials, including gender and racial wage differentials, and policies that aim to influence wages and income such as comparable worth and welfare reform. She has also published on topics related to health, social security, the federal budget, and tax policy. She has served on many committees and advisory boards and has regularly made media appearances. Dr. O'Neill has served as an expert witness in a number of cases involving claims of gender discrimination.

Dave M. O'Neill is an adjunct professor at Baruch College, City University of New York and is a research fellow at the Institute of Labor Economics in Bonn, Germany. He has also taught at the University of Pennsylvania and Pace University. Dr. O'Neill worked for many years at senior-level positions in economic policy analysis at both nonprofit research institutes (the Center for Naval Analysis, the American Enterprise Institute, and the National Academy of Sciences, where he was staff director of the panel to review labor productivity measurement) and government agencies (Bureau of the Census, the General Accounting Office, New York Federal Reserve Bank). He received his Ph.D. in economics from Columbia University in 1966. Dr. O'Neill has published articles on productivity, the effects of work and training programs, evaluation of employment tax credit programs, education, the underground economy, and racial differences in teenage unemployment. He has collaborated with his wife June O'Neill on publications dealing with affirmative action in the labor market, wage differentials and discrimination, welfare reform, the effect of health insurance mandates on employment, analysis of the uninsured population, and comparison of health status and health care in Canada and the United States.

Sam Peltzman
Ralph and Dorothy Keller
Distinguished Service Professor
of Economics
Booth School of Business
University of Chicago

Jeremy A. Rabkin
Professor of Law
George Mason University
School of Law

Harvey S. Rosen
John L. Weinberg Professor of
Economics and Business Policy
Princeton University

Richard J. Zeckhauser
Frank Plumpton Ramsey Professor
of Political Economy
Kennedy School of Government
Harvard University

Research Staff

Ali Alfoneh
Resident Fellow

Joseph Antos
Wilson H. Taylor Scholar in Health
Care and Retirement Policy

Leon Aron
Resident Scholar; Director,
Russian Studies

Michael Auslin
Resident Scholar

Claude Barfield
Resident Scholar

Michael Barone
Resident Fellow

Roger Bate
Resident Scholar

Andrew G. Biggs
Resident Scholar

Edward Blum
Visiting Fellow

Dan Blumenthal
Resident Fellow

John R. Bolton
Senior Fellow

Karlyn Bowman
Senior Fellow

Alex Brill
Research Fellow

James Capretta
Visiting Scholar

Lynne V. Cheney
Senior Fellow

Steven J. Davis
Visiting Scholar

Sadanand Dhume
Resident Fellow

Thomas Donnelly
Resident Fellow; Co-Director,
Marilyn Ware Center for
Security Studies

Mackenzie Eaglen
Resident Fellow

Nicholas Eberstadt
Henry Wendt Scholar in
Political Economy

Jeffrey A. Eisenach
Visiting Scholar

Jon Entine
Visiting Fellow

Rick Geddes
Visiting Scholar

Jonah Goldberg
Fellow

Aspen Gorry
Research Fellow

Scott Gottlieb, M.D.
Resident Fellow

Kenneth P. Green
Resident Scholar

Michael S. Greve
Visiting Scholar

Kevin A. Hassett
Senior Fellow; Director,
Economic Policy Studies

Robert B. Helms
Resident Scholar

Arthur Herman
NRI Visiting Scholar

Frederick M. Hess
Resident Scholar; Director,
Education Policy Studies

Ayaan Hirsi Ali
Visiting Fellow

R. Glenn Hubbard
Visiting Scholar

Frederick W. Kagan
Resident Scholar; Director, AEI
Critical Threats Project; and
Christopher DeMuth Chair

Leon R. Kass, M.D.
Madden-Jewett Chair

Andrew P. Kelly
Research Fellow, Jacobs Associate

J.D. Kleinke
Resident Fellow

Desmond Lachman
Resident Fellow

Adam Lerrick
Visiting Scholar

John H. Makin
Resident Scholar

Aparna Mathur
Resident Scholar, Jacobs Associate

Michael Mazza
Research Fellow

Michael Q. McShane
Research Fellow

Thomas P. Miller
Resident Fellow

Charles Murray
W. H. Brady Scholar

Roger F. Noriega
Fellow

Stephen D. Oliner
Resident Scholar

Norman J. Ornstein
Resident Scholar

Pia Orrenius
Visiting Scholar

Richard Perle
Fellow

Mark J. Perry
Scholar

Tomas J. Philipson
Visiting Scholar

Edward Pinto
Resident Fellow

Alex J. Pollock
Resident Fellow

Vincent R. Reinhart
Visiting Scholar

Richard Rogerson
Visiting Scholar

Michael Rubin
Resident Scholar

Sally Satel, M.D.
Resident Scholar

Gary J. Schmitt
Resident Scholar; Director,
Program on American Citizenship;
Co-Director, Marilyn Ware Center
for Security Studies

Mark Schneider
Visiting Scholar

David Schoenbrod
Visiting Scholar

Nick Schulz
DeWitt Wallace Fellow;
Editor-in-Chief, American.com

Roger Scruton
Visiting Scholar

Sita Nataraj Slavov
Resident Scholar

Vincent Smith
Visiting Scholar

Christina Hoff Sommers
Resident Scholar; Director,
W. H. Brady Program

Michael R. Strain
Research Fellow

Phillip Swagel
Visiting Scholar

Marc A. Thiessen
Fellow

Stan A. Veuger
Research Fellow

Alan D. Viard
Resident Scholar

Peter J. Wallison
Arthur F. Burns Fellow in
Financial Policy Studies

Paul Wolfowitz
Scholar

John Yoo
Visiting Scholar

Benjamin Zycher
NRI Visiting Fellow